Signs of Agni Yoga
HEART

HEART

1932

Agni Yoga Society
319 West 107th Street
New York NY 10025
www.agniyoga.org

© 1934, 2013 by the Agni Yoga Society.
First edition published 1934. Third edition 2013.
Reprinted November 2016. Updated September 2021.
Translated from Russian by the Agni Yoga Society.

After our daily labors, let us gather in conversation about the heart. It will lead us through the earthly domains to the Subtle World and thereby bring us closer to the realm of Fire.

HEART

1. To see with the eyes of the heart; to hear the roar of the world with the ears of the heart; to peer into the future with the understanding of the heart; to remember past accumulations through the heart—that is how the aspirant must boldly advance on the path of ascent. Creativity embraces the fiery potential and comes to be saturated with the sacred fire of the heart. Therefore, on the path of the Hierarchy, on the path of the Great Service, on the path of Communion, synthesis is the one luminous path of the heart. How can seekers radiate the rays manifested if there is no flame affirmed in their hearts? It is precisely the quality of a magnet that lies latent in the heart. The loftiest creativity is pervaded with this great law. Thus, every consummation, every unification, every cosmic union is achieved through the flame of the heart. In what way can a foundation be laid for great steps? Truly, only by way of the heart. The arcs of consciousness merge in the flame of the heart.

So let us keep in mind the wondrous attraction of the magnet of the heart, which links all manifestations. Indeed, the silver thread that connects the Teacher with the disciple is the great magnet of the heart. The unification of the Teacher and disciple affirms the essence of all aspects of evolution.

2. Many legends tell how wishes were fulfilled, but they do not speak about a basic condition, about the main character being in a quandary, a situation with no way out; and this condition sharpens desires until they become immutable. Even a small detour takes the

edge off the arrow of immutability. But just as a person who is not used to the water is able to swim when in danger of being drawn to the bottom, so the solution that fulfils a wish is found when every path has been cut off. People say that a miracle has occurred, but often it is only a sharper focusing of psychic energy. The heart, the sun of the organism, is the focus of psychic energy. Thus, when we speak about the heart, we must keep in mind the law of psychic energy. It is wonderful to have a sense of the heart as the Sun of Suns of the universe. We must understand the Sun of the Highest Hierarch to be our Banner. How wondrous and beautiful is this Banner, like an invincible force, once our eyes have assimilated its radiance—the radiance reflected in our hearts!

3. Whether people call the heart "the abode of the Elohim" or "the synthesis of syntheses," it remains the focus. Even those who only see the heart in terms of its lower, physiological functions regard it with care. How much more deeply, then, should a person listen to the heart, when he knows about the magnet and the silver thread! That is why the Teacher draws you away from everything narrowly physical, so as to remind you through each organ about the spiritual world. It is a festival for Us when pure thinking is transferred into the sphere of invisible existence. People should be led into the abode of the Elohim with great urgency, as if danger were on their heels. You can recognize that the chosen ones are on the path if the Invisible World has become real and accessible to them; you may then notice that the consciousness is growing and the very organs of the body are being transformed, nourished as they are by the link to the Hierarchy.

4. The heart is a temple, but not a hall of idols. So while We have nothing against the construction of a

temple, fetishism or bazaars are unacceptable to Us. Likewise, when We talk about building a temple in the form of a heart, We do not have in mind a heart-shaped building; We are indicating the temple's inner significance. A true temple cannot exist unless there is awareness of the infinite chain; similarly, the heart is in contact with all the sensations of the Cosmos. The heart's anguish or joy resonates to the distant spheres. Why, then, is anguish felt more often than joy? Of course, the constant perturbations in the Cosmos agitate the heart that is attuned to them. That is why the service of such a heart has great weight on the scales of the world. Help out in the construction of the world! There is neither a day nor an hour when the world is free of danger! To discern the dangers, not two eyes are necessary but three, as shown on the Banner of the Lords. One should understand that the temple of the heart gives rise to an urgent sensation. It was no accident that the heart was marked with the sign of the cross. Indeed, the sign of the cross is an eternal companion of the temple of the heart.

5. New circumstances will reveal the path to the future. Truth is always the same, but combinations are different, as they depend on the consciousness. So much that is beautiful ends up being destroyed due to ignorance of the temple of the heart. But let us adamantly strive to be aware of heartfelt warmth, and let us start feeling ourselves to be bearers of this temple. That is how we can cross over the threshold into the New World. How inconsequential are the people who imagine that the New World is not for them. Bodies may differ, but the spirit cannot evade the New World.

6. Doubt means the downfall of quality. Doubt is the tomb of the heart. Doubt is a source of ugliness. Doubt must be touched on in every talk, because where will we end up without quality? What will we understand without the heart? What will we attain without beauty?

People will ask, "Why does *Infinity* come first, then *Hierarchy*, and only then *Heart*, rather than the reverse?" But first comes the direction, then the link, and then the means. One must not mar this sacred means with doubt. Let us observe the quality of a person's pulse when he is experiencing doubt and also when he is engaged in faithful striving. If doubt is able to change the pulse and emanations, what physical deterioration it may work upon the nervous system! Doubt devours psychic energy.

After thinking about doubt, let us recall treachery itself, for who is more intimate with doubt than a traitor? One can overcome this darkness only through communion with the Hierarchy, with the most inevitable, partaking of It as one would the radiance of the sun. True, it does burn, but without it there is darkness!

7. The heart may be the focus, but it is the least egocentric of all. Not egoism dwells in the heart, but a feeling that embraces all humanity. Only reasoning shrouds the heart in a web of egocentricity. Kind-heartedness is measured not so much by good actions, which may arise from so many different causes, but by one's inner kindliness, which kindles the light that shines in the darkness. In this sense the heart is truly a transnational organ. If for us light is a symbol of the aura, its parent will be the heart. How necessary it is that one learns to feel the heart not as one's own, but as something that belongs to the entire world. Only through this feeling can a person begin to liberate himself from egoism while preserving the individual nature of his accumulations. It is difficult to embrace both individuality and universal containment, but

there is good reason for the magnet of the heart to be connected with the Chalice. You can understand how the heart radiates a special light that is refracted in every possible way by the substance that composes the nerves. The crystal of psychic energy can be colored in so many ways.

8. It is very difficult to purify the heart if the web of egoism is making it fat. The fat of egoism is a bestial inheritance. The pure accumulations of individuality can explain things of which the reason cannot even conceive. It is especially difficult to impress someone with a notion that has never entered the circle of his imagination. The heart is considered the palace of the imagination. How is it possible to move forward if the power of imagination is missing? But where will imagination come from, if not from experience?

9. Heartlessness is nothing but an uncultured state of the heart. Faint-heartedness arises from limitation of thinking. Intolerance belongs to the same family of abominations, all of which degrade the sacred vessel of the heart. You already know that a refined heart, whose energy is intensified, provides an impulse similar to that of an electrical generator; this shows that the heart is a vessel of universal energy. But the culture of the heart does not accumulate unless it receives proper nourishment. Likewise, the best accumulator will be inactive unless it is protected and connected properly. The heart demands constant nourishment; without it, the heart is deprived of the highest link and begins to decompose. In light of this, let us not forget how the ancients symbolized ascent by depicting an infant on the bottom of the chalice.

10. By conducting a rarely performed experiment, you can see how the heart reflects even distant earthquakes and other world events. You can note how not only cosmic perturbations but even reflections of the spirit's radiation act over great distances. We pay attention to the transmuter of prana, to the lungs, which pass the essence on to the heart as a way to establish universal equilibrium.

The new achievements being made in the subtle body are now being crowned with success. These achievements could no longer be deferred, because the foundation of the link with the Magnet of the Hierarchy was being violated. As an aid in restoration of the violated equilibrium, a new kind of subtle body is being developed.

11. When the treasures of energy exceed the treasures of the heart and straight-knowledge, a coworker-mentor is usually sent to establish equilibrium. A Professor actually was attached to Washington, and a Sage of the Mountain was with Genghis Khan. Many similar examples could be cited. You should regard this as something that enhances their activity, not as an absolute requirement. There are also many examples when men of action rejected such cooperation, thereby bringing irreparable harm not only to themselves but also to the Common Good. We have experienced such refusals time and again. Precisely, it was the heart's lack of development that prevented an increase in the possibilities that had been built up by past accumulations.

12. Our Hand will not get tired of extending the saving thread to the heart. Who can justly say that We were late in offering help? But We can cite many occasions when Our Messenger was frozen by people's heartlessness. It is so hard to bring into action the potential of the heart. One must manifest a flight over the abyss, as if soaring from the last shore into

the Infinite. How sacred is the courage of selflessness, which opens up the heart!

13. Can you picture what a humanity with healthy bodies and uncultured hearts would be like? It is difficult even to imagine such a feast of darkness. All the illnesses and infirmities in the world are unable to restrain the rampant madness of the heart. Truly, so long as the heart remains unenlightened, illnesses and infirmities will not be eliminated; were that not the case, the frenzy of the heart coupled with powerful bodies would horrify the worlds. Long ago it was said of a righteous man that "he walked before the Lord," which meant that he did not violate the principle of Hierarchy, and thus had purified his heart. Through even the slightest purification of the human heart one can derive a cascade of Blessings. Nowadays it is all right to act, if cautiously, but only in cases where the heart has not decayed. You should not get depressed about it, but you need to know that the darkness has intensified and many hearts are putrefying. The significance of the heart is an old truth, but this truth has never been so needed as now.

14. People will ask, "Which energy do you have in mind when you speak of the heart?" Of course, it is the very same Aum, the psychic energy of the three worlds. By studying this energy, you can ascertain that its deposits are multicolored. Certainly, the deposits may be red, purple, or blue, but as they approach the heart, they lose their coloring. The crystal of the heart is white, colorless. Naturally, this resonance of the heart is not observed very often, but you should strive toward it. The ancients used to advise people to place their hands on the needles of young cedars, so that the condensed prana might penetrate their fingertips. There are many ways to receive psychic energy from the vegetable kingdom, but the one regarded as the best is an open heart that knows the line along which to strive.

15. The ignorant, in their hypocrisy, may humiliate us, but the way is one, and nothing will obscure it if the heart is pure. It was wise to liken the heart to a ship, but where there is a ship, there is a helmsman. Courage is born of a pure heart. One might compare it to a rose, where the significance of the flower lies in the number of its petals. If they are torn off, the flower as a whole is injured. Therefore, guard the defenses of the heart. Wisely understand that only the lord of the flower has access to all its petals.

16. Here We are speaking about direct striving to Us. We are speaking about the advantage and success that flow from turning to Us in this way. It would seem enticing to try this remedy out, but how many people actually attempt to take this path? Yet every person who has put Our panacea to the test says that Our Advice is sound. He will confirm that when his thoughts resided with Us, he was always successful in everything. Every failure was due to a stain upon the silver thread. How beautiful it would be if everyone, on completing his day, would ask himself about the quality of his thought during those hours! How powerful he could grow by becoming aware of how his thoughts have strengthened the linking thread! Worthless thoughts could be eradicated as soon as they arise. But the way people are now, they hear without hearing and read without grasping the meaning.

That is why I am advising you again to turn the Teaching into a daily necessity. I advise you to observe the extent to which your surroundings and your associates become successful. Members of close-knit groups should be especially watchful regarding thoughts about each other, so that they do not burden or block the current. Many Teachings advise people to follow this simple discipline, but every book should give them still another reminder, because they are not putting into practice what is most urgent, most necessary.

It is a great happiness for Us when We can have the complete confidence in someone that We have in Ourselves. How secure is the stronghold of an open heart!

17. At all times the Teaching of Life is being poured forth upon the Earth without interruption. It is impossible to imagine earthly existence without this link to the Invisible World. As an anchor of salvation and a guiding light, the Teaching strengthens one's advance through the darkness. But amidst the unceasing shower of Grace, one can notice a rhythm like the swelling of the ocean's waves, in which a special expansion distinctly appears; it is then that the Teachings manifest. In this way you can explain the rhythm of the entire world as one of expansion and submersion; in other words, you can outline the evolution of Being.

18. The disruption of rhythm occurs because of many conditions, but the essential way to avoid this perturbation is to unite in directing yourselves to Us, turning to where there lies a solution for everything. Like a speck of dust that halts a huge wheel, interruption of rhythm cuts the current off. Right now, however, is a time of great tension. With the possibilities so near at hand, events are gathering into a rolling ball, and what seems terrifying will turn out to be salvation.

19. If people could sense the special nature of the moment even partially, they would be helping Us a great deal. Even if they do not discern exactly what is happening, just by sharing in a common mood, they would be strengthening the magnet of the will. People do not realize the extent to which unconscious vegetating complicates the world order. The heart, being a hearth of transformation, ought to give each person an idea of the pressure of the spiritual atmosphere. We should not suppose that the heart suffers only because of things that concern us personally; naturally, it aches on account of the agitation worldwide. You should attempt to unite hearts into a harmonious round, where all dance in accord, for even a hardly tested heart will add its precious energy to the common chalice.

The heart strengthens Our transmissions, pushing aside the new underbrush. There are many untested hearts, but there are still more that are buried under ashes. Many sparks are needed to penetrate those cold ashes.

20. If straight-knowledge is not awakened, then even reality, even the obvious, will remain inaccessible. You cannot force anyone to perceive what is in plain view, however striking. People will come to you saying, "If the Invisible World really exists, why don't I see it or hear it?" Something similar happens with sick people who turn down treatment. They are not averse to getting better, but at the same time they direct their entire consciousness in opposition to the doctor. So it would be useful to compare people who see with people who are sightless in spirit. You could discover the reasons why some gain success while others go to ruin. By comparing obvious manifestations in this way, one can solve many of the problems regarding how the worlds act on each other.

Actually, the Invisible World is quite visible when the eye is unobstructed. You do not need mediumistic phenomena to sense the Light of the Highest World; indeed, you can ascend only to the Highest. That is why all the ruses of lower magic, relying as they do on force, pale in comparison with the first light of the heart. Though not many people know the fires of the heart, these torches must provide light for all. That is why blasphemy of the spirit and rejection of the Teacher are such grave offenses. Let Me say it clearly: you may think a long time about what Teacher to choose, but once you have chosen one, do not fall away! Let us show understanding of the foundations of the structure.

21. Advise people to speak about the spiritual. You may notice a great many useful things in their spiritual recollections. Moreover, a spiritual conversation protects the participants from filth and irritation. Affirmation of spiritual manifestations will reduce the animosity people feel toward the Invisible World. A special aura accumulates where spiritual conversations are often held. They may be imperfect, but such conversations prove to be touchstones that test the nature of those present.

Different peoples contribute their particular transformation of the principles of spirituality, and according to this one can judge what their hearts are suited for.

Avoid disputes about the indisputable. I was recently amazed at all the controversies between the followers of Joan of Arc, Sergius, and Moses. Each disputant claimed that his Protector was not in agreement with the others. But for anyone who knows the Truth, it was sad to hear such fabrications, cooked up to cause disunity. And even if there is no unity, let people at least avoid butting foreheads—otherwise, horns will grow!

Just imagine what would happen if those who know the Truth were to join in harmony and unite their thoughts. What a power would come into being here on Earth, in spite of all the pressure of the atmosphere! Whoever triumphs in spirit is already one of Our own!

22. Advise people to cultivate the ability to think and to observe. The heart cannot carry out its mission if there are fleas instead of a thought and a mole instead of observation. Nobody gets very far traveling with companions like those. Now is the time to deepen the current of thought, for otherwise the masses will not find any way to apply the treasures they receive. Overproduction is a sign of superficial thinking and lack of observational power. It has been said that schools should start holding classes for training in observation and thinking. The heart cannot just be nourished from without; one must also support it by making practical efforts. Steadiness of striving will also come from developing vigilant insight.

23. All of you are familiar with a certain type of preacher who gathers up the bones of various writings and departs with them into oblivion. Reason prompts such people to gather detailed arguments, but the purpose of this conglomeration remains undisclosed, for the heart is silent. That is why we call them the "silent of heart." And although these preachers dole out all kinds of advice to other people, they themselves fall into faint-heartedness as soon as they run into opposition. Truly, only the heart bestows immortality. An affirmation of the heart is itself a revelation of the future. Those who fear the instructions that their own reason has gathered are far removed from the heart. The Ancient Teachings speak about the holy madness. Think of it as a countermeasure to the coldness of calculations; think of it as a vital source that lies beyond all lifeless conditions.

People who deny the Teaching are not far from falling into the abyss. Those who affirm the Truth, even in an imperfect way, are already on the path. When they cross over into the Subtle World, they will not regret that they have called the heart to life.

24. We are fighting a great battle. You should not fear the approach of a time that was proclaimed long ago. When We see a battle for Light before Us, you should not think that it is misfortune creeping up. Nor should you forget that persecution accompanies the greatest success. Only a taut string can resound.

25. It can be said without exaggeration that the majority of heart diseases issue from wealth. That is why those who have embraced the Teaching pull away from wealth or remain its mere custodians.

26. You know that a suggestion can be given in any language; this clearly demonstrates that the meaning and essence understood are not dependent on the conventionalities of various dialects. I believe the manifestation of a heartfelt understanding is a necessary step in approaching Us. The language of the Subtle World brings into actuality the dream about mutual understanding. You have to become fully aware of this possibility before you can make use of it.

27. The Philosopher's Stone is something real. It can be understood both spiritually and physically. The spiritual state that is called "the Stone" corresponds to a harmonious blend of all the deposits of psychic energy. Physically speaking, this preparation is quite close to a preparation of Paracelsus', but he made a substantial error to which he futilely adhered. As for the rest, the Arabic sources on which Paracelsus drew were quite correct.

28. Suggestion can be transmitted by thought, by sound, or by a glance, and it can be reinforced by deep inhalation. What opportunities for scientific observation lie in these actions! It can be observed how inhalation strengthens sound and the emanations of the eye. The various properties of the human glance were noticed long ago. By conducting a series of experiments, you could observe the distance over which the radiations of the eye act. During the experiments it would be instructive to watch how the power of thought combines with the physical emanation of the eye. Only by observation can you begin to appreciate the invisible world of human influences. The web woven by the unconscious activities of thought is so complicated! Do not be surprised that thought lives on in space. Similarly, the physical particles of the glance do not disappear. As we learn to observe, we shall once more remember about the heart and understand the symbol of the piercing arrow.

Many arrows pierce the heart, as shown on ancient images, and on the very same images we see the flame of the heart. Could it be that without arrows a flame is impossible? One can affirm that the basis of the flame's manifestation is a blow; it is like the birth of a new rhythm. The Teacher desires that the rhythm be *accelerando*—this applies to everything.

You should not decide beforehand what is possible. Precisely, what is impossible today will be possible tomorrow.

29. To approach Us, you need an understanding of full freedom. How terrible are the consequences of fear or profit-seeking! Unobscured striving, freed of all burdens, reveals the true path. Only a heart from which no cunning or corruption can be concealed is able to judge where such freedom begins. But the boundaries of the heart's freedom are subtle ones. What things do people manage to pile up around this subtle web! If the heart resounds to a distant earthquake, if our skin senses the warmth flowing from a hand, even over a considerable distance, then how much more strongly must the heart vibrate in response to human radiations! It is precisely this property that contemporary science fails to note sufficiently.

30. Why do so many experiments fail to yield results? First of all, because of impatience and unwillingness to accept responsibility. Sometimes people upbraid Us, saying that help did not come in time. But instead of reproaching Us, the person who asked for help ought to recall how before things were ready he veered off the path or started thinking that his load was overly burdensome. It is very sad for Us to see cowardly deviations or unwillingness to place oneself on the edge of an abyss. How can one intensify energy if not by an extreme situation? Such situations should be regarded not as end points but as beginnings. Likewise, for the exercise of patience it is useful to grasp the concept of a beginning. For some people everything is definitely an end, but for Our students everything is a beginning.

31. How are We to explain, when the heart is silent? How are We to speed things up, when the heart is heavier than iron? How are We to move a heart that has died in spirit? Yet it is possible to learn to value every reverberation of the heart, when the secret flower manifests a multitude of petals that guard the treasure deep within the spirit.

32. "The channels of Grace and the receptacles of the earthly poison"—that is what the chosen ones are called, those who are ready to offer themselves for the benefit of the world. Nobody could bear to take the poison unless he had the Power of Grace; but without the earthly poison, the Power of Grace would carry him away. In this sense, upward striving has an earthly foundation. Of course, many people lack the strength to take the poison; but also, for Grace to be firmly established, the heart must be tempered through actual testing. We consider it a treasure when the heart, having been freed of stress, is ever ready to resound to its environment. This is not easy to achieve unless the energies have been transformed into harmonious crystals, in which case *Ringse* forms, something quite accurately noted in Tibet in the Teachings of the Himalayas.

33. Who would insist that it is easy to follow the Teaching even if one's accumulations are inadequate? But if one's Chalice is brimming over, then the path of the Teaching is inevitable. We can understand the difficulty of accepting the earthly poison, for each of Us has taken a measureless amount of poison. In the same way that a magnet attracts certain metals, the heart accepts Grace. And in the same way that a sponge absorbs water, the pores of the skin take in the earthly poison. But prana, when consciously absorbed, alleviates the flow of the poisons.

34. People are divided not only according to organic characteristics but also according to the elements; certain attachments live on in their consciousness. Nobody will be able to discern as many gradations of flame as the people of fire. Nobody will be as fond of the water as the people of that element. Naturally, the people of fire will also be especially drawn to Agni Yoga. They will feel the absolute need for it. They will approach the Teaching of Fire not out of reasoning but because it is the sole solution. People are able to understand the need for the Teaching when they are at an impasse with no way out.

35. The most difficult thing for people is to combine extreme spiritual exaltation with tireless action. Success requires a high degree of spiritual tension, but in each action a certain reserve of energy must be maintained. An exhausted action loses its beauty and the magnetic power that comes from being convincing. A singer who has exhausted her vocal reserve primarily arouses pity. The manifestation of extreme spiritual tension should not express itself in acts of desperation, for in that case the manifestation of inner energy would dissolve in activity that is alien to the spirit. You should have a firm understanding of this law, in order to avoid turning into a windmill. I advise you to gather all the forces of the spirit, so that you do not scatter them in unrestrained actions.

36. If you notice signs indicating that someone has been chosen, do not interfere with the activities of this Emissary. One can learn to recognize the signs of Agni Yoga and in accordance with them recognize the path of the chosen one. So the manifestation of an Emissary lies not in externals but in the special character of his action. It is only natural that actions of special significance should strike people's consciousness; both sides, in their own way, show understanding of these actions. We cannot name a single Emissary around whom a wondrous accumulation of energy did not take place. Just as clouds come before a thunderstorm, clouds always emerge before the affirmation of Truth. But you already know the meaning of these spiritual phenomena. One can establish how over the centuries the glad Tidings are repeated and how they spread among the multitudes. From the spiritual Summit one can perceive the rhythm that conveys the echoes of the Teaching.

When you notice even the slightest signs that a person is being called, be careful not to interfere, for an Agni Yogi's foundation is fire, and you must not put it out. And who would dare to turn the fiery element against himself? Every flame extinguished resounds, which is why the karma of an extinguisher is like the fate of a murderer.

38. An Agni Yogi is economical in everything, not out of stinginess but because he knows the value of the energy that is poured forth from above. Thus, he conserves his own energy as well as the energy around him. People usually fall into error by assuming that energy is only in great actions; they forget that expenditure of the very same energy, so precious in its essence, is far greater in small matters. Small actions and small things clog life up. You should be especially careful of dust, which mixes with the emanations of objects and scatters the personal energy that should be preserved in a single channel. Thus, we shall safeguard everything connected with the energy of the Hierarchy.

38. How necessary it is to get used to understanding everything spiritual! We can expect nothing from the heart if our thought does not find cause to rejoice in the very mention of anything spiritual. Indeed, we must attain the stage where we radiate light from our innermost being, for it is then that we are true coworkers with the higher worlds. Radiating the light of Grace, we are at the same time doctors, creators, and protectors on the descending line of the Hierarchy. First we see the outer light, and then we come to know the light within ourselves; but only after the kindling of the "torch" can we radiate Light.

39. It is extremely important to speak of the spiritual. The path of the spirit, like nothing else, develops the consciousness and makes life pure. Look upon conversations about the spiritual as practical training for the heart. You need to undertake purification of the consciousness as a path to success. Again I am not speaking abstractly but am telling you something

to be put into practice. Try an experiment in which you administer medicines to an intelligent person or animal and one devoid of intelligence. It is instructive to compare and see the extent to which consciousness intensifies all the manifestations and processes. Besides, a conversation about the spiritual directs the A-energy upward along a definite channel. Precisely, *Ketub* is a unifier of energies. So you should not waste time seeking after the commonplace, when there are so many possibilities that draw you upward.

The heart's joy lies in striving upward.

40. The Invisible World takes part in the earthly life much more than is generally supposed. Advise people to pay attention to the multitude of small phenomena that usually go unnoticed. What build up unforgettable results are not striking or blinding manifestations but those that the limited mind calls "coincidence" or "accident." If we consider all the unexplained manifestations of the heart, even an unprepared mind will notice an unusualness that contradicts the conclusions of medicine. Let us take, for example, the so-called double pulse, where an external influence creates two focuses in the organism, as it were. But the concept of cosmic energy explains with perfect simplicity how closely we are linked with the Higher Forces, and the external fires and light will remind us of the same thing if our minds allow them to be seen.

One has to understand the immediacy of these manifestations without losing the ability to think rationally. That way one can replace magic with the Teaching of the Heart. Everyone has a heart, and everyone has an energy potential contained within that heart, which means that the New World is not prohibited to anyone. We say that the New World is cognition of the Invisible, even if that cognition is at a rudimentary stage. Even that degree of understanding would set life on new foundations.

The unifier of energies, the unifier of knowledge, the fiery *Ketub* is understood by an Agni Yogi. When people strive to cognize the Invisible, it will become clear how imperceptibly the strata of the new consciousness are being formed, and how this consciousness is changing the essence of life.

41. Sometimes let your heart converse with the Higher World. This conversation can be held in various languages. It could be that the heart will gather together memories of hours from many lives. Or perhaps the conversation will be a silent one without instructions or advice, one that only ascends and grows stronger in that ascent. And there may be the silence of gratitude or the silence of the power of readiness. The flame of the heart flares forth in striving to unite with the Highest World. Only the heart will find the path to the Hierarchy. The heart will strengthen itself with the Power of the Highest. Only the heart will serve as a stronghold in battle.

42. Vast, tight, and intense is the battle. We know how the heightened intensity of some people leads to the strengthening of others. When I advise you to conserve your energy, it means that the forces have been gathered for battle. The conflagration is spreading across the entire globe. In comparison with the present conflict, the former one is nothing. Conserving your energy is just a sign that you are fit for action. Similar caution is necessary in everything, since We Ourselves have approached with measures that have no precedent for the present race. But it is impossible to leave the world to decompose! Consider this time to be extremely serious! And knowing this, strive to Me!

43. Magic is like a massage. A massage artificially

limits and restores the body's features and blood circulation. In a similar way, magic artificially links people with the Invisible World and restores communication with it. A normal organism does not need massage; a developed spirit has no need of magic. Massage works on unhealthy organs and limbs. Magic offers a Teaching about conditions and palliatives without revealing the simplest approach to the Higher World. Once massage therapy has begun, it is necessary to increase the amount, or else the tissue may be threatened with abnormal growth or destruction. As for magic, it is necessary to go on increasing one's mastery of it, or else the elements will start to press hard on the retreating practitioner. So we find the same laws in effect when we compare the physical and spiritual worlds. The same laws reveal that the simplest paths are much closer to a developed consciousness. So long as moderation is practiced, the stomach will not grow larger. So long as the spirit is being refined, the heart will not fall silent.

44. It is necessary to establish once and for all that Yoga is not magic. First of all, there is nothing artificial in Yoga. The kinship and harmony of the laws of Being are opposed to coercion in any form. A Yogi will not disturb the Primary Energy unless there is a dire necessity. With a Yogi, complete cooperation with nature is created. So a Yogi's knowledge is based primarily upon straight-knowledge. It is upon this pure surface that the signs of experience are inscribed.

45. The process by which energy is compressed or intensified is similar to the workings of a pump. Thus, the upward impetus of energy is sure to be conditioned by downward pressure. People usually regard this pressure as misfortune or failure, whereas it is the physical threshold of ascent. Oppression, of course, manifests in an entirely different way; but any person who has attained ascent is able to determine moments of inner or outer compression. It is sad to see how uninformed people, not understanding the law of the pump, give way to compressive forces. This situation is especially serious nowadays, when a mass consciousness is being molded, when it is urgently necessary to harmonize thousands of consciousnesses that are disorderly, uneducated, and ignorant of the simplest and most unshakeable laws. It would be so easy for these masses to lose sight of the fact that intensification is the gate to ascent.

46. A guarantee is a concept of tremendous significance. It creates a chain of hearts and turns Chaos into the conscious arteries of Space. The symbol revealed to you at night was highly significant. The serpent of darkness is going to devour your friend if he does not enter into conscious communion. The responsibility of the guarantor is also great. Not without reason is it said that the hand burns! Indeed, it is no exaggeration to say that a fiery pain shoots through the guarantor when the one for whom he vouched makes mistakes; but there cannot be any other way of carrying on constructive work. Therefore, learn to be cautious and attentive.

47. In what does happiness lie? In being able to sit still without daring to stir up the Primal Energy with one's thought? Or in directing one's thought toward a new construction of life? I first spoke to you about action, but now let us affirm the significance of thought. Even the loftiest action impinges on relatively low strata; only thought, on account of its nature, is able to act upon the Primary Substance. First I spoke about action as something accessible and evident; but now that the consciousness has broadened sufficiently, it is time for the significance of thought to be affirmed. On the surface of existence subsist multitudes of actions performed without thought, actions indistinguishable from those of the animal world. But if we are speaking about straight-knowledge and the heart, then we have to affirm that thought is a power and co-creation of Existence. Notice that I speak neither of debate nor of intellectual speculation but of thought, which sweeps over the surface of Substance with an individual rhythm and thereby creates without limit.

48. Yesterday we began discussion of a new approach to the Era of Maitreya. Thought is the manifestation of true happiness. Thought that is divorced from the heart will not penetrate the surface of Being, while thought that issues from the heart is like an unstoppable arrow! You should not get upset when a thought is conceived during a powerful influx of energy. Thoughts so conceived are like a battering ram that will penetrate into the depths of Being. So after discussing outer action, let us learn to value the actuality of thought's creative power.

49. The note sounding from Space is amplified still more, and the new rhythms are like a new armor that the dark ones do not expect. You can constantly create new vibrations and thereby repel darkness.

50. A weaver has his warp before him, for without it even a master craftsman would be unable to embody his thought-creativity. To create with thought, the Cosmic Thought-warp is also necessary; that is what We call the Primary Substance from which fiery thought strikes the spark of creation. This same work can be performed by practiced thinkers and also by children who are aflame with an indispensable desire. One cannot judge the character of an anchorite or an ascetic unless one knows the level and quality of that person's thought. Nor can one judge a singer or a poet without knowing what sort of thought-creativity he or she radiates. We gradually wean ourselves from the habit of criticizing, because only thought-creativity is the Creator's coworker. So let us carefully gather all the existing thoughts that can bring benefit by penetrating Akasha and reaching the essence of Being. The greatest comfort lies in the fact that no one is devoid of thought, so once they are aware of its significance, everyone can cultivate this inborn blessing.

51. Sometimes people say, "I got so carried away with my daydreams that my heart began aching." The heartache comes not from evil fantasies but from the intensity of luminous desires. The heart's anguish, first of all, fills our essence with the substance of power. Naturally, the sculpting of Akasha is not always connected with heart pangs, but in any case, the feelings of pain indicate tension and cooperation with the Primary Thought-warp. Thus, one should not fear that anguish is a sign of evil.

52. Those who are entering the path of Great Service sometimes fear that their spiritual reserve may not be large enough for them to go on giving constantly. Although they know that the giving hand does not grow poor, it is difficult for them to apply this in its spiritual sense. But the same thing is said about the birds of the heavens that have plenty of grain for the morrow. Truly, when one cooperates with the Hierarchy, the spiritual store will not run out. The heart that cherishes the Image of the Lord will not fall silent. So nobody need fear that the spiritual store will be used up, for it is inexhaustible. You can hand out these treasures—just hold tight to the silver thread.

53. A warrior of the spirit who lacks experience sometimes falls into perplexity: "If the battle really is that fierce, how come my hands and feet are still intact?" As though the intensity of a battle is measured only in broken bones! But often the ordinary people participating in the earthly battle do not feel its intensity; only the leader realizes what is taking place.

54. People are rightfully asking, "How will the significance of thought be different in the New Era? Since the importance of thought is being affirmed so persistently, does it mean that thought is being given a special role in the regeneration of life?" This is perfectly reasonable. During the Black Age, Kali Yuga, thought has revolved around man, and magnetism has only extended over small distances, while in the New Era thought means Space! That is why we must not think personally but spatially.

55. For the majority of people, spatial thinking is quite difficult. To think spatially, you first of all have to retain your personality while liberating yourself from egoism. This antithesis will strike many people as absurd; for them, egoism and personality are the very same thing. The concept of a powerful personality devoted to the Common Good is something that surpasses the imagination of most people, but without personality thinking would have no potency. Thinking generated in egoism adds one more dose of poison to the planet's infected aura. Many people also find it difficult to realize that the substance of thought is indestructible and not linked to certain strata of space alone, which means the responsibility for each thought is great. An arrow can reach a bird of prey, but what can destroy a vile thought?

56. A wise householder does not light all the fires unless he has a special reason. Likewise, ancient legends mention a mountain surrounded by flame, but it does not say anywhere that the fire burned

continually—it rose according to the degree of necessity. Your fires also shine forth according to the degree of necessity. Whether it is the Eye of Brahma, or the wings, or the rays radiating from the larynx, or any of the other twenty-one principal fires, one has to let them flare forth according to their natures. It needs to be pointed out that the fires act through the power of the bond with the Hierarchy. It is impermissible for the centers to flare up in uncontrolled burning. In the Great Service solicitude and caution are the first principles of the Higher Cooperation. Every particle of the energy of Elohim and every *Urūcī* We protect from the Fire of Space. This accountability is especially needed when an intense battle is raging.

57. One needs to develop a firm understanding of the Great Service. Pure hearts can show steady support for the Great Service without fatigue or carelessness. How destructive is the dull nature of carelessness! And how many people, even among those who know, are unable to avoid it! In ancient times it was called the "grey serpent." Let friends adopt the manifestation of vigilance and attentiveness.

58. Over the years the significance of the laying of magnets and the importance of travel through various countries have become clear to you. This is not some superstitious remedy but the application of rays and magnetism, a subject already familiar to science to a limited extent. Even skeptics do not deny the special significance of personal influences. From there it is but one step to the concept of a strong magnet connected with a Center of manifested energies. Nor is it difficult to understand the significance of a human organism passing through a certain space, for the organism is an extremely powerful chemical battery. Even dogs feel the power of a person's tracks. How much more fully does this emanation develop when awareness is being applied! That is why the significance of envoys is very great and they continue to be dispatched.

Truly, you can observe where the foot of an Envoy has stepped and how a magnet has attracted an entire region into an orbit of activity—such has been said of the Angels of Life and Death. That is why you should keep a steady eye on events and discover the vast system underlying them. Since even ordinary astrologers can note the correlation between great events occurring at a distance, how instructive it could be for you to follow how the paths are being fulfilled, seeing that you know where they lead!

59. There are three circumstances that may place a special burden on a person's karma. The first—rejection of the Teacher; the second—suspicion that the bond with the Hierarchy may bring misfortune; and the third—evasion of a responsible mission. Only the heart can whisper that rejection or suspicion or evasion has begun. A person who has betrayed the Teacher many times is insisting, in his madness, that he has never even thought of treachery and never considered evading anything. A darkened mind can come up with a thousand justifications in order to conceal what long ago was inscribed on the scroll of karma. Better to not approach in the first place than to manifest apostasy! For an apostate, the night never ends! But this is no punishment; it is only the consequence of what has been sown. The heart is able to discern the seed of treachery.

60. People pay little attention to the Invisible World. You need to consciously accustom yourself to understanding its presence in everything. You can look upon Space as a conducting wire to the Invisible Worlds that are observing us.

61. One has to live through the difficult hour that is called "The Dragon of the Threshold." We call that hour "The Tearing of the Veil." That is how We designate the time when darkness intends to tear the veil but ends up only revealing the distances. But courage is needed; indeed, how else can the accumulation of courage come to light?

62. Just as the sun is the heart of the system, the human heart is the sun of the organism. There are many sun-hearts, and the Universe represents a system of hearts; that is why the cult of Light is the cult of the heart. To understand this abstractly means to leave the heart out in the cold; but as soon as the Light of the sun-heart comes alive, the need for the magnet's warmth will make it shine forth like a true sun. It has been said: "Let your heart lead you in crossing *Santana*." That is how you can make the concept of the heart resistant to the cold. You can look upon the rhythm of the heart as the rhythm of life. The Teaching about the Heart is as bright as the sun, and the warmth of the heart speeds as swiftly as a sunbeam. Everyone has felt astonishment at how a ray of the rising sun can instantly insulate everything from the cold. The heart can do the very same thing!

I am speaking of the warmth of the heart now that it is especially necessary. A thought surging forth in aspiration sets space on fire, while the warmth of the heart is a constant hearth. Courage dwells in the warmth of the heart—remember this! The manifestation of the dark forces acts like frost on a sown field. Only the heart's warmth provides a radiant shield. But just as we conduct tests on light waves with delicate care, we should approach the heart with caution and solicitude.

63. A heart that has dedicated itself to goodness

radiates grace unceasingly, without depending on intentional transmissions. Likewise, the sun sends forth its rays without premeditation. A heart that has pledged itself to evil sends out arrows consciously, unconsciously, and unceasingly. The heart of goodness sows around itself health, smiles, and spiritual wellbeing. The heart of evil destroys warmth and, like a vampire, sucks away the vital force. And so the activity of hearts—whether it be good or evil—goes on without pause. The conditions of good and evil have a different meaning on the lowest plane of Being and in the Highest World. You can picture a radiant furnace of light and a yawning abyss of darkness. It is terrifying when the swords of the demons and the Archangels are crossed! Amid the flashes of battle, so many hearts are drawn to Light or to darkness!

64. One needs to clearly visualize the ceaseless radiation of the heart. It is necessary to understand why the presence of evil hearts is so painful to good hearts. Neither the smile nor the forced grin of evil can conceal what the heart is radiating. The establishment of good in the heart in no way excludes righteous indignation, but irritation is the domain of evil. Only by striving to the Hierarchy can a person determine the boundary between many feelings.

65. The crossing of currents is as hard to bear as the sound of swords being whetted. Since even the sound of paper being torn places a burden on the heart, what a powerful contraction of the nerves is induced when all kinds of tensions and currents cross! Once more let us turn to the panacea. Only an intensified striving to the Hierarchy can weaken all the arrows of the currents.

66. You know about the influence of human emanations on plants, and you also know about the influence of color. Now it is necessary to recall the significance of sound. The similarity of these various influences is quite remarkable. Since an open, brightly resonant heart is needed to increase the potentials of a plant, then when it comes to the influence of sound, consonance and all the combinations of the dominant tones are necessary for the same purpose. A manifestation of dissonance cannot strengthen the flow of energy. Dissonances may be useful in the way they affect people, for as an antithesis they can reinforce the rhythm of consciousness; but with plants, where consciousness is minimal, dissonance is only a condition that retards growth. With minerals, dissonance may be a source of disintegration. Truly, a rose is a symbol of consonance, and the dominant chord of the rose's radiation is linked with the glow of the heart. Few experiments have been conducted on the effect of sound on plants, but the ancients believed that the finest flowers grew by the temples, where the harmonies of voice and music often rang out.

67. Seek out and commune with everything that is refined and subtle in its substance. I am talking not only about objects but also about people. Among people, do not choose those who desire only material manifestations. Even people who recognize spirituality are not worthwhile if they are seeking after crude manifestations. They will not be the first to draw near the Kingdom of the Heart. Perhaps others, who have not seen the Subtle World but have understood it in their hearts, will leave the wizards and magicians behind. The establishment of the inner eye and the unfolding of the fires depend upon refinement of the consciousness; only these gates lead to the Kingdom of the Heart. Skeptics who want to touch the wounds of Light with their own fingers are unable to open their hearts to the cognition that flashes forth as fast as lightning. Certainly, test everything that exists! But without the glow of the heart, these tests will be like the embers from yesterday's fire.

What is being said about the cognition of the heart is not abstract. If someone is unable to understand this refinement, how can he perceive the higher strata of the Subtle World? How can a person who lacks this spiritual cognition accept the subtle Ether, which nourishes the higher body? It would be pointless to direct one's cognitive powers to phantoms that envelop everything with their shrouds of decay. So test the World with your heart.

68. After all the demarcations have been made, we inevitably arrive at the synthesis of the heart. We need not mention that silence arises from an intermingling of all the sounds. So let us learn to correlate the heart with silence. But this silence will not be a void; it will saturate space with the synthesis of thought. Just as a heartfelt prayer has no need of words, a saturated silence has no need of formulas. An intensified silence requires creation of many strata of thought as well as many benevolent desires. So the heart, intensified by silence and full of energy like an electric generator, beats out the rhythm of the Universe, and personal desires are transformed into the all-guiding Universal Will. That is how cooperation with the distant worlds develops.

69. Complaints about insufficient guidance are the usual thing. People are used to covering up their peculiarities with complaints. But if there is anything that has not been grudged to humanity, it is Guidance; people just need to pay attention to everything that is being given! The multitude of impulses that spring from spiritual influences may vanish without benefit, but they also may work harm by remaining misconstrued in the pantries of a person's consciousness. It can be safely asserted that only a very small fraction of spiritual influences find a proper application; especially obstructive are the habits that drive the consciousness into conventional paths. They also enfeeble the faculties of the heart when it is ready to resound to the Highest Guidance. Precisely, it is the heart that knows the highest from the lowest; but when enfeebled and befogged, the heart itself will reside at the lowest level, where even the lowest will appear to be the highest. Purity of heart is the most essential possession. There is no room for wisdom, courage, and selflessness in a beclouded heart. But Guidance will whisper about deeds of *podvig*, and this advice should not seem terrifying or harsh.

70. Multitudes of extremely urgent transmissions end up calling forth only vague hesitations. You can observe how even worthy spirits often fail to carry out in time an Instruction they have been given, and how trivial are the circumstances that prevent them from doing so. Compared to the transmissions from Above, their actions and habits seem so petty, so incommensurate with the urgent Instructions. Again, people should not be dreaming about magic formulas as a way to attract Guidance, for It is near at hand, and the magnet of a pure heart will clear the path. The most substantial thing a seeker obtains will be this magnet, which attracts and opens things up.

Truly, it is joyous to be in the presence of the pure of heart!

71. True solemnity is built upon the highest degree of tension. Solemnity is not rest, not satisfaction, not the end; it is, precisely, a beginning—that is, resoluteness and a march forward on the path of Light.

Hardships are inevitable, for they are the wheels of striving. Terrible pressures are inevitable, for without them the explosion lacks power. How could joy arise from frivolity? Only lust lies in frivolity, while joy abides in the solemn victory of the spirit. And the victory of the spirit lies in affirmation of the unshakeable principles from which everything begins. When the Banner of Peace is being raised, you should be full of solemnity.

72. Though already on their way, a multitude of possibilities go unrealized because of personal complaints arising out of self-pity. When people begin to weigh how much they have sacrificed and how little they have received from the Teacher, the meaning of the Teaching disappears. People calculate what they receive like a day laborer counting up his wages; they do not commeasure what they receive by comparing it with eternity, that for which they exist. The idea of getting paid for good intentions is so totally inapplicable to what the process of perfection means! But it has to be said: a lot of people prefer posing as a day laborer, not because their hearts are depraved but because their imagination has been poorly cultivated. With many people, the straight-knowledge of Eternity is cut off because they turn to self-pity.

All Teachings repeat about the burden of the flesh in order to direct attention to the superiority of the spirit. The Teaching ought to be accepted as the source of true privileges, which are inalienable. One should value how the Teaching deepens the consciousness and provides life with true possibilities, so long as these are not rejected. This simple consideration is rarely paid much attention. People would rather send their complaints out into space, thereby calling down upon themselves a shower of stones. But let us not frighten them, or else they may accuse us of lacking love. People ascribe such strange conditions to the manifestation of love that you would think their love was coined in a mint! But you need love to travel the path to the Infinite. A Guide is so absolutely necessary! When in the state of final tension we clamber up the slippery rocks, seeking out the thread of salvation, the Guiding Hand will touch us.

73. Even in the most ancient times people understood the significance of the heart. They regarded the heart as the Dwelling of God. When they took oaths, they placed their hands on their hearts. Even with the fiercest tribes, they drank the blood of the heart and ate their enemies' hearts in order to acquire strength. That was how the significance of the heart was expressed. But now, in our enlightened times, the heart has been reduced to nothing more than a physiological organ. The ancients drank from the skulls of their enemies; the chalices used in sacred rituals were fashioned out of the parietal bone. Those who knew about the "bell center," the Brahmarandhra, understood that magnetic intensification transmutes the substance of the bone. But nowadays people just laugh at these powerful curative substances. The most trivial discovery attracts hordes of people eager to make use of it, while laboratories full of the most powerful chemicals are forgotten. But a natural union of the three kingdoms of nature is what provides the most effective compounds. You should first of all remind people how important the heart is as a unifier of the worlds. Is the fire of the heart any different from the very Fire of Space?

One can get a deep grasp of the constant communion with the distant worlds that the ancients were said to practice, for the magnetism of the distant worlds brings imponderable power. And doesn't the heart sense the subtlest of vibrations?

74. The various concepts of the will should be thoroughly thought through and delineated. The will of the brain has become the citadel of the West, while the East still has its stronghold in the heart. When conveying a suggestion, a Western hypnotist uses his will, straining centers in his extremities and eyes; but the emanation thus transmitted not only exhausts itself quickly but also brings on fatigue and, in any case, only acts over very small distances. Spatial attainments are not possible through transmissions of the will of the intellect. But the heart of the East has no need for tension in the extremities, nor does it needlessly intensify energy; rather, it sends forth its thoughts without any limitations regarding place. Heart suggestion, as a natural channel of communication, does not bring harm to the person who issues the suggestion or the person who receives it. The Western method is always obvious from the outside, while the Eastern method has nothing external about it; quite the contrary, the person issuing the suggestion does not look at the receiver, for he has the image of the destination in his heart. The advantages in heart activity are numerous and beyond dispute, but to obtain them you first of all must realize the heart's significance.

The power of the heart overcomes absolutely anything. The heart is able to know the meaning of events that happen far away. The heart is able to soar, thereby strengthening the necessary connections. The heart is able to partake of the distant worlds. Try this simply by transmission of the will of the brain, and you will perceive what is different about the will of the heart. The Epoch of Maitreya is the Age of the Heart! Only with the heart can you fathom the value of Maitreya's treasures! Only with the heart can you understand how greatly all accumulations and all straight-knowledge are needed for the future.

75. Love, *podvig*, labor, creativity—these summits of ascent maintain the upward momentum regardless of the order in which they develop. And what a multitude of attendant concepts they encompass! What is love without sacrifice, achievement without courage, work without patience, or creativity without self-perfection? And over this entire host of beneficial values rules the heart. Without it the most patient people, the most courageous, the most intensely striving will be nothing more than cold coffins! The heartless ones will be weighed down with knowledge and wingless. It is distressing when someone does not respond to the Call in time! It is distressing when someone does not fully follow the Hierarchy! Often people try to hide from themselves their own rejection of the Hierarchy. Traveler, can you in all sincerity acknowledge that you are ready to follow the Hierarchy? Could it be that your readiness is just up to the first bend, up to the first stage, where only the Hierarchy can help out? Could it be that when the times get tough you will forget, that you will remember the Hierarchy only in affluence?

From the very beginning, when the Teaching was first being transmitted, you were often amazed at the twists and turns and deviations made even by people close to you. You can understand the sorrow of seeing how a student on the threshold often rushes off into the forest. My Hand stays with the traveler who strides onward with complete readiness.

76. A very tortuous line runs between the worthy and the unworthy. Only the heart can find its way through all the folds of the brain. But now is the time to pass onward into the knowledge of spirit-creativity. Perhaps it seems strange to many people that even the Subtle World is invisible to them, although in the gradation of the various worlds it is still rather dense. This means that the physical eye is so crude that it cannot even discern the next stage of bodily transformation. If people are trying to improve even scientific instruments, then how desirable it is to refine the human apparatus itself! But unless the help of the heart is attracted, work on this achievement cannot move forward. A person who can feel through the heart is already able to advance beyond the limits of the body.

An apostasy that renounces spirit-creativity retards a person for many lives to come. It is inexcusable to enter a low state when your eyes have already been unsealed. Let us recall what work it is to break through the physical shell, what measures are used to move the consciousness forward after it has undergone tension! After all that effort, can you just turn back?

77. Many people are suffering from possession during humanity's transition to spirit-creativity; it is as if somebody had made spare keys to loose locks. It is especially necessary to examine people with care. Moreover, you need to remember that the possessed have a peculiar way of thinking that is full of contradictions. Someone who wants to help them can use the power of suggestion to drive out the possessing agent, or he can leave such people in peace and even, if possible, completely isolate them. That works because the possessor is in need not so much of the subject himself as the ability to exert influence through the subject on the people around him. The worst thing is to pester the possessed person by urging him to show the good judgment of which he is incapable. It is bad to start showing pity for the possessed person

out loud or begin finding fault with his contradictions. The expression of a command, strong and striking, or else isolation, can lighten the lot of a weak heart. It is through weakness of the heart that possession sneaks in. The fire of the heart singes the fur on the shaggy visitors.

Rejection of the Teacher puts an end to all possibilities, especially when the rejection has entered into the student's consciousness long before he or she is possessed. So it is that people often awaken dormant denials; of course, rejection of the Teacher is the primary consequence, because anything chaotic is first and foremost outraged by creativity and cooperation. In the chaotic lurk the seeds of evil, which are crushed out only by hard experience. But nowadays an unprecedented number of people are possessed. Darkness also wishes to express itself.

78. Originally the boundary between the physical and the Subtle World was not so clear-cut. In the most ancient annals you can find fragmentary indications about the very close cooperation between these worlds. During the densification of the physical, the focus of the heart was needed to maintain a balance between the physical and the subtle energies. The corporeal world itself was necessary as a way of reworking matter and thereby increasing energies. But as you know, the intellect strove for isolation, which ended up impeding evolution. The time of Kali Yuga has been a difficult one; Satya Yuga must once more bring together the worlds, which were separated by force. One has to wait for this time in solemnity, wait for it as the return of the perfection ordained. So let us agree to pay the proper attention to spirit-creativity. We can grow used to thinking about things from this perspective. Thus, we need to concern ourselves with what is most significant in giving life its direction. Whoever schools himself in maintaining a balance between the worlds is making his path a great deal easier.

79. Since the heart is an accumulator and transmuter of various energies, there must be more favorable conditions for arousing and attracting these energies. The most fundamental condition is work, mental as well as physical. In the motion of work, energies are gathered from space; but one must understand work as a natural process that enriches life. Thus, every kind of work is a blessing, while the vagaries of inaction are extremely harmful in a cosmic sense. Love for the endlessness of labor is in itself an initiation of considerable degree; it prepares you for the conquest of time. Being in a condition where you have conquered time guarantees you a place in the Subtle World, where work is an unavoidable condition, just as it is in the body. A complaint about having to work can only come from a slave of the body.

80. Connecting the consciousnesses in the Subtle World with the consciousnesses of incarnate people will be the next conquest. Indeed, Being is in spirit, in space, and between the worlds, while on Earth there are only envoys of the transmutation of energies and the transformation of matter. Thus, the lifespan of the incarnate is nothing compared to that of the entities in all the other states of existence.

The belt of labor has to be drawn more tightly, and this should be regarded not as a misfortune but as a means of attaining the next step. The plowman who directs his energy to transforming the earth's crust is often able to extend his hand to the Rishi himself, the Rishi who watches over humanity, blessing it with His thought. You were right in remarking that every reaper was a sower, and every sower a reaper.

And since the temple is in spirit, the justification is in spirit, and the victory is in spirit, you can adorn life with a splendor that is constant and true. Get used to the beauty of labor and the creativity of thought, for with them we shall conquer darkness.

81. If you meet a person who is truly aspiring to build on a grand scale, you will not start talking about your morning porridge or some trivial things that happened the other day; in line with the dimensions of your companion's thought, you will show striving to the future. In the same way, We outline in Our conversation a future course that extends like a cable attached to an anchor, a cable upon which you pull yourself up in safety, a cable that you reach out to with growing desire. That is how We train the heart to build the rhythm of the future, because without such slight shifts forward people will find it difficult to enter into the reality of the future, just as they find it hard to realize the harm of so much that they do. Obviously, if someone throws trash into a carefully prepared chemical mixture, the reaction will be different from what was expected. There is no power that can restore the original combination. In the same way, evil deeds cannot vanish into thin air; that is why it is easier to avert evil than to rectify it.

82. It is difficult to wipe away an evil act. You would have to build on so many extra stories and towers to muffle the howling of a vicious prisoner who tries again and again to get through any door that is not shut all the way. Ask people about how they are relentlessly pursued not only by their evil thoughts and deeds but also by their unsuccessful ones. The path of life is covered with the marks of actions that manifest as indelible spots; that is why it is wise to strive into the future. In flight to the future there is no time to get

spots on the white wings.

83. Distinguish tension from fatigue. These conditions differ, but there are many similarities. You should sense when it would be beneficial to put a stop to them by transferring attention to another center. The golden balance is especially applicable here. How many entities in the Subtle World are waiting for fatigue to take place! Not only evil entities who, in their own way, tense the will, but also a multitude of featureless disincarnates are trying to cling to the magnet of the heart. People complain that their thinking becomes confused during fatigue. How could this not happen when the incoherent thoughts of the Subtle World's lower strata are percolating through a person's consciousness! The lower strata are not steady in their thinking, and the flakes of their fragmentary thoughts litter up space. In terms of the tension of energy, a clear-cut thought imbued with hatred is more valuable than the muddle of unconscious thinking. It is very distressing for an Agni Yogi to come in contact with a swarm of ghostly grey thoughts. First and foremost, the Teacher is concerned about the direction of thought. The highest degree of speed and focus is developed over great distances.

84. The spiritual battle causes an influx of blood into the extremities. An Agni Yogi with a fiery Chalice is not left behind; help is assured when a flaming heart gathers brave spirits around it. The Battle is not on the physical plane. It is not small earthly forces that vie with each other; rather, Forces with ages of experience have gathered to determine their destinies! The earthly reflections of the Battle swell out like unexpected blisters! But the fiery heart does not act according to earthly signs. The tension is very high!

People dream about freedom, yet they keep their hearts in a dungeon!

85. Freedom is precious as a way of protecting the personality and individualizing the energies attracted. But it is freedom that is the most distorted concept of all. Instead of being suffused with freedom, life is filled with tyranny and slavery, the very features that exclude cooperation and respect for personality. So it is that some people manage to form their existence from an exclusive combination of tyranny and slavery. Of course, people talk repeatedly about freedom, but they are not even sure what its characteristics are. But when they firmly understand the real meaning of freedom, their consciousness will be raised. Intense quests for freedom reveal that the spirit, in its potential, is longing to attain new heights, but nobody has taught it how to handle the treasure of freedom.

86. Cooperation can be an adornment for a conscious spirit. What conveys the concept of cooperation is neither coercion nor, still less, competition, but rather an increase in energies. Those who have understood the Hierarchy with their heart also clearly understand what it means to work together. A person who teaches freedom is a manifestation of the Hierarchy, because first of all it was said to take the shortest path, gather up your forces, and ground yourselves in an understanding of individualization, a rainbow being fortified by each of its rays.

We only cast out manifest traitors, as cosmic litter; with everyone else, We find the ray that they have transmuted into action.

87. Vengeance is rightfully condemned by all the Teachings. The original wrong may have been committed with only partial awareness and even on the spur of the moment, while vengeance is always thought out and consciously intensified in the heart. Vengeance is like a megaphone that amplifies the wrong, which is why its harm, in the spatial sense, is very great. Vengeance does not bear much resemblance to indignation. Like the urge to threaten, indignation may come and go quickly; but the premeditated acts of vengeance poison the atmosphere far and wide. It has been said that the intention is equivalent to the action, but it should be kept in mind that this applies to the action of thought. It is extremely difficult for humanity to get used to considering such things. For contemporary humanity thought has turned into an insignificant cerebral contraction. For most people nowadays, since the eye does not see the consequence of thought, it means that the consequence does not exist. At this rate we will come to a point where the whole process of thinking is denied! The heart is in a more advantageous position; it moves and makes noise—and so the heart is able to knock.

88. When an overflow of psychic energy manifests, it gives rise to many symptoms in the extremities, as well as in the throat and stomach. Soda is useful in bringing on a discharge of energy, as is hot milk. The Teacher is watching over the fires. The fires not only illuminate the aura but they also stay on in space, which is what makes them so very important. These manifested fires, in their turn, focus the energy and give birth to new nodes.

89. Be on your guard against senseless criticism. Not only does it contain a quality that causes decay, it also delivers a weak person who criticizes into the power of the criticized. A weak but cruel heart may give rise to a hostile reaction in the aura of the person criticized. Moreover, usually the person doing the criticizing is not strong himself, or else he would not find time to indulge in judging others. The unjust nature of criticism, like that of any other lie, weakens the already insignificant consciousness of the self-appointed judge, thereby causing him extensive harm; whereas the person unfairly judged only gains by strengthening his magnet with the attractive force of new auras. Readers might ask, "Why these ethical discussions in the book *Heart*?" First of all you should remind them about the hygiene of the heart. The hygiene of the heart ought to be regarded as an absolutely necessary activity. You should discard all discussions about abstract ethics. Everything is good that is healthy in every aspect. We insist that anyone who has entered the path of the Teaching shall, first of all, be healthy in spirit. Can a person walk in evil toward the Light? Truly, the Light will detect every grain of evil.

90. Look upon the hours of Communion as a prayer, as a casting away of everything evil and destructive. If a person's thought does not run counter to the good, it means that the Gates of Wellbeing are open. This is the hygiene of the heart that is most necessary.

91. Let us pay attention to certain actions that seem unsuccessful but actually have a special significance at their basis. Sometimes you can observe how a person performs some action or another with almost no prospect of success, something compelling him to act in just that way. Such actions are usually not bad in their essence, but they are often repaid in a very unfair way. These are all karmic payments. Of course, the person who receives these payments has forgotten all about the debt, and on the way has gradually lost many spiritual accumulations; but the person who is paying still strives to discharge the debt, even if the garment he is returning no longer fits. The debt will be paid off, even if the payment cannot be accepted.

You can also observe how people make payments for others, those close to their hearts.

92. A very old story tells how a certain king, desiring to free himself of all outside influences, asked a sage for advice. "In your heart you will find liberation," said the sage, but the king waxed indignant and replied, "The heart isn't enough. A good guard is more reliable than that." So the sage took leave of the king, saying, "Then the main thing, Your Majesty, is that you stop sleeping." The story indicates that the heart is the sole source of protection. With good reason do all Teachings enjoin prayers before sleep, in order that the beneficial bond be strengthened. Humanity does not like to think much about the fact that it spends over a third of its life in sleep, a state subject to peculiar, unknown influences. Science pays little attention to the significance of sleep, this sojourn in the Subtle World. Are we not in need of a strong bond with the Hierarchy when we are at the threshold of something unfamiliar to our everyday consciousness? Just think, almost half of life passes outside of earthly existence! Of course, the heart being ready for all three worlds helps the consciousness to continue on into the next region. Who would want to share the fate of the king who pinned all his hopes on a sentry?

93. All scriptures tell stories about hermits and saints who compelled demons to serve and work for something useful. Certainly, this is quite possible when the motivation is free of selfish considerations. I can attest to what an extent the dark ones serve constructive activity when the power of a selfless command protects the heart that issues it. But one condition may be dangerous, even disastrous—irritation full of imperil opens up access to the dark ones. All sorts of uninvited guests head for wherever there is irritation, seeking to make the most of it and enhance the efficacy of the poison. How much tissue is torn, how many tests and experiments are ruined, much to the joy of the malevolent entities! Advise people to accept this not as a fairy tale but as a dangerous reality. The source of good and evil does not disappear.

94. Health is a consequence of one's past, which is why it is wiser for the owner of the house to carefully avoid creating negative consequences. You should understand the essence of the Teaching, which transfigures the heart. If the essence appears unimportant and does not suffuse your life, then all the words and signs will turn into useless rubbish.

95. In terms of its consequences, gratitude is one of the most practical concepts. Even regarding small things, a person can learn to feel grateful. Once people feel gratitude, they can talk about it in schools as something that guarantees human wellbeing.

96. "Sickness from sin"—so says Scripture. We say that illness arises from the imperfections of past and present. You should know how to approach illness. Much to the regret of doctors everywhere, the true preventative measure will be perfectment—the process of becoming perfect. People can understand that perfectment begins with the heart, and that it has not only a spatial meaning but also a strictly material one. Mothers carry their children close to their hearts as a panacea for calming them down, but they are usually unaware that holding somebody close to one's heart exerts a very powerful influence. That is why in the Subtle World we gather people close to the heart so they can be strengthened and healed. Naturally, the giving heart loses a great deal of energy through application of such a powerful remedy. Often a mother's heart has been depicted as pierced by swords and arrows, a symbol of the absorption into her heart of all the pains manifested.

Treatment by the heart can heal illnesses with clear symptoms, but it is particularly effective with diseases at an early stage. Now this remedy is almost forgotten, but it is no less powerful than a blood transfusion, for the subtlest of energies is transmitted by the action of the heart—only without the admixture of blood, which is disagreeable and lower in its quality. In thinking about perfectment, one must not forget to be solicitous of the heart that gives.

97. After two weeks of superficial striving and apparent effort, a person comes to the conclusion either that he is unsuitable or that the Higher World does not exist. Yet the very same man will tell a servant who has worked for him a year, "I can't promote you yet. You haven't been on the job long enough." With commonplace worldly affairs people understand that the period of time matters; only when it comes to considering things of a higher order are they reluctant to learn what is essential for attaining mastery. It is difficult to speak to people who have not matured in heart or those who have managed to extinguish its fires. It would seem that the fires of the heart are quite natural and simple in the way that they manifest; but long periods are necessary for the understanding of the heart to appear in the physical world—the understanding that links the lowest plane with the Subtle World. Of course, the multitude of fires demand that one adapt to them, in order to bring what seems to be chance into a chain of rhythm. Few are the people who strive to be citizens of the Universe. Earning this title requires a great deal of solicitude, keen observation, vigilance, and, first and foremost, indomitable striving.

98. How can you get across to people who are

unprepared that the topic of the Higher World deserves a heartfelt attitude? It is hard when somebody does not know anything, but even more difficult with people who have swallowed the Teaching like a spoonful of gruel; from them you can expect a special degree of betrayal and distortion. There is no sign strong enough to persuade a consciousness gone astray that it needs to look more at itself than at the people around it. How can someone see any fires when his eye is searching for a wrinkle on his neighbor's face? Someone with a cold heart may be surprised and harbor doubts about the achievements of other people, and thus cover each spark of the heart with ashes.

You are amazed that people can swallow poisons without harm; won't you consider where that immunity comes from? Not from the structure of the stomach walls, but from the innate fire of the heart.

99. To those who have not paid attention to the so-called "phenomena" that have been corroborated by photography, x-rays, and the testimony of witnesses, it would seem that a new Subtle World could not possibly come into being. Let us recall: someone responded to cosmic manifestations; someone heard distant voices; someone saw the Subtle World and took part in it; someone gave off light; someone levitated; someone walked on water; someone walked on fire; someone swallowed poison without harm; someone had no need of sleep; someone had no need of food; someone could see through solid objects; someone could write with both hands; someone could attract animals; someone could understand a language without having learned it; someone could read thoughts; someone could read a closed book with his eyes shut; someone did not feel pain; someone surrounded by snow generated the heat of the heart; someone could go on without feeling fatigue; someone could help by healing; someone could manifest knowledge of the future. In this way one can recount all the phenomena that have manifested and enumerate a multitude of instructive examples that actually happened. Gather, for a moment, all of these qualities into a single body and you will have the transfiguration of the old humanity into a new one, a process referred to in many Teachings. The main thing to note about this transfiguration is that all its various parts have already manifested, even in the midst of an imperfect existence. This means that with a well-defined effort one can impart to humanity a powerful impetus to transfigure life in its entirety. Therefore, let us remember about the great Fire and the fiery citadel—the heart. This is no fairy tale—the heart is the dwelling of the Spirit!

People want evidence, but there is plenty of proof right in front of them, which means that first of all they should call that to mind, and understand the power of thought and the power of the heart's fire. Think! Thinking shows a person the significance of Culture!

100. Healers fall into two groups: one heals through laying his hands on the patient or looking directly at him, while the other sends a heart current over a distance. Naturally, in building the future the second method is preferable. When you use the heart's radiation, it is not necessary to impact many of the patient's centers; rather, you can just work on the diseased part without burdening his attentive powers, thereby supporting his organism in its battle to restore balance. You know how intangible Our touches are, so that We can avoid infringing upon the person's ability to act independently. You also recall how We have avoided physical manifestations, allowing them only to the extent that was necessary in providing evidence of a particular step. We hurry beyond that as soon as We see understanding. We say that a lazy person is a violator of the laws of life. Those who heal through the heart are acting in the subtle body as well as the physical. Attention should be paid to the phenomenal side of life; it is far more substantial than it seems.

101. You should commeasure the use of your forces when they are being demanded in every direction. The significance of the battle can be understood when one sees tired warriors returning for a new battle. Truly, the first task of a Yogi lies in the distribution and economy of his forces. There are good reasons why the generous of heart refrain from uselessly waving their arms about. You especially need to be cautious right now, for you must not strain your energy by expending it needlessly. You should be on guard.

102. While even the loftiest Yogi acts and heals consciously at times, he or she may also do so in accordance with a Higher Ray, without making personal decisions. If only people understood that the Higher Rays exist, they would protect themselves from intermingled influences. Space is filled to overflowing with all sorts of rays and currents that cross and clash. Where there is no aspiration to the Hierarchy, how many irregularities, incidental or ill-intended, can put a stop to striving! We have gotten used to the fact that people have recourse to Us only when they confront some obvious danger, but they cannot hold on to the link with the Hierarchy when threatened by the most formidable dangers, the invisible ones! Therefore, you should bind yourself to the Ray of the Hierarchy, actually merging with it as an integral part. Indeed, even the loftiest Yogi sometimes acts in accordance with a Higher Ray.

103. How can one protect people if they themselves do not wish to hold on to the thread of salvation? To keep on going in the right direction is in itself a victory. Our help is ready to pour forth, but it must stream to someone and into something. Who, then, is able to aid Us with straight, simple striving? The heart will help seekers find this channel and discover the true path.

104. People do not want to observe the manifestations of the Subtle World, which are scattered everywhere. Similarly, they cannot conceive of ethics as being a practical pharmacopoeia for attracting the spatial energies by the simplest method. Do not tire of repeating about the vital need to realize that by making use of the heart one can attract the loftiest possibilities. People forget to apply the simplest method of disinfecting life. A lot is said about the significance of fire, but it is completely forgotten that the living fire is the best purifier. People received access to electricity, but the essence of the energy had to be left out, and they wound up with a dead light. A bonfire, some firewood, an oil lamp, or candles purify space and clear it of many contagious diseases. You can see that people with knowledge not only use electricity but also have a real fire, which quite easily attracts the spatial flame. Ask a doctor what role a lighted candle plays in disinfection. He will probably think your question is silly because it has never crossed his mind that fire might be a living thing. But why have there always been oil lamps in temples, if not for the purpose of purification? What is the origin of the ancient custom of surrounding a sick person with fire? Thus, fire can be a doctor and guardian. The living fire in a furnace or oven often prevents workers from getting ill. Indeed, the bonfire as a symbol of purification expresses a medical concept.

105. Even such simple matters as living fire must be spoken of in the book *Heart*. Some of the best people are satisfied with electric lighting, forgetting how many illnesses have been brought on by energies that once were deliberately bottled up. The same thing goes for rays. Why do people fail to notice that X-rays affect the heart? Nor do they care to note the influence of metals on the heart. A great many experiments are necessary in learning to control the surrounding conditions even to a slight degree. Though people wish to be freed from illnesses, they are in a hurry to increase them. We should not be regarded as musty old opponents of inventions; quite the contrary, We are summoning people to new discoveries.

It is essential to take into consideration the special conditions of the present time. Understand the shifting of the peoples and the formation of new fiery manifestations, which may have a profound impact. Whoever is able to maintain a mood of solemnity is acting correctly. Harmony and cheerfulness are needed—take very good care of the heart.

106. Usually one of the main things that puzzle people is their inability to see the Subtle World with the physical eye. Naturally, it is because the eye is not yet able to master the transmutation of ether. Imagine taking a photo right up against the window of a room; you could never succeed in getting a clear image, whether of the objects inside or of the distant contours outside. Similarly, on going from a dark place into sunlight, we sometimes are blinded and struck by the force of the blue light. By intensifying these manifestations of light to an infinite degree, we obtain the light of the Subtle World, which appears as darkness to an

unprepared eye. People sometimes are also puzzled as to why a seemingly limited person has visions of the Subtle World. First of all, although that person may have fallen to a lower level now, in the past he possibly performed some purifying action; in other words, there once was a time when his heart was awake. It is especially remarkable that the quality of the heart does not disappear; it may manifest in a very one-sided way, but it continues to exist as a potential force.

Also, why is it that women are often awake to the Subtle World? It is because their hearts are far subtler, which makes transcendental perception easier for them. Truly, the Epoch of the Mother of the World is based upon the cognition of the heart. It is women, and women alone, who can solve the problem of the two worlds. And so you can summon women to understanding through the heart. That will also be beneficial, primarily because the quality of the heart is everlasting. Already women have performed heroic deeds of all kinds, but now they are being given the flame of the heart instead of the fire of the stake. Let us not forget that for every important achievement, the Feminine Principle is absolutely necessary as the foundation and essence. The heart cannot be open to the Subtle World if it is not understood through a special *podvig*.

107. So much has been said about the language of the heart, yet for the majority of people it remains an inapplicable abstraction. Let us not insist on the highest forms of this means of communication; rather, let us try to master the basics, which ought to be revealed immediately without requiring any special preparation. The first and foremost purpose of every language is mutual comprehension, which means that you should try not only to understand the person with whom you are talking but also to speak in a way that is clear to him. To do this, acquire the ability to speak in your companion's language. Speak with his words in the way that he speaks; that is the only way he will remember and accept your thought into his consciousness. So we shall learn to accommodate the words of the person with whom we are talking, and imperceptibly we shall go beyond words to the very nature of his thinking. The highest form of communication will be the grasping of thought without sound.

108. One has to learn many, many modes of unfamiliar expression. Every expression of ours perplexes an adversary, but if we use his habitual expression, it enters at once into his consciousness as his very own thought. In this way you can accustom your consciousness to suppleness of expression. We call this process "the translator of the heart." In other communications of the heart the main thing is to avoid egoism, which could be called "the unkind eye." It is essential that the Teaching be put into practice not as the whim of a single day but as an ongoing exercise, one that is free of irritation and vexation.

109. The wounding of the subtle body ought to be an object of scientific study. Such wounds happen much more often than people may think. During battle or in experiencing the discomforts of returning to the physical body, you can observe the injury, which is always reflected in physical pain. Moreover, the feelings of pain focus on the most stressed part of the organism. Naturally, the heart suffers most often. One can understand that the heart is a life-giver, and for this very reason the fiery heart above all else aspires to battle. Among the various physical sensations the most precious are the pulsations of the heart when they are connected with the advanced work of the subtle body. Another highly instructive manifestation is the change in weight that occurs when the subtle body leaves the physical.

110. Numerous experiments could be conducted in connection with the subtle body, but first of all it is necessary to assimilate the sensitivity of the heart and understand the instantaneous nature of the subtle body's activity. If in order to research the heart a doctor applies his skill at amputating legs, he will, of course, be a murderer—something that actually happens quite frequently. Especially outrageous are cases in which people have administered poisons to the heart, forgetting that the heart cannot withstand poisons and the subtle body is injured by such criminal practices. How much simpler it would be to stop the suffering by applying suggestion or a vegetable remedy; but to do this, you need people who understand suggestion.

111. Truly, the successful development of the heart rests entirely upon moral foundations. These foundations transform the physical nature and vivify the spirit. Of course, people may ask you, "How does this condition apply to the dark forces, seeing that their hierophants possess certain fires?" It is correct to understand that the dark amorality is based upon a discipline of fear. You should realize the cruelty of this discipline! While We very cautiously take into account the law of Karma and value individuality, on the opposite side are disharmony and destruction, and their foundations rest on tyranny. Of course, on the lower steps fear appears to be a reliable approach. Thus, the dark intimidator comes across as a stern creditor. But you need to keep in mind the solidarity of the dark, amoral destroyers. Ill-prepared warriors often do not want to know the enemies' strength, but the heart can be pierced as effectively through the breast as through the back. Therefore, be skillful in learning all about the enemies' methods.

112. Not only the currents but also the calls coming from space disturb one's physical equilibrium. The multitudes are drawn to the magnet of a flaming heart. They call out in their suffering, and the generous heart is unable to reject their calls. So when people turn to the magnet, its energy gets depleted, but this is an unavoidable condition to which every magnet is subject. Naturally, the potential power of the heart will only increase thanks to such exercises. But the manifestation of such calls has another important significance, for space is being penetrated with threads of the noblest aspirations, and these rays are weaving a luminous net—the net of the World. Those who understand the net woven of the best calls will understand the *podvig* of an anchorite's life. It is not a life of solitude; quite the contrary, it is service made accessible to those who suffer.

113. Humanity is terrified of everything "supernatural," forgetting that nothing can be supernatural—that is, beyond the real. Therefore, strongly insist that Agni Yoga and the Teaching of the Heart cannot contain anything supernatural. Be especially cautious with people under thirty, since they are still at an age when not all of the centers can function without harm to the heart. It is essential that you make clear that Our Yoga includes no coercive magic and would never generate chaos. You need to light the fires of *podvig* in the young, to kindle heroic achievements that will transform their essence and, imperceptibly to them, prepare their hearts for future perfectment. Thus, with as much joy and simplicity as possible you should set sail to the White Island, as We sometimes call Our Dwelling.

114. Participation in Agni Yoga happens simply, just as many significant experiments were conducted and many achievements attained quite simply. Every step is valuable when it is simple and direct in its steadfast striving. We undertake so many specializations, only to fuse and transform them in the heart. Who, then, will not ignite when the bonfire has already been kindled? How many hearts are already prepared to flare forth in the future!

115. Do not reject, do not be horrified, and do not be surprised—these rules will make it easier for the phenomenal side of life to unite with the ordinary. Of course, you ascertained from your own experience that the phenomenal side could enter your life with perfect naturalness, in no way disturbing your productivity and even enhancing your ability to work. What I am saying has all the more significance inasmuch as it is commonly thought that perceiving the phenomenal in daily life tears one away from productive activity. Quite the opposite, the manifestation of striving to the Infinite teaches the vastness of human possibilities. Likewise, there are many misunderstandings around the concept of testing. Certainly, people are familiar with the idea that even whole worlds are being put to the test, but their brains are accustomed to legal and academic tests, so they are always able to imagine examiners full of schemes and ruses whose sole aim is to convict the unfortunate who fall into their hands. Actually, there are no examiners, but there are observers who watch how a person makes use of his or her knowledge. Naturally, one should put the blame for failure not on the observers but on oneself.

116. For the disciple tests become like milestones on the path, which he notices when he crosses into the Subtle World. That is how we learn to be tested in various states, and that is why we must understand the essence of the work we are doing. How much work that goes unnoticed in the physical world yields splendid results in the subtle state. That is why a broad outlook is necessary in evaluating work. Often the production of something that seems quite abstract results in extremely concrete findings, while calculations that appear perfectly precise yield nothing more than an exercise in patience. The process of testing is wonderfully beneficial and is included in the system of the ancient Teachings.

117. Intolerance is a sign of ignobility of spirit. Intolerance contains embryos of the most evil activities. There is no place for the manifestation of spiritual growth where intolerance nests. The heart's potential is unlimited; how impoverished a heart must be to deprive itself of the Infinite! One has to eradicate every sign, every indication that might lead to the idolatry of intolerance. Humanity has invented all sorts of obstacles to ascent. The dark forces are trying in every way they can to restrict evolution. Naturally, their first assault will be an action against the Hierarchy. Everyone has heard about the power of a Blessing, but out of ignorance they have turned this beneficial action into a superstition. And yet the power of the Magnet also lies in its ability to strengthen someone with a Blessing. Much is said about cooperation; thus, with every creative act it is necessary to assert awareness of the Higher World. And what strengthens the power with more immediacy than the Ray of the Hierarchy!

A person who understands the essence of continuous labor, who grows strong through concentration on the Hierarchy, who frees himself of complicated formulas in order to transfer concentration to the heart—that person will understand the essence of the future.

118. I affirm that because we human beings serve the transformation of matter into energy, nobody should belittle our significance or the importance of our passage through the lower strata. As the essence corresponds so little to the form that it happens to take in life, one might even think of the existence of human beings as that of envoys in disguise. Indeed, the essence may be very beautiful!

I am affirming the striving to construct a temple of the heart. That is what we shall call the awareness of cooperation.

119. It is a great gift if one can awaken clairvoyance by touching a person's solar plexus. This process can be undertaken in the physical body as well as the subtle, because it is one of several indestructible processes; but in order for it to take place in the physical, one has to develop a strong magnet of the heart. In this way one can, at a certain stage of development, inspire useful actions that uplift the spirit of humanity. Naturally, the consequences and expression of clairvoyance are quite diverse, but its potential directs the organism to an environment in which, under various circumstances, humanity is led to perfection. There are good reasons why the gift of awakening clairvoyance and clair-comprehension belongs to the Mother of the World.

120. Certainly, deposits of psychic energy are perfectly real, both in the animal kingdom and the vegetable. You might recall that *Ringse*, which I mentioned before, contains a deposit of psychic energy that possesses the qualities of indestructibility and vitality.

121. When I call out, telling you to strive to Me, it means that in the midst of the battle a dangerous moment has arisen, and the unification of hearts is necessary. It is impossible to imagine a complete victory in Infinity, but by the same token utter defeat is just as impossible. Often a doctor shifts the pain to another part of the body in order to demonstrate its relativity, but with cooperation such examples are not needed. When the builders of a vast plan have been summoned, there can be no relativity. In a dangerous hour, the heart aches. One can come up with all kinds of causes, but the basis of anguish and alarm is the same—namely, a severe phase of the battle. Nobody could imagine a battle to be a march forward that faces no obstacles. So We stand on guard and call upon the coworkers to stand in tight formation.

122. The world's convulsion is like a convulsion of the heart. Just as nothing can make the threatening forces abandon their assault, nothing can free the sensitive heart from quivering when something precious to it is subject to assault. But you should tell everyone not to feel terrified, for as long as the formation stands firm, nothing can penetrate. However, the quivering of the heart is unavoidable on the Tower, as well as anywhere there is devotion. Let us distinguish this feeling from those caused by atmospheric influences, which even in time of tension cannot give rise to the sort of reaction that the psychic reflexes convey. I affirm that you should be as calm as possible, because We are keeping vigil.

123. Praise doctors who give the patient a strong tonic at the beginning of every illness. It is too late to try and overtake the illness when the heart has already grown weak. The doctor's job is to catch the illness at its inception and pour in new strength to help fight it off. That is why We first of all direct your attention to musk. But since there is not enough of this precious substance for everyone, We once more turn your attention to the plants that make up the diet of musk animals. Of course, a vegetable compound will not be as strong, but it will still serve as a curative substance with a wide array of applications. That way doctors can avoid a major enemy of humanity—all narcotics. It is not very hard to find out the composition of the diet of musk animals, and ways can also be found to get musk without killing them.

124. You should pay attention to the spasmodic sigh that typically accompanies certain kinds of spiritual exaltation. The experience of getting goose flesh during conversations with Us is also quite typical. During the course of experiments undertaken to discover psychic energy, each of these sensations will be found to have its particular significance.

The speed of an uninterrupted transmission is equal to the speed of light. It is characteristic of the domains of Fire that they all can be contrasted and compared, so one can find remarkable analogies that may prove the unity of the foundations. Where should one turn, when from every direction the unified signs are being indicated?

125. If we do not learn to separate the useful properties from the harmful right here on Earth, where are we going to acquire this experience? In following the law of the heart, you must clearly distinguish the useful and the harmful aspects of every manifestation. Seldom are all the properties of a manifestation good or bad, but the heart understands where there are sparks of light and where there is the dust of darkness. The new cannot be built according to thoughts and intentions that are conventional, prejudiced, and worldly. But you should remember that grace flows far and wide; its sparks are swept into many different hearths by the cosmic whirlwind. You yourselves see how unexpectedly the seeds of plants establish themselves. Similarly, there are all kinds of differences among humans, which is why I always speak about containment.

126. It is good that you are discerning the distinctive features of expressions. Precisely, the music of the spirit is contained in these features. None of the shades of speech are there by chance! How much psychic flame is coursing through the nerves and coloring speech!

127. Every thought generates action. The most insignificant thought creates a tiny action; therefore think broadly, so that even if you meet with failure there remains a potential large enough to generate substantial results. Even if people often do not know how to act in the right way, they could at least cultivate broad, benevolent thoughts within themselves. I am emphasizing cultivated thoughts, because the dark dust is destroying the beauty of creation. It is difficult for someone to start thinking about beneficial construction when a mist of blood is fogging up his consciousness, but sooner or later he will have to turn to the power of purified thought. Therefore, it is better to begin sooner.

128. The process of conceiving ideas is deeply rooted in the foundation of Being. Without ideation there cannot be striving to knowledge or creation. How can a spirit create if it has not been persuaded to do so by ideation? How can a spirit speak about the Highest Principle if no ideation has been laid in the foundation of Being? The values of the spirit are distinguished according to this criterion. Without ideation this manifestation would be nothing more than the dance of a skeleton. But as you see, a balm is now needed to heal the putrefying portions of humankind.

129. It is harmful to keep in one's living quarters

the skins or body parts of man-eating animals and other instruments of necromancy. A person who has grasped the significance of magnetism in the human organism understands the vital power of the organism's fluids and how unnatural it is to mix the fluids of a human with those of animals in various forms; that is why any sort of man-eating is a festival for the dark forces. Moreover, the bodies in the lower strata of the Subtle World are especially drawn to necromancy.

130. The most sublime experiments are reduced to the tricks of fakirs who, instead of inducing the growth of a mango tree with the power of thought, adroitly attach some fruit to a branch. The best human achievements are debased by similar means, but We shall continue on the true, primordial path so as to not violate the law of Being.

131. I am now advising that scientists pay attention to the organism's sensitivity to all sorts of inexplicable phenomena—the sensation of goose flesh is one example. Of course, this can be explained as a nervous contraction, yet it is instructive to pay attention to whether or not there is something alien in the surrounding atmosphere. Such observations are quite useful when one is investigating psychic energy. Something makes the physical atmosphere tense and acts on the surface of the skin and the nerves. This physical reaction should be investigated from a chemical point of view as something that accelerates nervous contractions. Rays and currents are so close to the Subtle World! But the people conducting these investigations should first of all learn to pay attention to sensations. Doctors themselves pay less attention than anyone else to the great variety of sensations. They divide complex organisms into primitive parcels, and that prevents them from making their observations more subtle.

132. Think every day about the tasks that the New World poses. Strive to the New World as if it were something standing right on the other side of the door. Nobody should just leave it to others to take care of the New World, since every one of us has to grasp what it means.

We ought to gather, even in small groups, so that we get used to being part of a community.

133. Use every means to spread the Good. It is a shame to see how at times a speck of something brings a whole wheel to a halt. A great heart has a great capacity, while a petty heart mainly fills itself with petty things. Evil must not be allowed to spread unimpeded. The example of a garden and weeds makes this sufficiently clear. Invite the sweet-sounding singers for a walk among the weeds, and their mellifluent tunes will fade. But the ardor of the warriors of Good will not cool as they progress on the path! Thus, let the heart be the judge of where the Good begins!

134. I beg you not to abide by conventional divisions when you delineate good and evil, because the boundaries are so sinuous that they cannot be subjected to earthly standards. The main difficulty lies in the fact that the Subtle World is drawing very near and exerting a constant influence, but its lower spheres, being chaotic, strike out at every consciously constructive group. Naturally, the greatest manifestations are especially bespattered with refuse.

135. Thought-reading flows from straight-knowledge. Not artificial magic, not staring into someone's eyes, not holding his hands, but the fire of the heart is what links up the subtlest apparatuses. There are two difficulties: the thought-reader may be surrounded by several different currents, or the person whose thought is being read may be thinking so unclearly that he himself is unable to establish his basic thought. But the reading of thoughts is instructive not only as a phenomenon accessible to the consciousness of contemporary humanity but also as a physical, scientific investigation into the transmission of currents. So many important experiments are waiting their turn! All of you are familiar with luminous manifestations, but scientists have yet to investigate what causes these lights. Are they purely a matter of that person's optical apparatus, or do they have some spatial and chemical reality? Might this condensation of energy lay the foundation for a new kind of lighting? All of these manifestations are related to investigations into psychic energy. Why should people assume that humanity is destined to limit itself to just one kind of cosmic energy called electricity? There may be many channels for the various manifestations of energy. Of course, it is easier for people to first pay attention to their own microcosm, the heart, where all the energies of the Universe are slumbering.

136. If clairaudience and clairvoyance exist, there must also be clairalience—the ability to smell distant or subtle scents. Of course, in the manifestation of psychic energy it has a special significance; psychic energy is found in condensed form in the aroma and, moreover, brings on the spasmodic inhalation that I have already mentioned. It is helpful to recall the odd way in which the ancient wisdom was transformed, how it degenerated into absurd ceremonies. When you read about the customs of Egypt, China, and other ancient peoples, telling how they greeted each other by means of smell and inhalation, it may be difficult to discern therein a recollection about psychic energy, a memory passed down from vanished races. But even now, open straight-knowledge reveals the essence of the surrounding atmosphere. It is not a question of smell but, precisely, of essence.

137. It is known for certain that some aromas arouse tension in the psychic energy on the skin surface near nerve endings. Certain varieties of roses as well as the ingredients of the ointment known to you as the "balm of the Mother of the World" are useful for this purpose. The beneficial effect of the balm is greatly enhanced by the manifestation of the psychic energy aroused. That is why various types of skin disease and the breakdown of organic matter are so much subject to the balm's action. Of course, still better results are attained when the clarity of consciousness is increased, so a proper suggestion is useful even when the very best medicines are being prescribed. Let us not forget that these instructions could be useful in investigating psychic energy.

138. Incomplete sleep does not mean insomnia, which is harmful because it tears the insomniac away from the Subtle World. Quite the contrary, incomplete sleep sometimes gives rise to a necessary result, that of restraining the ardor of the subtle body in time of spiritual battle. True, sometimes there may be no need for sleep, but that is a special condition. During sleep the heart can yield quite remarkable observations. One can gradually bring to light the activity of the heart in connection with its participation in the life of the Subtle World. One can explain how, on the one hand, the heart depends upon and reflects the cosmic pulse, while, on the other hand, it takes on a peculiar tempo from the Subtle World when it is directly participating in that domain. So by making a series of careful observations, a person can establish the connection of the Subtle World with the Cosmos and the physical world. The role of the human heart is to accumulate energies and transform them, but it is important to use experimental means to show humanity the significance of vibrations.

Who could believe that by taking part in a battle in the Subtle World somebody might get a heavy feeling and tension throughout his or her organism? But even doctors can confirm the degree to which various kinds of depression are being observed nowadays.

139. The approaching Era must free humanity from all forms of slavery. This can be attained by cooperation with the Hierarchy. We shall not grow tired of repeating about cooperation. A person cannot perceive the significance of the all-embracing heart if, instead of cooperation, he is dreaming of all sorts of slavery. So when we take up the study of magnetic currents, we shall find that awareness of cooperation increases all of the unifying currents by a factor of ten. It may strike someone as strange that cooperation, which is usually thought of as an ethical concept, would influence currents, which are usually considered physical phenomena. That is how someone who is ignorant of true science thinks. But you know quite well how the domain of spirit is inseparable from physical laws.

140. One can discern Manvantaras and Pralayas in everything. This majestic law can definitely be seen everywhere, from the tiniest manifestation to a change of worlds. One can understand the precise progression by which the smallest is connected to the greatest. Likewise, the sensations of our organism and consciousness alternate in a uniform manner. We can either get a sense of understanding or else end up on the edge of a precipice of ignorance, as if facing a vast void. And on the crest of a wave of cognition we shall recall our former lack of it. Likewise, when facing the void we shall be conscious that this is the Maya of Pralaya, an illusion, for there is no void. Therefore, remember that the mirages of the void give way to the inexhaustibility of the spirit's treasures. So what have I said to you today? Only a single word—inexhaustibility. Let this word be a covenant, a testament to the Future.

When you are cognizing the Infinite, you must get used to its properties, the first of which is inexhaustibility, a quality that will gladden every brave heart.

141. Even the most knowledgeable people find it hard to translate the activity of the Subtle World into physical time! People can hardly conceive of the fact that almost no physical time is needed to absent oneself and go into the Subtle World. One can take the farthest flights into the Subtle World, but earthly clocks will mark them off only in seconds, because the measurement of the Subtle World is so different from that of the physical. Along with this you should note that when the subtle body is forced to leave the physical, the words of the sleeping person do not correspond to the impetuosity of his subtle actions and are still subject to the law of the physical world. So the physical mind always acts according to the law of the physical world; only the psychic energy of the nerves is subject to the law of light.

Those who are working with the Subtle World often rush to cooperate without noticing that they have absented their physical bodies. Only a feeling of vertigo sometimes lets them know that this phenomenon has taken place, because cooperation with the Subtle World is thought of as unusual. But soon this situation will change.

142. I wanted to show you how the cosmic pulse grows stronger during the division of the spirit. It is impossible to assimilate all the tension of the surrounding energies while in the physical body. Only occasionally, for a short period of time, can one make use of favorable conditions to give somebody an idea of how complex the surroundings are. Only ignorance can assume that the Cosmos grows in a primitive way! The extremely subtle process by which energies are interwoven offers a field that requires investigation; the chief obstacle to doing so lies in impatience and mutual distrust. How can unrepeatable manifestations be discovered if the person who is sensing them forgets to give the sign and the investigator does not keep the instruments ready?

We strongly advise that a biochemical laboratory be built; naturally, it would be for the purpose of conducting serious, lengthy experiments. All the signs here on the heights should be observed with particular attention. Nowhere else have so many special conditions been gathered: nowhere else have the Highest Paths been correlated with the multitudes of people at the foot of the mountains. Nowhere else are there such glaciers and underground hot springs. Nowhere else are there such deep gorges, such powerful eruptions of gas and magnetic flux. Expansive ideas should be found, ideas that enable scientists—even those who do not know about the essence of psychic energy—to apply the results of their experiments to all the kingdoms of nature. That way they can discover many long forgotten treasures and purify life. They should pay special attention to psychic energy as a key to the future. A great many investigations have gone off on a false track. One must grasp the overall situation and find the place for each detail within that big picture.

143. The spark between the poles of the magnet shows how thought is transformed into a physical transmission. We tirelessly transmit the details of the heartful, flaming experiment. Moreover, many things that concern this supernormal plan are becoming more physical, thereby following the course of evolution.

144. Regarding the battle indicated, one should not think that the predictions of its length are overstated. Since even physical battles have lasted months and years, the highest battle cannot be settled right away. Where is the lightning that can shoot through evil instantaneously? Yet even if such lightning were gathered, it would be unwise to hurl it, because, first of all, the entire planet would suffer. Only the ignorant can allow a basic law to be violated.

145. A great deal is said about creating through vibrations, and when these words are spoken, eyes are raised heavenward; what is forgotten is that every person is not only a transmuter of energies but also a creator of subtle vibrations. Since the heart is a transmuter of energies, its psychic energy makes vibrations more subtle. With their refined rhythms, the classical Mysteries reminded the participants about the significance of vibrations. Likewise, every job that is performed with sincerity becomes a source of subtle vibrations, which is why I speak about the quality of work. The ancients took note of auspicious and inauspicious days. This was a reminder about alternation, about the same Manvantaras and Pralayas, but applied to earthly existence. With vibrations, each rhythm, each alternation, each quality will be a foundation for cooperation with the Cosmos. When I tell you to seek closer at hand, I also have in mind the quality of each work as a true act of creation. We do not like hypocrisy, because there is deception in it; in other words, it has neither intensity nor quality. So in all things let us remember about cooperation with the Cosmos.

146. You should remember that while the spiritual

battle rages there may be unusual vibrations, and of course you should not expect that they will all be in harmony.

You may ask Me what I need of you right now. I need devotion, a devotion that is purified of all additives. When space shudders, we need to purify our feelings, just as an archer removes the tiniest particle of fluff from the tip of his arrow. Our Battle is moving forward, so plant your feet firmly and cast aside every impediment.

What kind of help is possible when a battle is going on? First of all, it is possible to create new circumstances; therefore vigilance, and still more vigilance!

147. Tell doctors again and again that they should observe people when they are in a so-called healthy state. For physicians the most interesting manifestations will not be those observed when patients have contagious diseases. The principle of contagion is somewhat reminiscent of possession, but the most instructive manifestations of psychic energy will not, of course, take place during a contagious illness. Even so, this fact is never taken into consideration. How can we expect rapid discoveries when the most important factor, psychic energy, goes entirely unnoticed? When it is not even subject to dispute or denial but simply paid no heed, as if it were among the least significant manifestations? The most successful approach will be to repeat about psychic energy. Someone will lock himself up in his room and secretly read about it. He may not confess the fact to anyone, but he will be thinking about psychic energy all the same.

148. Again someone will come up with the question, "Why is so little said about the Subtle World in all the scriptures?" You can be sure that a great deal is said everywhere, but people do not want to take notice of it. Upon ancient icons you can see green spheres that represent the earthly next to red spheres that represent the fiery realm—in other words, the Subtle World. On one image you can see a whole scene in green tones and next to it a red world of angels. What could be more graphic than that? The various prophecies are full of messages about the Subtle World. The Koran also makes mention of the Subtle World. You cannot name a single Teaching in which no place is given to the life of the Subtle World. Because they feel terror before everything invisible, people stuff their ears and close their eyes, preferring to remain in ignorance. But can a person think about the heart or ponder psychic energy without remembering about the Subtle World, a vast realm so inseparable from the dense world?

149. Do not be surprised that even in these days of great tension I speak with you calmly about the mystery of the worlds. This comes out of long experience, and it is the only way to lead the warriors in spiritual battle on a battleground where countless abysses yawn wide! The times are so tense that if we think in a worldly way we will walk about in despondency, but the supermundane law leads us upward. Thus, the person who does not go down goes up; but only by spirit do we avoid descent. So above the earthly decision is the heavenly one. And above the brain is the heart.

150. If I say, "I am always with you," will many people believe it? They would even be afraid to believe in a unified consciousness. For them each such unification means a violation of their selfhood, and as such is utterly impermissible. They will never appreciate the tenfold increase in energy that arises from the cooperation of consciousnesses. But without such cooperation the entire Teaching of the Heart would be impossible. Why give out all these details if a mutual reinforcement cannot take place? But if this principle is attainable, then it is likewise possible to extend it until it blossoms into the full unification of consciousness called *Paloria*. In the case of those who have acknowledged the unification of consciousness and gone on to attain it, how greatly can they expand their work for the Common Good! Of course, I am speaking about the inner spiritual work, which the blind can neither perceive nor appreciate.

A summons to unification of consciousness is necessary everywhere, because this is the simplest way to introduce the life of the heart. This is not sorcery but rather a physical law that can weave a net of salvation around the planet. So everyone who follows the law of Being can rightly consider himself to be a citizen of the Universe.

151. I am saying, "Strive full tilt into the future." I am saying, "Direct your steps to Me." I am saying, "Gather everything that will project you above the crossing of the currents." The poison of the past—that is what We call immersion in the past, and it can stir up the dormant tendencies that karma has built up. The past can temporarily deprive a person of the accumulations he possesses in the present. So our power increases when we transfer our consciousness into the future. Every past symbol turns us back and transmits the power of the crossing of the currents. You should especially keep this law in mind when the atmosphere is becoming increasingly tense. Reincarnations are little mentioned in some Teachings so that people will be given a still stronger impetus into the future. It is good that you do not pronounce some names, and even try to forget them. One should not revive the vibrations outlived long ago.

152. Naturally, We have nothing against ancient

objects so long as their aura is good, but a person should not look at them through the prism of his past. We are well aware that perfection is attained not by plunging into the past but by irrepressible striving into the future. Especially now We are advising that seekers transfer their entire consciousness into the future and thus avoid the many snares set by past existences.

153. In hoary antiquity incense was used in order to ascertain the aura of an object. It was assumed that objects with good auras would be saturated with incense, while bad radiations would block absorption of this botanical manifestation. Later on, incense came to be used in temples as a means of strengthening the Subtle World and bringing it nearer. Actually one of incense's properties is its ability to strengthen the vitality of the Subtle World. It is used at funerals to help the deceased, who has just crossed the borderline, to maintain consciousness and also to free him from the drowsy condition usual for someone who is unprepared. Such details of the ancient knowledge have been totally forgotten, as has the significance of various fragrances. Not only has the manufacture of perfumes lost the meaning it had in ancient times, but also out of ignorance extremely harmful combinations are often being used. The knowledge I am conveying, when elaborated by extensive research, will open up an entire domain for useful application in everyday life. In antiquity the use of aromas was joined to a knowledge of healing. The priests explained how to make use of aromas and in what cases to apply them. So without resorting to sorcery, one can follow a whole system of healing based on inhalation and nourishment of the nervous system by rubbing aromatic substances into the skin. In this sense the ancients saw far deeper than the skin's surface.

Inseparable from the subject of aromas is the concept of our emanations, but this field has hardly been studied either. Every time research on various emanations is made public, it invariably encounters the charge of "charlatanism." Likewise every subtler sensation is sure to meet with mistrust—as if all the diversity of nature were not calling out for greater refinement!

154. Let us not forget to sound the call to battle. Let us not grow tired of summoning the warriors to the sword, the sword that will give peace to the world. We are not thereby affirming intimidation; rather, the manifestation of achievement is necessary as nourishment for the spirit.

155. There are many occult books, but the majority of them cannot serve much purpose now. The main reason is that in everything they only take into account some special "chosen" people. But Our Teaching has in mind all, all, all! Only these calls to all the world can replace abstract ethics with the Teaching of Life.

156. When the world becomes tense, the spiritual armor of the closest coworkers grows stronger, and their radiation grows purple and fiery. So the cosmic armor comes to correspond to worldwide conditions independently of personal feelings and day-to-day work. Thus, one can get a sense of the cosmic influence so long as things are unfolding according to the law of Hierarchy.

One should note how the spiritual armor is being forged at the same time that the consciousness is expanding. We can help make this armor stronger, but unless there has also been growth of the consciousness, such intervention will be tantamount to destruction. So the Mysterious Hand can be seen when people are acting according to the law of Hierarchy. This needs to be remembered especially now, for even a tempered heart may feel distress when sensing the unprecedented tension.

157. The flaming sword is a ray of the spiritual armor. The symbol of a sword-like ray, which has appeared in every Teaching, is an extremely challenging sign. Even the most peace-loving images have affirmed a sword. This does not express a desire to coerce, but it does indicate a readiness to defend the most sacred. So in the midst of the raging fire one can see a thin sword above the brow of a warrior of spirit. It is a shame that on the earthly plane the process of impressing the aura's radiation on film is still so imperfect. Clear evidence of rays and other fires could be presented.

158. You should be wise in understanding the final collision between the two worlds—the one that is departing and the one that is being born. You can see signs of madness in the former and daring in the latter. I have been saying for a long time that the world is dividing, and you can see how deep the split has already become. You need to understand how close at hand is the decisive time and with what solidarity it must be met.

159. Even dogs are aware of the Subtle World, but people are unwilling to pay attention to reality. The Subtle World is a lofty sublimation of the earthly sphere. Fire is one of the basic manifestations in every process of sublimation. But if people are so far from accepting the idea of the Subtle World, what can one say about the Fiery World, where Fire is the very essence of all Existence? After the writings about the Heart, about the Subtle World, We will need to write about Fire, about the Fiery World. How far that World will be from the contemporary understanding of life!

But a person who knows about the Subtle World will also want to ascend to the World of Fire.

160. It is right to remember that even the passing shadow of a person leaves behind an ineradicable trace. How, then, to describe the impact of thoughts and words! The light-mindedness of humanity is astonishing, for with its every step it leaves behind the most frightening deposits. Humanity supposes that words can wipe away the traces of past thoughts. But who, then, creates the impassable labyrinths that bring on the destruction of destined manifestations? When you realize that the fiery sphere retains the remnants of all the thoughts carelessly cast into space, you may recall the old riddle: "What cannot burn away?" — "A thought." Humanity generates thought that is lodged firm in the strata of space. You should know with what complexity space resounds when it is shot through with thoughts, often ones that are insignificant and filthy. But if you start talking about the chemical reaction of a thought, people will consider you mentally unsound. Neither threat nor fear nor counsel will help unless the traveler in the Subtle World runs up against his own thought barrier. As an inscription on an ancient stele reads, "Traveler, do not stand in your own way!"

161. Condensed thought may be extremely harmful for the heart. Just as a heavy gas may burn away blood vessels, thought may weigh upon the heart. There exists an expression, "a serpent lying under the heart." Urominai is the name of the serpent that gnaws away at one's forces. At one time people knew to be cautious in their thinking. Heavy thoughts hover on in the atmosphere. So remember about the Battle and show caution.

162. It is not enough to firmly establish the

consciousness; one also has to get used to guarding it under various circumstances. You need one blade for cutting paper, another for wood, and a completely different one for metal. You might liken the physical, subtle, and fiery worlds to the resistance of paper, wood, and metal. Truly, one has to constantly accustom oneself to being conscious of the Subtle and Fiery Worlds; various exercises can develop that consciousness. So one must get used to a state of constant work, endless and untiring. There is no substitute for such tension of the consciousness in its usefulness for the Subtle World. People usually work only for rest, not for the limitless process of perfection; so when they find themselves in the Subtle World, before the very face of Infinity, they fall into confusion and fog. Likewise, to approach the Fiery World you must accustom yourself to going forward without fear, as if walking on the edge of an abyss. Only the highest self-mastery and readiness for danger can prepare a person for the fiery spheres.

163. People must prepare for higher cognitions; only through such thinking can a new consciousness be brought closer to humanity. The great reality must be purified once more, in order that it may become like a lodging for the traveler. So unavoidable is this reality, and so beautiful, that it would be madness to remove it from the great, destined ascent. The various ages, each in its own way, foretold the future reality. Out of ignorance even beautiful chambers were filled with horrors, but it is only ignorance that dwells in horrors. If the spirit has chosen a beautiful path, then its dwelling will be beautiful.

164. Dissatisfaction is a characteristic suited to the Subtle World. In it one can discern eternal motion, for without this motion it is impossible to go forward in the higher worlds. You can satisfy and satiate the stomach and muscles, but what will satiate the heart? Though it may fill you with rapture, even contemplation of the Highest Light will not give you satiety. Flaming heart, insatiable heart, only the very pain of the world will propel you forward! The mist that obscures sated eyes will turn into the radiance of the kindled heart's flame. So let us guard the fiery treasure. Let us help the people to understand the precious heart. And in doing so, let us call to mind all the milestones needed on the path. Let us not forget the wise words, "And this, too, will pass." An impetuous motion will never bring one back to the same place.

165. To understand the common aspiration means to construct the Temple of the New World. To strive and aspire, thereby nurturing each other, will in itself constitute an understanding of the Teaching. Such striving will pave the path to the Fiery World, but the seeker must have the courage to turn his eyes to Fire, to acknowledge it as his sole nurture.

166. You may calculate the rupees correctly but get confused in adding up the annas, and the total will end up in error. To avoid such error, you will have to force your way forward by adopting the full measure. To be completely devoted means to propel your consciousness along the line of the Hierarchy. Just as a taut sail propels the precious cargo onward, an intensified consciousness bears one beyond the boundaries of danger.

167. When you place the needle of a pendulum above a sandy surface for the purpose of observing cosmic vibrations, you do not try to force the needle to move faster by pushing it with your hand. To force it would, first of all, be stupid, since that would only yield false results. The same thing goes for the pendulum of the spirit—you should not force it to come up with predetermined results. The outlines etched by the needle of the spirit are complex, and only the heart's striving can vitally and truthfully corroborate what the pendulum indicates. A Teaching of ancient Tibet speaks about the same pendulum of the spirit. A magnet is placed above the head of the person being tested. Not only is the inner reaction noted, but also, as the magnet begins to sway, it is observed whether the movements are abrupt or quivering. They may also be circular, this sign being the most striking indication that the condition of the consciousness is a correct one. Naturally, this experiment is extremely lengthy and even quite painful, for it requires complete immobility, and you know how hard that is to attain.

168. It is impossible not to notice what strong opposition every conscious movement toward Light encounters. Besides the usual counteractions from the dark ones, the work of Chaos may also be noticed. In being aware of this law of the opposition from the Unmanifest, we find self-consolation and experience in cultivating patience.

169. People may be so savage in spirit that they can only exist by criticizing one another. This is not an inspection of someone's armor for the purpose of helping him out; quite the contrary, criticism becomes the very meaning of life. If one were to deprive such a critic of his tongue, he would wither away like a plant without water. Such a phenomenon could be examined from a medical point of view. One can find in this criticism a sort of vampirism involving possession, in which obtaining more active, vital fluids is necessary to nourish the possessor.

This phenomenon of life can and should be investigated with a scientific purpose. Of course, it is difficult to overcome possession, especially because after possession the gates remain open to visitors for a long time. With someone who has admitted a possessor, very intense observation is necessary to protect him from irritation, which leaves the door wide open.

The heart is the best guardian against possession, but you have to make sure that the heart does not fall asleep.

170. If you wish to make a speech in a language you do not know, it is unwise to start preparing the night before you deliver it. If you wish to perform on an unfamiliar instrument, it is unwise to start practicing the night before you go on stage. If you wish to cross into the Subtle World, it is unwise to begin preparations the evening before you depart. It is horrible when a person who has turned away from thought about the Subtle World his whole life behaves like a negligent student and only on the eve of his crossing begins in confusion to repeat words he has never really understood. The time of crossing is sure to come—this is an unavoidable fact that every Teaching proclaims. It has been said, "We shall not die, but change." Is it possible to speak more concisely, to speak with a greater sense of affirmation? It means that one must know the language of the Subtle World. It also means that one has to acquire the right of entry with full consciousness, but all this is impossible to attain on the eve of departure. There are those who instill terror, instead of joy, in the person about to cross over, and this violates the law of life. But as you know, the best guide forward is the flaming heart. When you have such an inextinguishable lamp, there is nothing terrifying about crossing the skies and meeting the Guiding Ones.

171. A heart may hear the call of victory even while the battle is raging. Such a heart is worth cultivating, and the work of refining one's consciousness will be an extremely beneficial activity.

172. Fire is closest to sound and color. There is a good reason why the sound of a trumpet so powerfully attracts the Fire of Space. It is not by chance that some paintings seem to glow, for the very same fire of the heart is ablaze in them. You should envision the manifestation of fire not only as a reality but also as something inseparable from us.

173. The Teacher has joined in an eternal oath about establishment of the New World, so follow Him with your every effort. Humanity needs to purify its existence, so reconstruction must begin from the hearth, from everyday life. You should not wait for whole nations to start moving; on the contrary, the life principle will undergo a worldwide reformation on a personal basis, quite apart from nationality. So you should first of all remember that it is not the narrow old boundaries that will partition the world. The foundation of psychic energy is not limiting itself to a specific nation, but will discover a completely different world pattern.

174. The flaming pentagram is a shield in times of battle. A person in the midst of special tension is just such a pentagram. With his larynx burning and his hands and feet ablaze, he rises like an invincible shield that protects the works manifested. Naturally, a condition like that is especially dangerous in the midst of life, where so many small betrayals occur. I recommend silence as a way to avoid setting fire to several centers, especially the heart. A selfless, flaming heart is a special joy for the Higher World. Such hearts blaze forth like torches, shining above all the pressures of the world.

175. A sealed glass vessel can only be opened by

a harmonious vibration, a resonance. This is fairly well known, but the harmonic ratio of the resonance with all its amazing diversity has yet to be considered sufficiently. Isn't it strange that the same glass vessel resonates to glass, metal, and wood—to bodies of the greatest diversity? Such resonance reminds us once more of the diversity in the harmonic ratios of various combinations. This example is a useful one for human leaders. What tremendous harm is inflicted by monotony, which penetrates every human stratum! The law is one, but its vibrations are as varied as the Universe is manifold. Those who know this law can hardly look upon humanity as a pile of homogeneous stones that happen to resonate to different vibrations. We should rejoice in this multiformity, for it is what opens up the path to refinement. What would become of the human heart if it only resounded to a single note? So let all leaders remember about multiformity and diversity.

176. Armageddon has already begun—the end of 1931 saw the start of the Great Battle, and I did not conceal it from you. So the Battle cannot end now, but must reach a victorious conclusion. Of course, when the flaming pentagram must be uplifted as a shield, all the sensations of the Battle affect the heart. You should not be surprised that events are piling up, for the earthly battle is following the heavenly. A great deal has been said about the Heavenly Host, about Michael the Archistrategus, the Supreme General, about the manifestation of the affirmed Leader, and about all the perturbations. That is why I say, "Caution!"

177. Do not neglect anything. In neglect lies the cause of many misfortunes. Advise people to understand that even the greatest of manifestations may be the least visible. Cosmic significance is not dependent on physical dimensions. A seed provides the best example of this. Now especially we are pointing out the need to respect the diverse manifestations that have filled life. Does a messenger necessarily have to be a giant? And must a ray be nothing less than blinding? And wouldn't a voice of deafening volume be harmful? Right now a multitude of manifestations, insignificant in appearance, are traversing the world. Every seeker needs to sharpen his attention. A person who can train his attention to observe the smallest will also understand the greatest.

178. The ability to have respect for even the smallest will help you to acquire the ability to be patient as well. And what patience is necessary when facing Infinity, especially when we realize that it is unavoidable! Besides, we know how much every murmur of protest impedes the path. The burden created by disrespect for the small should be replaced with the joy that is found in observing the multiformity of creation. We can help each other by speaking the very simplest words.

179. Who, then, will help out when the Battle is raging? A person who, having acquired patience, accepts the armor of courage. You know what courage is necessary to go forward on a dangerous course. Two paths can be offered, a dangerous path and a safe one, but a flaming heart will choose the former.

180. No sooner is the beginning of the Great Battle mentioned than someone starts to feel tired. What will he have to say, then, when he confronts countless hostile warriors? Every Yuga has a preparatory phase of considerable length, but there may be periods of acceleration when all the forces must be intensified to an unusual degree. People should not understand the great, decisive Battle as just a war. The manifestation of the Battle is something far deeper. Its torrent will flow through the entire Subtle World as well as the earthly. It will express itself not only in armed conflicts but also in unprecedented clashes among peoples. The boundaries between the belligerents will be as tortuous as those between good and evil. The earthly eye will not have access to many of the decisive battles. The ominous clashes in the Subtle World will express themselves as catastrophes on the earthly path. Similarly, earthly courage will have an impact on the Subtle and Fiery Worlds. The Great Battle will be the first link in the unification of the worlds. Thus, one can expect quick actions to arise from every direction. Cooperation has enormous significance in this Battle. Even now the star of the flaming heart is bringing tremendous help. Since this help may not always be visible, you can illustrate it by citing the example of an author who exerts great influence even though he does not know his readers. The same may be said about cooperation between the two worlds. One has to maintain a high degree of tension in the days of the Battle. Of course, this does not rule out doing all kinds of everyday work, but in performing each job you should remember to send it off with a thought for the benefit of Light. Likewise, whenever you are pierced by a hostile arrow, you should be conscious and receive each blow in the name of the Great Battle.

181. The restriction and ossification of the consciousness are the main reasons for the disunity of the worlds. The course of the Great Battle is often impeded because of a complete lack of harmony between the consciousnesses of the earthly world and the Subtle. Those who have passed into the Subtle World with a consciousness imbued with monarchism cannot reconcile themselves to the present condition in their countries if the regime has changed. So even where a great deal of unity exists, differences regarding one matter may throw the forces into confusion and division. And when we recall how many spirits crossed into the Subtle World during the war and how many changes have taken place in recent years, it is easy to picture how little correspondence there is between the worlds. One can also imagine what significant work is presently being carried out by expanded hearts who strive selflessly to broaden consciousnesses in both worlds.

We know how hard it is to expand consciousnesses, and how many attacks such beneficent work is provoking. It is impossible to estimate the amount of pressure that the black lodges exert against these leaders. Glory to them, the Light-bearers!

182. The golden light that fills the inner essence is a characteristic sign that the heart is being armed. Just as the outer reaches of the aura turn from purple to ruby, the silvery Lotus of the heart flashes with a burst of red and gold when the spirit dons the ultimate armor. That is how an inner condition is attained that allows participation in the fiercest battles without harm or risk of the subtle body being severely wounded. The results of this armoring of the heart were already evident when the warrior stood up to the dark forces and, in spite of their overwhelming numbers, made them tremble. She left them with their threats, and the empty threat of an enemy is in itself a victory. Naturally, the pure golden light is not easily attained; it requires a lengthy achievement.

183. Although many conditions of the heart, ranging from soft-heartedness to hard-heartedness, have been noted in people's observations, fiery-heartedness has hardly ever been mentioned. But it is precisely this quality that ought to attract our attention and occupy it. It is hard to be unafraid of the black assembly, but no one can overpower the fiery heart. Let them come up with all kinds of threats; one pillar of Light will put all the darkness to flight.

184. All the crusades in humanity's past are nothing in comparison with the March of Maitreya. I affirm that the Great Battle means the renewal of the Earth. The future should be understood not as a battle but as *podvig*. One can expect battles not only in the usual sense but also as a reconstruction of life. There may be various periods, but in them one can sense a strengthening of life's tempo. You already sense this acceleration of rhythm. Everyone can perceive this in accordance with the condition of his nerves, but he will be sure to sense a new cosmic condensation. One can feel a direct intensification of the rays. One can feel anxiety or feel striving into the distance. All of these details will indicate the existence of the same new accelerated rhythm. You can understand how the intensification of energy is laying a new step for the planet's progress. No one should be surprised that Chaos breaks through, for the Battlefield is enormous. Let us not forget to notice even the smallest manifestations. There is so much diversity in the clashes between the fundamental forces of the Universe!

185. People are so far from recognizing inner manifestations that only a few will understand the special meaning of My Indication to join together in silence. For them silence means inaction, since they are so unwilling to learn about the interaction of energies. For them only a broken nose or an injured eye is a sign of energy. Yet an intense silence constitutes a fiery barrier that, when reinforced by the number of those who are uniting, becomes a genuine stronghold. Therefore, in an hour of tension you can gather together and sit in silence. Naturally, you may think of the single path in which salvation lies. And so I am sending you all strength.

186. The work of the subtle body is carried out with much greater influence when it is far away from its physical body. The subtle body can develop its power to the greatest extent where the physical currents cannot reach. Of course, from a physical perspective it is incomparably more difficult to carry out work at a distance, and by no means do all subtle bodies have the courage to venture out on distant flights. You can see the difficulty with which the physical body responds to distant flights by observing how much it sweats even in a cold environment. I commend those who have paid attention to such physical manifestations. Even doctors usually overlook many typical signs, but true science can only develop by confronting and comparing facts. When I spoke about tension, I had in mind not muscular tension but that of the heart. When the heart does not manifest significant pains after undergoing such tension, you can count it a remarkable success. This sort of adaptation of the heart is not easily attained. Foolish people assume that the training of the heart and consciousness can be accelerated at will, but when we are aware of Infinity, we must adapt these apparatuses with great wisdom and patience.

187. People should know that when the subtle body is working thousands of miles away, it is already free of the burden of physical fluids. Of course, for the subtle body these thousands of miles are nothing, but physical influence is measured in earthly units.

It is true that the brain cannot always retain the instructions given, but even when a person's consciousness is dim there still remains an unusual sense of disquietude that forces him to give special thought to specific dangers. In the same way, one should also think over everything connected with the Teaching.

188. The immediate duty of everyone who knows about the Subtle World is to affirm the existence of this invisible but real world every time the opportunity presents itself. Some people may respond by getting angry, but it will give them an opportunity to think about reality. If research on human physiology were supplemented by the study of the Subtle World, which connects all the various conditions of existence, our world would at once enter into a distinctly new era. I can affirm that the commotion arising from the present turmoil has attained unprecedented proportions, because the bond between the worlds is totally ignored. Let nobody claim that he has not been warned in due time. Let the traveler not forget that he cannot return to the house that he left behind, that it is only by his own efforts that he can reach the Luminous City to which he has been summoned. Let the traveler remind everyone he meets at the crossroads that paths are irreversible.

189. The appearance of Our trusted messengers can be acccpted as a sign that the New World is now being born. I criticize all those who are failing to notice the myriad of signs appearing everywhere in the world. The Teacher can tell a person to look, but He cannot force him to see. Do not be surprised that in the mosaic of the book Heart so much is included about the Subtle World and the Great Battle. Many hearts sense both of these realities, but often they cannot express them in words. Yet the thought born in the heart with the swiftness of light will express itself in words.

Remind your friends that there is a good reason why their hearts are aching.

190. In order to sharpen the senses of taste, hearing, and smell, people shut their eyes; in order to concentrate the sense of sight they accompany their gaze with hand gestures. So people adopt all sorts of artificial methods because they cannot balance the effects of psychic energy. Likewise, people do not know how to strike a balance between indignation of the spirit and equilibrium. Both concepts are indispensable for attaining perfection, but how can one reconcile militant indignation of the spirit with wise equilibrium? Usually these concepts seem incompatible, but what allows indignation of the spirit to avoid turning into irritation and creating imperil if not the response of equilibrium? And far from giving rise to imperil, an enlightened, selfless indignation creates the most precious, ruby-colored armor. So it is only when psychic energy has been given the right direction that a treasure takes the place of poison. But what is the judge of true selflessness? Of course, it is none other than the heart. And not just any heart, but precisely the heart that is facing Infinity.

191. I want to accustom you to the scales of Infinity. Understanding of these scales develops slowly, as does the ability to use them in commeasuring events. A neophyte cannot grasp the universal context and dimension of various events. To him it is difficult and unusual even to rearrange his room. How, then, is he to think about universal wings! He is also held back by his concern about the pettiest possessions, and he does not see the stage at which any condition is acceptable because it has been weighed on the scales of Infinity.

192. A disease may nestle inside a person for a long time, but if it does not manifest in gross physical form, no ordinary physician will recognize it. Ten prophets and clairvoyants may testify to the existence of a hidden disease, but they will be looked upon as liars because it has yet to appear at the grossest level. Similarly, humanity has schooled itself in the coarsest forms of everything, having banished refinement and straight-knowledge. Even the most importunate signs of the Subtle World have been consigned to oblivion. Nobody wants to know about or count up the multitude of words that speak quite definitely about the Subtle World—words found in every language. Let us take, for example, a favorite word, inspiration. It means that somebody "breathed into" or "instilled" something, that inspiration came from somewhere else. With perfect clarity the word presupposes that something came from without, but people go on speaking about inspiration without any awareness that what it refers to is a manifestation of the Subtle World. Just think of all the signs scattered everywhere in the world, yet something shuts people's eyes to them. What is it, if not darkness?

193. A similar inability to commeasure is shown when people make the usual comparisons between the earthly and subtle worlds and speak of dates, suggesting that the Subtle World formulate its foresight in earthly terms. But earthly standards of measurement do not exist in the higher worlds. Certainly, there do exist cosmic dates and periods, as is established in astrology, but the future of the Subtle World cannot be expressed using earthly standards. The same thing goes for other comparisons of this kind. Therefore, the rapprochement of the two worlds requires refinement and flexibility of consciousness. It is in the book Heart that people need to be reminded about the Subtle World. The laws of the Subtle World will first of all be assimilated by the heart.

194. Antennas can be adjusted to receive various

waves, but that does not undermine their fundamental character. Similarly, hearts may pick up various currents, but their essence will be one. You can especially observe this fact in regard to premonitions. Comparative analysis can demonstrate the remarkable spectrum of human hearts. You can observe how a single event may trigger what is unquestionably a state of great excitement, but such states are so diverse in terms of their length and character! One event might provide material to fill an entire volume with observations. One heart will grasp the template of the event in the Subtle World, another will require the appearance of a physical current, and yet another will respond only after the event has actually occurred. One heart will evaluate an event according to its merit, another may exaggerate its importance, and yet another may do no more than unconsciously record it in the rhythm of the pulse. Most certainly, the response of the heart is far more substantial than is generally thought. A premonition is not a superstition or an act of imagination, but a physical fact. By making a slight observation a person can foresee an event; what is important is not the background of the event but its potential. So the heart resonates to waves of the greatest diversity. Would it not be helpful to give deep consideration to these phenomena?

195. Let us not be surprised if nowadays hearts are being burdened by currents of extraordinary tension that are crossing and clashing. The currents of nations, the currents of the world, the currents of powerful personalities intersect each other, but through them run the currents of the Subtle World, which is where so many actions are taking place. Only now are events taking shape; you can imagine how the universal consciousness is acting upon feeble brains!

196. Imagination is the result of the accumulation of experience. This is quite well known. Yet there may exist a tremendous accumulation, and instead of imagination only lust and irritation are in evidence. Affirm that the imagination cannot be developed without the participation of the heart. That is why the creators, both inner and outer, will be those who have wisely combined accumulations with a manifestation of the heart's fires. This should be explained to all the children in every school, so that not a single tenet of the Teaching remains an abstraction. You yourself also see how the manifestation of the spirit unfolds in a logical progression. You know how at first the fiery sword begins to shine and completes the aura, but later it penetrates one's entire being. The symbol of a sword is especially appropriate to the Great Battle, when all the spiritual forces are gathering under the Banners of the Lords of Light. The golden light also grows stronger at this time and thereby grows closer to the golden deposits of prana. All of the forces are expressed in the flaming heart.

197. Isn't it amazing that in the days of the Great Battle we can still speak about the imagination? For the Battle is not a work of imagination but already the clash of hordes! So one more page has been turned. I insist on great caution, great care, for the time is a great one. We are also gathering in the Tower in order to oppose all the evil ones. You ought to be ready for great battles, for only the inconsequential are not called to battle.

198. To desire means to find the gates to the Subtle World. But precisely learning to desire is what people find difficult. They cannot bring their feelings into equilibrium and are therefore unable to create a steadfast, unshakeable desire. Yet in the Subtle World desire is a creative lever. This power came from the Highest World, but it also requires the clarity of the Highest World. When We direct you forward on the line of the Hierarchy, We are preparing you for this regal quality, the clarity of desire. Amidst the intersecting currents of the lowest spheres it is not easy to find a purified desire that is like an arrow. You can overcome the pressure of the earthly atmosphere by aspiring and striving to the Highest, which is why the Hierarchy is the goal. The flaming heart that can reduce useless rags to ashes is also able to lead onward to the Hierarchy. You can notice from your own experience how the outer becomes the inner, the inalienable. First the Yogi hears the music of the spheres, but later he himself begins to resonate to this harmony of the Higher World. But for this to happen, a flaming heart is necessary.

199. Cosmic energies may become so intense that grave consequences will arise unless a compress of prana is applied. The heart radiates with a tense light, like incandescent gold. Yes, the earthly realm can be distressing.

200. I cannot sufficiently stress the importance of this moment. After lengthy preparations, both sides have finally clashed. One can observe this happening on all the planes, in every field from the spiritual to the military. The food of the Heavens has been turned into manure, and the sacred Fire into a torch of arson!

201. Courage can only be found in the heart. In the reasoning that arises from the convolutions of the brain one can find an intelligent distribution of forces, but the courage that proceeds on the straightest, most luminous path cannot live outside the heart. Judge this fact by the antipode of courage, fear. Fear first acts upon the heart and from there flies to the extremities. Most certainly, every trait is measured by the heart. A doctor would be able to study all the qualities of human nature through the heart by observing all the nuances and tones of the pulse. Of course, as a general rule a double pulse will not be observed, because contemporary science completely fails to recognize the fiery condition of the heart. You might go to physicians and beg that they pay heed to obvious manifestations that only require a little attention. Let them get angry, but also let them see who is coming to them and begging. In ten years the blows of fate will force people to read the Book of Life with respect.

202. The accumulation of experience, which has such great importance, always reminds us of an example from early childhood. A child does not know what fire is like until he has burned himself. Of course, adults may respond to this example with a supercilious smile, but they conduct their own experiments using the very same methods. Nothing will induce humanity to apply more sensitive methods. Naturally, people will be perplexed as to why the consequences of many of their misfortunes last so long and are so painful. They can be sure that every effect is deemed necessary for their redemption. Again, this is not a punishment but the accumulation of experience, and one may marvel at the exactitude of the karmic scales—its great equilibrium leaves no room for reproach. The way in which the tension between the cups of the scale is established depends upon the heart. It may fill the cups to overflowing, it may lift one cup up, and it may appraise the value of the accumulations in both of them. So let people keep sharp watch on the process by which they exonerate themselves, a process that takes place in the heart. It is with good reason that one of the definitions of the heart is "the vindicator."

203. How, then, are you to go onward? Precisely,

by holding fast to Me and picturing yourself in the midst of an ocean where you are kept safe only by the Khata of the Mother of the World, the sacred scarf that She extends. During the battle with darkness, an unparalleled pertinacity is essential in opening up all the wondrous possibilities.

204. Truly, cooperation may open up every possibility, but one needs an understanding of where such cooperation lies. Often people relegate cooperation to the domain of governmental matters, whereas cooperation is a condition that underlies one's entire life. Precisely, all acts of mutual assistance, however slight, contain a cooperation that has a cosmic significance. When consciously utilized, every glance, every handshake, every thought becomes a sign of cooperation. How precious it is for people to feel that they are constantly generating consequences! Like giants, they set the world -atremble. But where are the people who will direct the cooperation of their energies to the Subtle World? Where is courage? Where is solicitude about the Invisible? Where is determination to also help out in that realm, where the earthly bonds are not completely forgotten, where monsters menace just as they do here? That is why the achievement of cooperation in the Subtle World is so very great. Just as here on the earthly plane, there one must call out to people and lead them upward, courageously defending them from wild boars and savage dogs. Truly, such cooperation is selfless. You can gradually train yourself to bring benefit to all the worlds.

205. It is commendable to defend the Sign of the Lords. It is useful to train oneself in understanding how close the Lords are. Just as it is impossible for a person to do without food, he cannot live rightly without holding close to the Hierarchy. Let the seeker not resemble a log that just lies there, leaning on something else for support, but rather be like a vigilant guard who increases his powers by being ready to rise up in defense at any moment. Though you are sufficiently aware of the One Light, I am speaking about it again, so that you can increase your powers. Even the cross itself is powerless without the heart. Even the purest prana will not penetrate a spiteful heart. Even Aum will amount to nothing in the face of a deceitful, treacherous heart. Let us keep this in mind, so that no form of possession may penetrate the heart. Having examples of possession right before you, you see what is being lost during these days of shameful weakness.

206. You can understand that the ritual aspect of Yoga was required in ancient times, but now one should move forward by taking the path of direct communion with the Higher World. The Yoga of Fire leads the aspirant on this shortest path without abandonment of life. In this lies an important distinction, a new understanding of the ways in which the worlds are coming together. We have before us an example of a significant step in attainment of the so-called Samadhi, a step taken without withdrawing from life. One can well understand that this manifestation of the Mother of Agni Yoga is not easy to attain under the conditions created by the Great Battle. The value of such a manifestation lies in the fact that the usual rules of concentration are completely transcended. Precisely, the entire significance has been transferred to the heart—in other words, all the significance of the rapprochement of the worlds has been focused there. In this connection, one should note that her heart has borne this saturation beautifully. Of course, the sensation being felt right now does not arise from Samadhi. I have already advised you several times about the need to be cautious—as in spirit, so in matter. I beg you to protect your heart from both inner and outer disturbances. Exceptional measures need to be taken in order to repulse all the attacks. You must understand that tomorrow is completely different from yesterday, for the rotation of events is without precedent. Never before have there been such heavy clouds, and you should be of good cheer when facing them.

207. Many of the observations drawn from life are so instructive! You can study how the success of outer actions depends upon the striving of the heart. You can also study exactly which deviations from strivings act upon the outer waves of the currents. At times one can see how a condition that is insignificant from the perspective of everyday life may have a tremendous impact upon inner action, or, on the -other hand, an unworthy desire, even a very slight one, can destroy a structure that is ready for use. But paying attention to the activity of the heart is not generally accepted. People are ready to doom themselves to any misfortune rather than think about its causes. We are also concerned when we see how people permit an intolerable train of thought near the magnetic centers, how they are unwilling to keep in mind that it is precisely near these centers that a special vigilance is necessary. Naturally, everyone is allowed to think about himself, but where the pace is being measured in millennia, it is inappropriate to flit about like butterflies. In the final analysis, people must learn to commeasure! Thoughts about the Highest must give rise to the highest.

208. The happiness of the world is dependent upon the cross. The draining of the cup of poison is what insures a future for humanity. Only out of its own ashes does the phoenix rise again. The pelican nurtures its young with the blood of its own heart. That is

how the highest energy is transmuted, the energy that lies at the basis of the birth of whole worlds. So when I spoke to you about shouldering an excessive load, I was already pointing out the fact that the higher energy is developed only under tension. And when I spoke to you about the salutary courage of despair, I was already pointing to the shortest path. So let us comprehend the salutary energy, for that is the only way for us to avoid all the malicious threats. Who, then, would prefer slow decay to luminous flight? Only by flying far and wide can we reach the shore of Light! But foolish are those who suppose that ruin is unavoidable. The ultimate degree of tension is only necessary for distant flight. Thus, We speak of victory, not of downfall.

209. An understanding of the grace and benefit of tension impels the heart to the Higher Worlds. Only on this path does the blue flame glow. Some parts may burn up, but the essence will shine brighter. Do not feel frightened when the great days are approaching. When you are examining armor, you should be aware that victory is made possible only by trust and the heart. It is where the forces have gathered that you can find true successes for yourself.

210. "Aren't there some elements of egoism in the state of ecstasy and the state of Samadhi?" an ignoramus will ask. But then, how could he know that this supreme state not only has none of the characteristics of egoism but is entirely antithetical to it? How could someone who has never known the highest tension realize that precisely such tension conveys the power of lofty Grace for the Common Good? Nothing generates such pure self-renunciation as a heart brimming with ecstasy. Which of the human energies can compare with the energy of the heart, and which of the energies can act at such great distances? For the heart, the worlds have no boundaries and the consciousness knows no restrictions. With the heart a window can be created that opens onto the Invisible. But as was once said, the Invisible will become visible and we shall be ready to accept the Fiery Baptism in life. Therefore, let us be fully aware of the significance of the experiment that the Mother of Agni Yoga has performed here without withdrawing from life. Having recorded everything from the first spatial sparks through all the fires up to Samadhi, she will leave writings that will form a threshold into the New World. That is why I speak not only of tension but also of great caution. Armageddon does not make the conditions of ascent any easier, and that difficulty makes what has been achieved all the more valuable.

So I am saying, learn to listen to the fiery heart. Do not harbor doubt about something that has been purified with Fire. Wisely have the foundations of the heart been revealed in life. How deeply should the seeker rejoice in this rock of goodness!

Hold on to Me more firmly. Hold on to Me at every moment, at every step. The daggers of Satan are drawn, ready to plunge into your back, but if there is firm unity, each blade will break against the rock of goodness. Steadfast striving is necessary; it proves useful in all the worlds.

211. Let everything be done for the Good. Let every action lead to a new achievement. Let thought of the general welfare accompany every deed. Let the command of the Good influence everything, just as the vivid image of the Teacher does. Indivisible from the Good is the Teaching of the Heart. Besides the heart, who or what can justify or censure a person's intentions? The purity of the heart is manifested by

Fire. It is necessary to speak about this vital application of Fire again and again, yet nothing is said about the fiery purifier either at home or in school. And could a teacher who has never even thought about reality speak about Fire? Just because somebody makes an affirmation about Fire does not mean his own consciousness is firm. That is why we have to be so assiduous in observing and examining the manifestations of our own lives. Quite often important signs surround us and reveal the significance of our future, but because our power of attention is undeveloped we are unable to discern the cogent reality.

212. Patience is a gift of heaven—so said the ancients. Why should patience be something from heaven, when one would think it ought to belong exclusively to the heart? But how are we to intensify patience if we do not know about the Higher World? It is only when the silver thread that extends from the heart to the Higher World becomes strong that understanding of patience will arise. We revere this quality; close to it are tolerance and containment, the capacity to embrace—in other words, the opening of the Gates. Even though we may not feel close to something, if it opens up the heart of our neighbor, wouldn't we tolerate it in order that his heart might be kindled? Or would we prefer to please ourselves and end up embittering the heart of someone close to us? Rather, wouldn't it be a wonderful test to keenly observe just what will open somebody's heart to the Good? In considering the great diversity of attainments, one cannot but recognize the general harmony among the various spheres. It may be expressed in just a single sound, but each true note rings out with a cosmic consonance and must be accepted with care. That is why people are so

indignant at heart when this note is rejected. The test of patience is one of the very highest.

213. Possession must be very clearly defined. You should not be surprised to find a number of possessed people near the hearths of spirituality. The reason for this is that the dark forces are seeking to shore up their guard. Who, if not the possessed, is best able to assist the dark forces? Moreover, there are countless varieties of possession. First of all, you need to look into the essence and discern where there is Good and where harm. That is how the flaming heart will immediately discern where possession is concealed.

214. The guarantee given by the Forces of Light is the most powerful foundation for the New Life. I can assure you, the dark ones have a dreary road ahead. I am affirming the Light of the future, which through various voices will kindle fires all over the world. I am affirming that the Teaching is a manifestation of the New World. I am affirming that the most precious concepts are steps on the path of life. I am affirming that there is no darkness that could extinguish Our signs. I am affirming that something beneficial can be obtained from the turmoil. I am affirming that the forces of the Subtle World are striving to approach the earthly plane. I am affirming that this difficult hour is a clarion call. I am affirming that everyone who follows Us will attain salvation. I am affirming that the many scattered members will be united. I am affirming the path to the sunrise, a path on which there is but a single decision. I am affirming the date of happiness, a date that brings a promise of salvation to the world.

215. You should not fear the attacks of darkness. There exist a multitude of dark machinations, but they are like the branches of a torch. I affirm that it is the destiny of the dark ones to be adversaries of Light; but

I am sending out a call to unity, and therein lies a great experiment. One has to provide the world with evidence, and isn't the temple of the Spirit such evidence? I am affirming a new understanding of the Hierarchy. I am affirming that a new battle for the Banner of Light is beginning.

216. Right efforts wipe away the manifestations of contagion. A person who is striving actually has very strong immune resistance. The same goes for people who are walking along the edge of an abyss. The most powerful wings are woven of aspirations and striving. It even turns out that striving is the most effective antidote. The fire born of swift, intense striving is the very best shield. The ancients explained why arrows fail to reach those who are striving. Nowadays doctors could show how a special substance develops in the course of spiritual striving. Accept this fact as vital advice and put it to work in your life. I am pointing out how the striving spirit changes its position with the swiftness of light and becomes impossible to catch. So you should get used to striving and manifest it physically as well as spiritually. A teaching that does not instill striving is like a sack full of holes. You should embrace the essence of what is being said, because a study of the words alone will stop with the tongue. But beware of a tongue that moves rapidly while the heart stays deadly still. Let us not forget about the antidote of genuine striving.

217. Do not doubt that I have good reasons for speaking about striving. So much is in need of definition. Seekers also need to strive because the whirlwind is powerful and it is better to fly ahead of the cyclone. You need to strive to Me in thought—it is this striving that is the most essential. Learn not only to have My Image constantly before you but also to project your thoughts along the Hierarchical line. Just as a boat's anchor is cast so that one can move closer, in casting our thoughts along the Hierarchical line we move onward without wavering. Nobody doubts that the best way is to hurry to the best.

218. What I pointed out about possession and the Satanists is something that you are now observing every day. Avoid complaining and be strict in protecting yourself, and you will attain victory. Let that strictness be like a sharp sword. Thus, everyone who blasphemes must be punished.

219. There is tremendous tension; you should understand how closely the world situation is connected with the work. It is impossible to divide the two, when the overall situation is tantamount to a battle of unprecedented proportions. That is why I emphatically command that you stay undivided, that you be imbued with the tension of the moment. You must not retreat, but rather join together in putting pressure on the possessed. If a jest be permitted, one might call this phase of the conflict "the battle against possession." The dark ones try to strengthen themselves through possession, but such methods cannot last very long, for it is precisely through possession that they bring on their own disintegration. You know how possession gradually destroys the organism, for it inevitably causes the paralysis of certain nerve centers. In fact, doctors could do a great deal of useful work by directing their attention to possession. Ask Dr. L. whether he noticed certain peculiarities in the eyes of the possessed, for one can judge the duality of existence by the eyes. After he replies, I will make corrections in response. I do not have in mind just superficial manifestations, such as lackluster eyes or a shifting glance, for attention should be paid to other symptoms as well. One can also observe symptoms in the gait, the voice, and even in a change of weight. Do not ask psychiatrists about it, because their conclusions are already set in stone; but physicians like Dr. L. are able to observe without preconceptions. How urgent such observations are now that possession is reaching epidemic proportions! Sensing the weakness of human hearts, hordes of spirits, shrewd and ferocious, are rushing to capture the earthly odor.

220. I shall assign the first experiment in understanding My Instructions. I shall lay down the basis for beginning collaborative work. I shall issue the first explicit Command about launching activities for the next step. I shall send out the first call on behalf of the Banner of Peace, which is facing fierce opposition. I shall issue the first Command warning those who are working harm. I am establishing the first hour of a new creation, but unity is only possible if there is complete, conscious communion with the Hierarchy. Moreover, good must conquer evil, which means that good must be active. It is worthless if the spirit is good but the tongue is spouting blasphemy. For the next step, every blasphemy must be exterminated, for the karma of blasphemy is close to that of betrayal. This should be thoroughly understood, for a person who blasphemes cannot know the Hierarchy.

221. In the future when the photography of auras begins, the use of light filters should be considered. The presence of blue and violet tones suggests how difficult it may be to capture on ordinary film the shades that bear resemblance to the tones of the Subtle World, to which the aura belongs. Thus, an aura can be photographed if the space around it is filled with meteoric dust or if powerful psychic energy takes part in the process. So after doing what we can on a

physical basis, let us again return to psychic energy. But for the accumulation of this energy it is vitally necessary, first of all, to avoid blasphemy, which disintegrates everything.

222. We constantly insist that you learn to overcome every sort of fear. This requirement is not something abstract, but has in mind your immediate ascent. Once it has grown stronger, fear, like many negative features, forms itself into a sort of negative magnet. During the lifetimes that follow, this magnet will impel the personality toward the object of the fear that has been instilled. If someone is afraid of something, he will inevitably be compelled to cross the path of that very horror until he has freed himself of fear. That is why it is beneficial if a person, having realized the invulnerable nature of his spiritual essence, goes on to liberate himself from all fears, because all the objects of fear are really insignificant. Even an encounter with a powerful dark entity is not dangerous for someone who maintains a firm bond with the Hierarchy. Other negative qualities can also be terminated if a person is aware that reverting to them would be worthless, since he would have to experience their return blow.

223. "Catch the smallest devil by the tail and he'll show you where the biggest one hides." This ancient Chinese proverb points out the importance of small details in revealing the most essential. In fact, caution in details will be the most effective key to attaining great achievements. People mistakenly assume that details are unimportant on the path of ascent. Even the most beautiful, heroic actions rested on details that were foreseen in good time. What great attention does the follower of the Teacher direct to all the stones! Anything not intrinsic to the situation will come to his notice. Only a poor student will say, "Teacher, in

my exultation I smashed my nose." Such an inability to commeasure will show how far the student is from being vigilant. This Chinese proverb has another meaning as well: the greatest criminal is best detected by the smallest details of his conduct.

224. When We turn attention to details, it means that these are what can improve the situation. Quality of work depends upon correlations seen in advance. An approach that only paints with broad brushstrokes is reminiscent of the work of the giants, who had to leave the picture long ago on account of their crudeness. But the spirit knows neither giants nor dwarfs; it knows striving for a state of perfection in which all the bells of the Cosmos ring out. So let us recall the conditions for perfectment. We may have begun with the Asuras, but we shall conclude with the Devas.

225. You should keep close to Us in the Battle. You must learn to love the place close to Us, as if nothing else existed.

226. Snarling fills the spheres. Every one of you must help to maintain the equilibrium. The dark front is using every means available to penetrate our lines. We shall not tire of turning your attention to how much vigilance is needed in small details. Learn how to listen and look around. Not only can you catch the ruses of the dark ones, but you also can hear all the bells and other cosmic signs. They indicate how tense the atmosphere is and how close We are, and they also serve to remind one of the Hierarchy. You should not get confused if the bells and strings begin to resonate softly; there are many reasons that could happen. Moreover, they might be heard by people who should not yet hear such calls to battle. That is why now in particular I am turning your attention to details. It is very helpful to study these minute breaths of nature.

Besides being applicable to the Great Battle, these observations are necessary for further progress.

228. At a time when the atmosphere is polluted as never before, one has to speak about breathing. Depression has grown denser and even reached the mountains. Never before has there been such density in the lower strata. Researchers could investigate this phenomenon, and people could ponder the peculiar features of our times. So even relying on such elementary methods we could come to realize how unusual these times are.

228. It is no honor to be enticed by the dark ones. It is no honor to find oneself at a loss for words in speaking against the dark stratagems. Let us not imagine that the devices of our attackers are going to decrease. It is wrong to believe that someday a state of undisturbed rest will arrive. Every shock is but a touchstone. So you should look forward to each act of oppression as a source of the tension preceding a leap. If a depth of spirit exists, who can exhaust its depths? And who could measure the fullness of the heart, and with what measures? Truly, the heart answers for itself. Truly, only the language of the heart can convey the essence of existence. Therefore, we shall not be afraid when the oppression intensifies. Doubt may undermine every intensification, which is why doubt is rejected and its progenitor is called the father of lies.

The details of what is happening now correspond to the great significance of what has been destined. You may rejoice in these details, for they remind one of some glorious pages.

229. Who or what can substitute for the unity of hearts that, like a bonfire ablaze, conveys the calls to the distant worlds? Who can go on being afraid if he has touched the Infinite even once?

230. Since even the smallest accumulation of spirit is important for the future, shouldn't we fill the consciousness with an inflow of energy? Most certainly, everything positive determines the nature of the treasury we have in the future. Besides, for the sake of the Hierarchy, it would be inappropriate to become a pauper in spirit. And every conquest or discovery made can be brought to humanity. Naturally, personal gain has no place in the Hierarchy or in the flaming heart. The saturation of the heart may be of three kinds: personal and selfish, in other words, short-lived; self-sacrificing for something close and clearly defined—a *podvig* in the midst of life; or a universal saturation of the heart that extends to all humanity. The last type of saturation is both easy and difficult: easy because it liberates one from the Earth, difficult because it affirms a feeling that is beyond race and nationality. The universal saturation of the heart requires experimental research and exercise. Proposing such a saturation is like suggesting that the contents of an entire house be packed into a small box; but a well-tested spirit will have no problem choosing what is most precious.

A person who finds it difficult to bring along precious accumulations in following the path of Hierarchy has no understanding of values. So the wayfarer must get accustomed to not letting anything slip and be ready to offer his accumulations on into Infinity.

231. Sometimes the roots of a tree may be firmer than the foundations of a house. When the floor starts shaking, wouldn't it be safer to catch hold of the branch of a tree? The times are so difficult that you may find a branch more secure than the slabs that make up the floor. Even a small window may prove more useful than a door. In the midst of earth tremors, the supple, living branch will not break; that is why you should focus on studying the nature of things. It is silly not to make use of what is growing right by the window. Only a madman needlessly uproots a plant that he himself is unable to cultivate. Likewise, it is only creatures of falsehood that try to encircle the path and force the traveler to deviate. But on the branches of life one can leave the signs of the true path. So let us protect every branch that grows by the window. When necessary, let the leaves of the garden preserve our work and protect us from the whirlwind—this means that the whirlwind is raging.

I am explaining that you should not fear the whirlwind, for it is bringing flowers from every corner of the world. The roots that make up remedies often come from widely scattered places.

232. No wonder the heart senses what special measures are needed. Naturally, the heart knows how circumstances change a situation. But to await a change of circumstances is like waiting for a whirlwind to blow in from beyond the mountains. The whirlwind is already blasting away; is it heading toward us? Won't it rip the roof right off? Won't it sweep away the harvest? Who, then, will stay its fury? But the Invisible Guardian is whispering, "Call on Me."

What, then, will purify the atmosphere, if not the whirlwind? If even the purest snow on the highest mountains is full of meteoric dust, how dense the atmosphere of the valleys must be! There is no room in the bustling city. So let us turn our eyes to the sunrise.

233. A command of the will can change the pulse. One can almost stop the heart. You might carry out all kinds of psychophysiological actions, but if you ask Me how to act now, I will tell you, "Let your heart ascend." Picture your heart as if it were in a chalice from which a flame was rising. Thus, above the

physiological functions let us place the aspiration of the heart upward to the Hierarchy.

234. When the world is deep in confusion you may expect frightening whirlwinds that, like waterspouts, will pierce through the lower strata of the atmosphere and totally twist the way people think. You must be ready for assaults quite unlike anything undergone before, but to pass through them means to go forward on the path of knowledge.

235. It has already been said that once possession has been detected, one should either drive out the possessor or leave the possessed person in quiet and solitude, for then the possessor, unable to find a field of activity, will get bored and depart. Of course, it is better to prevent the possessed person from having access to weapons or alcohol, but to do so in a way that does not make him feel at all isolated.

236. If we look at a deodar tree, the tallest and most powerful, we will find many marks on the trunk where former branches have fallen away. Far from weakening the deodar, the departing branches leave the most powerful evidence of the tree's strength—even steel will break against these spots. No Teaching feels frightened about those who fall away. The Teaching knows that the lower branches must fall. In fact, when carried off by the wind, those that have fallen away may end up carrying out what they have been assigned to do. They may even give birth to new deodars. And their resin will have curative properties, all the same. Later, when they are joined together to support the corner of a house, they will unite in bearing the overall pressure. So do not be frightened when people fall away. They cannot go far from the resin of the heart. And if you observe from above, looking down upon the multitude of crossroads that intersect, you will even smile

upon the travelers who are meeting. When you realize the length of the infinite path, you will come to apply different standards of measurement. There is nothing frightening about people wandering; it is only immobility that is chilling.

237. A guarantee will make a good shield, but let us distinguish between falling away and betraying. Falling away may be due to some karmic cause or some peculiarities of the physical body, but there are no circumstances that justify betrayal. I can assert that the consequences of betrayal are the most impossible to avoid. Nothing can free the traitor from the fate of being betrayed himself. A betrayal of the Teaching is considered to be the most heinous of all. Human beings cannot blaspheme the Highest Spirit. In studying the activities of the heart, you can see what physical shocks are brought on by betrayal of the Highest. The disintegrative force that issues from a betrayal is not limited to the boundaries of the personality; it acts ceaselessly over vast expanses. Just as the highest spheres sense every benevolent ascent, every betrayal resounds like the stones of a crumbling tower. Following up the analogy of the deodar, one might say that betrayal is like a hollow tree in which bats have nested.

238. Human snarling is giving rise to a real menagerie. That is why people have to learn not to imitate animals. Of course, there are still plenty of human manifestations that bear similarity to animals, but a person who is striving forward does not have time to look back at the brutes.

239. If a mother does not attend patiently to the first wishes of her baby, she is no mother. If a Teacher does not show patience in dealing with the first steps of a disciple, he is no Teacher. If the Teacher does not understand the path of a disciple, he is no Teacher. If a

Teacher does not lay his hand upon the eyes of his disciple, he will be the one who deprives him of sight. So let us guard the path of the heart. Any form of oppression is foreign to the heart of a Teacher. The Teacher keeps an eye on what the student is experiencing, and will gently remove his hand if it touches fire. Patience is a gem in the Crown. It is evidence that one is drawing near to Infinity.

240. After courage comes calm. A coward cannot arm himself with calm. But how wondrous is the calm of truth's sword. That is why you should often remind yourself that the gate of courage is absolutely essential.

241. With every sensation of pity, the heart contracts. While pity for others eventually expands the heart with a new light, self-pity leaves the heart like a withered mango. The same principle applies to rapture and charitable deeds. It is time to draw a line between mercenary motives and universal Blessings.

When teaching history in the classroom, it would be useful to give the students the task of describing what they would have done in the place of various heroes. The teacher should not try to get the students to answer in a certain way; rather, the ground should be open to any and all considerations, so the students will embark on their first tests. Thus, from their earliest years children should grow used to being able to choose consequences freely. Naturally, the Invisible Hand of the Teacher will always forewarn about backsliding. Of course, this presupposes the existence of at least a thin thread of connection with the Hierarchy.

242. Regarding the various qualities of love, let us note the love that holds back and the love that impels forward. Essentially, the first type is earthly, while the second is heavenly. What a multitude of creations have been destroyed by the first, and what a similar number have been winged on by the second! The first is aware of all the limitations of space and consciousness, but the second has no need to measure things by earthly standards. It is unimpeded by distances or considerations of death. While the first views the world as a planet, the second is not hampered even by the possibility that the planet may be destroyed, because all the worlds lie before it. Actually, the second love extends to the physical world as well as the Subtle and Fiery Worlds. It kindles hearts, giving them the highest joy, and is therefore indestructible. So let us expand the heart—not for Earth but for Infinity.

243. Let us accept love as the motive force in the expansion of consciousness. The heart will not be aflame without love; it will not be invincible, nor will it be self-sacrificing. So let us bring gratitude to every receptacle of love, for love lies on the border of the New World, where hatred and intolerance have been abolished. The path of love unfolds with the intensity of cosmic energy. So on this path everyone will find his place in the Cosmos. Not as dried leaves but as lotuses aflame will people find kinship with the Highest World.

244. Where does the boundary of personal gain begin? The heart knows such boundaries, while the intellect is unable to pull apart the petals of the fiery lotus. When the guard is entrusted with protecting the entrance, when he is given a shield, and when he accepts in his shield all the arrows aimed at the Teacher, this will also be a personal action, but it will be the very opposite of personal gain. The heart is well aware of these beautiful personal actions in which every enemy arrow grows into a new petal of the fiery lotus. These personal actions—compelled by no one, ordered by no one, disproved by no one, but condemned by all

the evil forces—will be the true rays of *podvig*. Precisely such a condemnation, arising from malice and anger, will serve as genuine evidence of *podvig*. You should note that darkness does not condemn genuine selfishness; this also provides a true criterion. Not only should you know the standard that leads upward, you should also know the one that draws people down. That is the only way you can fully appreciate the shield of *podvig*.

245. Relativity and imperfection are manifestations that characterize every life, but it is these features that open the door to the future. People who create obstacles for themselves by dwelling on their imperfection, demonstrate their "completeness"—that is their unfitness for moving forward. Completion is impossible in the process of motion. Only the ongoing attainment of perfection amidst the fiery whirlwinds establishes the true path. It is to this same process of perfection that the various kinds of earthly martyrdom—*podvig* and heroic actions—lead, for it is amidst the extreme intensity of these achievements that the greatest fire of the heart arises. Of course, martyrdom should not just be understood as something physical, as the principal martyrdom is always spiritual. While the heartbeat may be nearly normal, the spiritual tension can be quite extraordinary.

So it is essential to establish the significance of achievement in spirit. Nowadays it is quite rare for somebody to be condemned to the stake, but martyrdom of the spirit is especially on the increase. This is the way things are bound to be when the Subtle World is approaching the physical. There is nothing astonishing about physical motion being transfigured into spiritual. Let us not forget the symbol of transfiguration, which shows the physical existence being transformed into the subtle. A great many symbols have been manifested to serve as milestones on the path of evolution, but humanity regards them as abstractions.

246. A multitude of mistakes have been made because the evolution of laws has been misunderstood. Whenever humanity approached fundamental laws on the basis of what the ancients had discovered, it usually forgot to take into consideration everything that had accumulated over long periods of time—though such stratifications are of no small importance. So if you take a stick and draw a circle in the air, it will return to its original position altered and full of new deposits. The philosopher who affirms that our planet is renewed with every rotation is correct. In any case, it changes with every rotation, as does the law, which, while remaining unshakeable at its core, is constantly being enveloped with the spirals of evolution. These envelopes are deeply significant, which is why it would be an error to adopt the law of past millennia in toto. And that is why we insist on constant study. We cannot be satisfied with the law that governed the planet during the Ice Age. Likewise, we cannot equate the spiritual equilibrium of a thousand years ago with that of the present time. Even in terms of chemistry the strata around the Earth have changed. Unapplied energies have been aroused, which is how chaos finds new ways to approach.

247. The present-day chaos is like a race between Chaos and the Manifest. The summoning up of new energies is leading to explosions of the elements. That is why one can no longer stop, but must instead stake all one's resources on making things manifest. So the white horses of Light must overtake the black horses.

This reminder has to be repeated; otherwise, some seekers may be enticed by the swift, dark steeds.

248. Each day brings new decisions. It is wrong to focus on today, for you may be left behind with the past. All the battles fought on the basis of today will be lost tomorrow. The Banner will reveal the path of the whirlwind!

249. Without noticing it, you yourself speak symbolically and conditionally, so do not be surprised that cosmogony also needs symbols. The language of the heart is the breath of the Supreme. Let us not hinder it with needless words.

250. A good deal is now known about the thread that connects the physical and subtle bodies during the projection of the latter. Likewise, clear awareness should be revived of the silvery thread that connects one with the Hierarchy. People should not imagine it to be something abstract, for it exists just like a tornado in which heaven and earth have been joined. Given its spiral structure, the very formation of the silvery thread resembles that of a tornado. Once the energy of the heart swells up with love and devotion, the luminous spiral will whirl out into space and, naturally, will encounter the Teacher's ray due to the law of attraction. You should get used to seeing and sensing this light-bearing link that burns hot and bright amidst the whirlwinds of space. Since many people have never even seen tornados, what has been said will just seem to them like empty sound. But let them begin to think more deeply, starting with the crudest and most obvious manifestations and then imagining Infinity, where anything is possible, where no rational thinking is capable of exhausting the totality of Being.

251. Some people deny everything invisible. Not only savages but also many "educated" people are unwilling to even think about the stars. The Teachings offer hints about countless heavenly dwellings, but evidently people do not wish to speed up their journey. It is just as in the theater where spectators sob with pity one moment, but the next thing are ready to go back to their grudges and pounce on each other.

252. The agony that the heart suffers in its striving to the distant worlds gives rise to a special kind of anguish. Hearts that have been tested many times cannot be confined to an aura that is fixed and earthly in its scope. And their experience confirms how powerfully the Teaching summons them to an expanded understanding. Nothing will erase the memory of the distant worlds in those who have approached them in the fiery body. Just as the stars are innumerable, the memory of the distant worlds is inexpressible in words. Likewise, the heart will not forget about the silvery thread, which extends like a ladder into the Infinite. The earthly body cannot withstand many fiery revelations, but the thread of the heart maintains an awareness of the distant worlds.

253. Keep your eye on the many events taking place. They cannot be thought of as chance occurrences; rather, they are spreading across the world according to a certain law. It is as if invisible hands were touching numerous strings. Moreover, you can notice that formerly silent strings are beginning to resonate again, and more powerfully than ever. Those who understand Armageddon to be a field in which signs of the highest energy manifest are correct. This battlefield cannot be something that arises accidentally; rather, it is like a magnet that attracts opposing energies. The field of the future City of Light is destined to act as a counterbalance to this battlefield. Just as the existence of the field of Armageddon is proclaimed by

the clash and clatter of arms, the existence of the field of the City of Light is proclaimed by the peal of bells. According to the contrast, one can judge the dimensions of the destined. So you might turn your ears to the din of the battle in order to hear the ringing of the bells.

254. A tower rests upon a steady foundation, built firm upon a rock. The tower of courage rests upon a steady consciousness, reinforced by the rock of the heart. But by what means will the heart verify itself? Only by the Hierarchy. Let the heart accustom itself to conversing with the Teacher. Like the wise ones of old, let the heart know only communion with the Lord, so that nothing trivial may intrude while the heart is talking with the Highest.

The conversation with the Teacher should be guarded as a treasure. A person who understands the sacred significance of this communion will not plunge into darkness. But how carefully must one protect the heart from the possibility of the silver thread being severed! Nothing can restore the severed thread. It is possible to show every kind of compassion, but the thread is forged out of a multitude of qualities. Just as ancient Images were cast out of many metals, the silver thread is made strong by many different qualities. Indeed, the heart's sweetest conversation with the Teacher is a forge in which a mighty fire glows.

255. You know that living fire is the best means of disinfection, but the nature of fire is the same in all of its manifestations. The fire of the heart will be a lofty manifestation of fire, which means that it will be the best purifier and protector. So instead of using all kinds of dubious, often poisonous antiseptic medicines, it is much better not only to have the fire of the hearth but also to kindle the fires of the heart. One can

find out for oneself how effectively the fires of the heart fight serious illnesses. Sooner or later our contemporary physicians will have to pay attention to the various states of the fires. Doctors will not make much progress in finding a panacea if they go on barking at truths that have been known for ages.

Your thoughts about the Vedic deities are perfectly correct; indeed, the microcosm resembles the Macrocosm. I affirm that the fire of the heart purifies the densest darkness. But along with this ability to purify, the heart is full of the qualities of a magnet, which is why it is the natural link with the Macrocosm.

256. One should understand the fiery path as a path to the Highest. Not words, not fear, not habit, but the communion of the heart is the most enduring manifestation, the one transmitted from time immemorial. So it is the rainbow bridge that will bring us closer to the other shore. How many controversies rage on regarding that shore, but it does exist, and one must find the path to it. Not dried up autumn leaves but the flaming heart will cross every bridge. A person who does not think about the birth of the heart's fire is ignorant of the upward path; he is unwilling to look upon it in a luminous way.

257. Let doubt fall silent, for it has put out the fires of the heart many times. One must rid oneself of this worm in order to avoid dealing with a dragon. Doubt is especially ruinous nowadays, for a warrior can only possess a single sword. Nobody can have two swords in a battle, nor does anyone throw two spears or shoot two arrows. A seeker can only attain with a single stroke, with the daring of single-minded striving. It is not easy, but success is found near the fire of the heart.

258. Dreams may reflect the past and the present. Dreams may reflect an already molded template of the future. But besides these earthly reflections, there may be reflections of the Subtle and Fiery Worlds. Of course, it is these latter two types that people are often unable to recall because such reflections are fleeting and, being of a different nature, can hardly be measured by earthly standards. Only the flaming heart is able to retain these sparks of the distant worlds in the consciousness. The same thing happens with visions. One may see stars belonging to constellations other than those seen through a telescope, but for this to happen the fiery body has to be sufficiently formed. Of course, the fiery body always exists, but it may be chaotic and unconscious. But when the course of striving runs through all the bodies, the triad begins to shine.

259. People should not think that lofty attainments will make them safe from the monsters of darkness. On the contrary, the Light will reveal new monsters whose fury is fathomless. We shall not grieve over this, for it is the monsters that provide the legs for the throne. There is a good reason why sacred objects are depicted as mounted upon animal-like pedestals. But this consideration does not mean that people need not be vigilant.

260. Since the so-called state of Nirvana is not rest but rather the highest tension of energy, one might ask whether rest even exists. Indeed, how is it possible to imagine rest if everything is in motion and exists on account of motion? The very concept of rest was invented by people who wished to flee from existence. They preferred immobility, forgetting that there cannot be a moment without motion. Equilibrium is the concept needed. The seeker should think not about rest but about how to maintain equilibrium in the midst of the whirlwinds. The silver thread is made taut by the power of striving, and for that very reason one should know what equilibrium is, so as to avoid burdening the thread of the Hierarchy by faltering. The thread will not break when it is tautened, for even a straw holds out so long as it is not bent. The silver thread is based on the very same law of connection, but if a person does not refrain from fluctuating in a disorderly manner, he usually cannot hold fast to the link. So let us not bemoan the lack of rest, since rest does not exist in the first place.

261. Nobody in the wrong will be able to hold out against equilibrium, which is why the stroke of the sword must be delivered in accordance with the law. So let us understand the way in which both the physical and the higher laws are focused in the heart. This center was called the crossroad, and was represented by an equilateral cross; the dorje, like the swastika, indicated the rotation of the heart's fire. Rotating and having arms of equal length are signs of equilibrium. In childhood someone tried to stand on a ball, unaware that this is a great symbol of equilibrium.

262. The external must not conceal the fundamental. That is why humanity should not litter up the path to ascent. One has only to let in a little dust and the most resonant trumpet will lose its tone. It is this tiny pinch of dust that is more dangerous than all the swords and knives put together. The same must be said about the fluctuations: they arise not from great works but from the same speck of dust of the spirit. Thus, a person who is successful in the great also keeps his eye on the small. And a heart destined for the great senses even the smallest. It is wrong to suppose that the great is blind to the small. Quite the contrary, the great eye can see the smallest, and the flaming heart detects the inaudible rustle. If we understand the sensitivity of the great heart, then we will also be well aware of

the significance of the world's structure. Let us not soar with intoxication, nor wilt away with lofty pride. Pridefulness struts in shoes of stone; intoxication flaps wings of wax. But the dignity of the spirit is the fire of the heart, the wings that ascend to the sun.

263. Let us not forget the forward offensive, even if we see that the usual tactics of the Lords are being employed. Let us not forget how we must hasten, even though we hear the roar of the Teacher. Who can say at whom the lion is roaring on the other side of the mountain? Oh, hunter, do not assume that the tiger has already gone into hiding; rather, deal a final blow to the leopard, because in doing so you will strike fear into all the beasts who are hiding. The sword is pointed not to friends but to enemies. So let us avoid being faint-hearted.

264. Beyond all the boundaries of the human world flash the sparks of space. Likewise, over and above all the worldly statutes calls come flying from far away. Do you not awaken at times with unusual words resonating in your consciousness? Do you not sometimes hear unearthly names? Not few are the encounters in the Subtle World. Not few are the channels to the fiery domains. And often we are called by those whom we are destined to meet sooner or later in the future. The earthly world is not barren so long as we ourselves do not limit it. The ancients teach us a great deal about the possibilities of transformation and the link with the Higher Consciousness. It would be inexcusable if we remained in an animal state, for although animals sense the Subtle World, they are not conscious of it. But people need to become aware of their link with the distant worlds; in this lies their distinction and their power. But if people close off their consciousness, they not only injure themselves but also harm the Existence that all beings share.

265. Understanding of the highest law of the heart follows affirmation of the milestones of the future. The brain is the past, the heart is the future. Thus, more fires kindle around the heart. It should not be forgotten that besides the usual fires every epoch lights its own torches, and of course the Era of Fire gives rise to a special combination. A concentrated pure golden color and golden purple will be close to the forces of Fire.

266. Have you noticed that there are many possessed people around? Attention needs to be paid to the unprecedented spread of possession, since doing so makes it possible to fight it. First of all one should understand with whom one is dealing, for to understand means to conquer.

267. You know the sounds of the music of the spheres, the spatial bells, and the resonating strings. Someone is sure to ask why the vast majority of people do not notice these manifestations. But why are the vast majority of people satisfied with false pitch, utterly refusing to understand the subtleties of sound? Although even the rustle of paper tearing punctures space, the majority of people fail to notice it. So it is with smells. The aromas of the Subtle World often penetrate to the physical world, but first and foremost people are unwilling to notice them. They do not even notice the smoke from a raging fire until it starts to suffocate them. Not only lack of sensitivity but also lack of mobility makes people blind and deaf. They are missing the rudiments of imagination, which is why they completely distort the very meaning of Being. So for these shallow thinkers the magnet of the heart is pure nonsense.

268. Uriel is the Lord of powerful action. One can turn to various Leaders according to the nature of the help needed. If Michael joins hands with Uriel, it means that a powerful offensive is necessary. With rigor and severity did Uriel master the elements on Venus. So it is possible to steel the power, tempering it by accepting the blows of the elements. These mighty Forces should be understood as realities.

269. Let us turn from the Subtle World and vigilantly follow the gross manifestations. Let us not assume that we are somehow insured against every attempt; We ourselves are constantly objects of attacks. The only difference is that everyone encounters an opponent commensurate with his powers. The dark ones make use of every opportunity to attack and strike with everything they devise.

270. Keep up your courage, for only courage will make possible the manifestation of motion. You have heard of betrayals being committed against the best and the most worthy. The present time will not pass without these signs manifesting, for they have accompanied every Teaching. Anything of great significance has betrayal, this supreme crime, as its counterweight. You cannot point out a single Teaching that was not subject to betrayal.

Teraphim may be artificial or alive. For events of worldwide scope living teraphim are chosen; people call them the anointed, because their link with the Hierarchy marks them with physical stigmata. Although these teraphim may not affirm anything out loud, the dark ones still sense the grace conferred in the anointment, and they commit betrayal in order to arrest the growth of the Good. You must courageously guard yourself from traitors and draw on energy from the heart. There is no need to worry over the growth of the Good—where there is a seed of Light, there are flowers and fruit as well. But you must hold onto the thread of the heart as the sole anchor.

271. The creative output of the dark ones is quite monotonous. People wrongly assume that they are highly refined, whereas it would be more accurate to think of them as skillful liars.

272. The case of X. is an unusual one. Certainly, the karmic debt has been paid, but there remains what might be called the "husk of karma," a situation that is highly valued by the demons. Nothing intensifies enmity as much as the mirage of karma. It constantly seems as if the one who has paid off the karma still has some debt, and this ignites enmity. We make a great number of differentiations regarding karmic ties. It can be observed how over the ages one personality rises and another descends; what, then, might happen with the connective thread when such a divergence is taking place? In any case, the demons make use of the karmic husk to launch still stronger attacks.

273. The karmic husk reminds one of another kind of shell, the shell of the subtle body that also brings about many disturbances. Actually, neither of these shells ought to exist in the first place. It is only human imperfection that allows these borderline formations to exist. Of course, the physical body undergoes transformation into a subtle body, but if the spirit lags in freeing itself from earthly attractions and lust, the subtle body cannot separate in a pure condition from the physical. In such cases, it bears a distinct deposit of earthly passions. Even if the subtle body frees itself of such vestiges, this shell will still linger for a long time, wandering and swaying about like a scarecrow—and often a very negative scarecrow. It is human ignorance that bestows these dregs upon the beautiful

Subtle World. If people would think of the connection between the worlds and the evolution destined them, they would not dare to encircle themselves with such harmful debris.

274. Because of the earthly attraction, the shells of the Subtle World are especially close to dense, physical existence. It is precisely these shells that roam the entire world in the form of phantoms, and all sorts of evil spirits love to take over these free lodgings. Great is the responsibility of those who pass over into the Subtle World while still harboring earthly passions! It is horrible to litter up the beautiful expanses of Space, for Space leads to Light and can resonate with the higher knowledge. How hideous is the husk of petty carnal desires, from which it is so easy to free oneself—one has only to think of the Hierarchy of Light.

The heart, the heart, the heart—the heart is what will always remind you about the Light!

275. The Teacher is in need of an especially clear consciousness in the disciples. But when darkness cloaks the consciousness, it does not allow a person to focus all the power that is preserved in the depths. Among the reasons why a task went successfully or failed, the condition of the consciousness occupies no small place. Even a slight blockage or carelessness in striving alters the result. For example, someone may come to you with the desire to help and only be waiting for some stimulus from your side. But you may be completely absorbed in some unrelated discussion, and the desire to help melts away like a sugar lump in a cup of tea. Moreover, the custom of the country demands that time should be filled with the most inconsequential communications, and in the midst of this rubbish the most precious seeds get lost. If only humanity would value time, then a great deal that is necessary could come about. Of course, this should be governed by the heart, so that the higher measures are harmonized.

276. Naturally, it is neither spring nor autumn that brings on fatigue; rather, it is the growing density of the currents, which is pressing upon the centers. It cannot be otherwise when legions of people, possessed and raving in rage, are rushing forward. So there is no reason to be surprised when possessed people on distant continents begin to utter the very same formulas. This is one more proof of an Invisible World Government that issues from a common Source. After all, both Light and darkness are monarchical. It is extremely helpful to follow the trend of world thought. Looking at both sides, one can see a definite division, since each side will make its own efforts and adopt its own decisive measures. So even from the perspective of the earthly plane one can observe this division of the forces and understand the movement of the armies.

277. A person can think with the heart or think with the brain. There was perhaps a time when people forgot about the work of the heart, but now is the era of the heart, and we must focus our efforts in that direction. Thus, without freeing the brain of its work, we are ready to recognize the heart as a motive power. People have thought up a thousand ways to place limitations on the heart. The works of the heart are understood in a narrow sense, and not even always in a pure sense. We must bring the entire world into the sphere of the heart, because the heart is the microcosm of everything that exists. A person who is not inspired by the great concept of the heart will end up belittling his own significance. We tell people to give up getting irritated, but only greatness of heart will save a person from the poison of irritability. We speak about the

ability to embrace, but where is there an all-embracing ocean outside of the heart? We remind people about the distant worlds, but it is the heart, not the brain, that can remember about Infinity. So let us not belittle the organ that has been bestowed upon us to be a receptacle of Grace.

278. Every feeling gives birth to an energy. When a feeling is shared, it multiplies that energy many times over. A collective feeling can create a powerful energy, but for that to happen the individual feeling must be intensified, and the collective feeling that everyone shares must be brought into harmony. In this lies the whole reason why contemporary feelings have such a weak influence; hardly a single state of intensified feeling is maintained nowadays. Yet what a great reality would be reflected in an upsurge of a multitude of harmonized feelings! The ancients called feeling the forge of power. Indeed, how majestic is the feeling of mutual love! And mutual gratitude is no less powerful. Invincible is the feeling of self-sacrificing heroism. With it beautiful towers and strongholds can be constructed. But from where will this harmonization come? Not from reasoning or the convolutions of the brain, but from the heart, from Light. To the dark ones we will leave only the feeling of rancor. In the midst of the smoking red sparks there will be no harmony.

279. Few people will accept feeling as a force. For them, feeling is a moth wing. With that sort of perspective, the entire structure collapses. We find comfort not in the fact that someone has vouched for our existence but in the knowledge that our most powerful transmission will attain its luminous goal.

280. Satanic fury may also prove useful. Someone may put to work the power of the air, someone else the power of fire, and another person the power of water.

Skill in driving the most furious horses can only bring the goal closer. So let us be strong in our mastery of the elements; it is the will of the heart, not reasoning, that masters the elements. Indeed, reason will always seek to persuade us that the fight with the elements is madness.

281. So feeling gives birth to energy, and energy can create so-called possessions. How is one to deal with these possessions? We know about renunciation, but if something already exists, how is it possible to regard it as non-existent? Besides, wouldn't looking at things in that way be destructive? So let us once again invoke the Teacher and in thought pass this cumbersome load on to Him. He will be able to transfer our mental gift still higher. That is how we can solve the problem of possessions. Thus, the very name of the owner disappears, and we remain the custodians of the property of the Hierarchy. Indeed, we are allowed to read the Teacher's books, and the Teacher grants us permission to live in His house, feast our eyes on His things, and feed on the fruit of His garden. Thus, the Name of the Teacher will constantly accompany us, and we shall smile as we dust off the manifested objects that the Teacher, out of confidence, has entrusted to us. People do not know how to deal with possessions because they do not wish to understand the meaning of the mental transformation of the earthly plane into the Subtle.

282. Let us not pass over in silence a single manifestation of life. Let us summon the heart to act as judge: are we sincere when entrusting our possessions to the Teacher? We may utter delightful words but be wishing for the opposite in our hearts. So let us avoid being like the old ones, and let us with our hearts

highlight the language of the Subtle World—people call this "conscience."

283. Pure thinking is the best disinfectant. It is high time that thinking was accepted as a chemical process. Likewise, the manifestation of Armageddon should not only be understood as a war in the conventional sense but should also be viewed in terms of all the events in life. The epidemic of possession is a phenomenon that characterizes the time of the Great Battle. Certainly, our convulsed planet is overrun with suicides as well as physical and spiritual calamities. Amidst humanity can be found unusual diseases of the brain and nerves, as well as every sort of perversion. The vacillations of the spirit may be truly astonishing. One may feel indignant about the way in which the finest people are greeted with threats and hatred. It is as if the soil itself were speeding to destruction! Of course, the mad ones do not see all the luminous warriors, and they allow the dark forces to drag them into the abyss. So every seeker must summon up all his strength in fortifying himself on the foundation of the Hierarchy. Even on an ordinary battlefield a warrior must not let his communications get cut off. In this way, one should realize the Great by turning to the simplest examples.

284. In churning butter the simplest dairymaid is already aware of a mystery underlying the formation of worlds. She also knows that you cannot get butter by churning water. She will tell you that you can churn butter or whip an egg; thus, she already knows about the matter that contains psychic energy. But it is this circumstance that will strike a scientist as unconvincing. Likewise, the dairymaid will know how useful spiral rotation can be, but to some people this stipulation will appear prejudiced. Though you may feel angry, think about your surroundings and apply the laws of physics to your own existence. That is the only way you will make it through Armageddon! Naturally, it would be a mistake to forget that the heart can be applied as a counterweight to all the confusion.

285. Command your heart to come as close as possible to the Teacher. If you have to affirm the Teacher in words, begin to converse with Him as if He were right beside you. You should not expect that the Teacher's reply only come in the form of ordinary words. The answer may appear in a multitude of signs, some of them obvious and near at hand, some of them occurring far away. You should embrace the entire scope of life, so that you are able to discern the signs pertaining to great creativity. People should realize how vast the battlefield of Armageddon is. They should think about the proximity of the Powers of the Higher World. Not being dependent upon the conditions of life, these Powers are able to stand at the shoulder of every striving spirit. Truly, we are affected by the gentle touches of the Subtle World, but we should feel these not only in the quiet of the night but also in the light of day. Human beings are wrong to notice all the subtle sensations only as dusk is falling. Right now is the path to the Light!

286. The mirror of the present hour shows an unprecedented confusion. There is not even a predominance of one color. The mirror of Armageddon shows an image of gold, blue, black, and red arrows in flight. There are no outlines, but columns of explosions and clouds, hanging like heavy shrouds over an abyss. That is how the beginning of the Great Battle has been depicted since ancient times.

287. If you notice that someone is overly focused on physical yoga, remind him again that such a limitation

is undesirable. Tell him once more that the horse which has learned all the exercises and gone through them many times is not the one taken for delivery of an urgent message. So do not lose yourself in the limitations of the body. Every bodily acquisition also results in a new limitation. Only the spirit knows no limits, and the teaching of the future will be founded on the conquests of the spirit. The bodily yoga must be transformed into a path of subtle fires. Bodily yoga cannot lead to a joining with the Subtle World, for it does not grant the heart an exclusive position. But the subtle transformation will only endure if founded on the heart. It maintains the fiery capacity that is the sole condition for transformation.

288. Let no one hope to attain success by following the bodily path. Karma is not in the body but in the spirit. You also correctly noted that blows upon the aura first of all react upon the eyes. The membrane of the eyes determines the essence of the subtle substance.

289. Flights in the subtle body are revealing a quality that is new for the Earth. To be precise, the subtle body is not bound to the Earth but is flying upward with still greater ease. The earthly body rises with difficulty and falls easily, but the opposite is true of the subtle body; in fact, it is harder for it to descend. It is difficult for it to break through the manifestation of the lower spheres. Of course, I am speaking about the higher state of the subtle body; for the lower bodies, it is the lower spheres that are more comfortable. It is instructive to see how the higher subtle body is already beginning to manifest the quality of the Fiery World. So starting from the earthly state one can see all of the worlds in embryonic form. To do so, one only has to purify one's consciousness, strive in harmony with the Hierarchy, and keep a sharp watch on what is happening.

290. Anyone who has even once heard all the roaring and groaning in space has an idea of what the lower strata above the earthly plane are like. True, one must rush beyond the boundaries of these domains where horrors manifest. Even when flying through them, one feels it almost intolerable to contact the unnatural condition of these intermediate planes. So seekers should accept the path of the Subtle World as a conscious effort to reach the Fiery World.

291. Sharpening the power of observation makes it possible to observe many scientifically significant phenomena. And it is possible to observe how blows upon the aura affect not only the eyes but also the sensitivity of the skin, especially around the area where rays issue from the shoulders. One might also notice light radiating from the most unexpected materials—from wood, linen, glass, rubber, and many objects that the commonly applied laws claim should not be radiant. Of course, you know that so-called electricity represents the grossest form of the visible energy of Fohat. But when the accumulator—the purified heart—acts as a conductor for the manifestation of the subtle Fohat, then light of a special quality may issue from any surface. Fohat forms strata everywhere; to demonstrate this, all you need is an apparatus of sufficient sensitivity. Only the heart can act as such an accumulator. Of course, this cannot be an easy task when the heart has to assimilate a multitude of energies—everything from a tiger to Fohat!

292. Whoever keeps watch on the manifestations of subtle energies knows how the heart is linked to them with unbreakable bonds. He knows how hard it is, when surrounded by tigers, to rise up and carry

others on into the higher spheres. But this is the labor that must be performed by those who are launching the New World. Yes, even the very beginning must be tangible.

293. Clarity of thought and expression should be among the qualities of an Agni Yogi. Few are those who strive to think clearly, and few who realize how many subtle imprints cannot be put to use on the earthly plane, even if they are quite ready for manifestation. How many of the mysteries surrounding misfortune could be explained as consequences of tangled thinking! Everything strives to clarity. The element of Fire, the subtlest of all, offers striking examples of fiery construction. Likewise, human thought develops along the lines that fire has laid out.

294. Certainly, belittlement is a bad adviser. Belittlement gives birth to the most insignificant. Let us not think of people who belittle as martyrs; they have sown rotten seeds and creep low on the ground, hoping to see the sprouts. On the other hand, by affirming, people rectify themselves and thereby create strongholds. You already have examples of how useful affirmation is. Works can only grow by words of blessing. Think about benediction.

295. It is said that envoys from the Sage of the Mountains came to Genghis Khan. A chest that they brought contained a golden cup and several multicolored cloths. An inscription read: "Drink from one cup, but clothe yourself in the garments of all nations." That was how the Hierarchy was revealed and the tolerance worthy of a leader was expressed. In the same way let tolerance also be affirmed by expansion of the Teaching of Light. Let us pay attention to the rhythm of the Teachings given. It can be seen how the process of conveying new knowledge alternates with the process of reiterating and confirming it. Thus, the time has come to bring together everything that has been gathered and to distil the teachings of the Foundations of Life. It will soon be possible to give scientists access to the cosmic paths, which means it is all the more necessary to affirm enthusiasm for the Common Good. Especially now it is essential for people to find agreement regarding how to live and make their way into the future. When every aspect of humanity's situation is subject to unprecedented danger, the thread must be woven without reference to the trends that are expected to arise. One can find fiery forces within and thereby avoid making something commonplace out of the true panacea, the essence of All Existence. It can be seen how for some people Infinity itself ceases to be frightening, how for them the Hierarchy becomes a thread of ascent, the heart turns into a throne of the Highest Light, and the Fire of Space itself begins to shine forth as the Supreme Kingdom.

296. Let us see not only how awareness of Fire speeds up one's journey to the Supreme Kingdom, but also how it can restore a certain equilibrium to our planet, an equilibrium that is sorely needed. The path of researching cosmic rays is a correct one, but unless there is knowledge of the heart and psychic energy, any discovery will only be approximate. Pay attention to how widely the net of the Teaching is being cast. Let people hide the source, if that is their way of doing things; it does not matter. It is useful that the Teaching is being disseminated by unexpected means to the various parts of the planet. We can already show that this growth is taking place, and this kind of affirmation is the crown most suitable to the contemporary situation. Let us not be surprised that the roots are growing beyond the visible; that is what guarantees their vitality. Is it really possible to keep track of all the paths that the Teaching takes? A magnet acts according to its own laws. But from the mountaintop I can see space being saturated, and therefore I can salute you.

297. The Teacher rejoices when the manifestation of the subtle body's sensations in the earthly shell becomes tangible. A person whose consciousness is being refined is perfectly right to feel that our essence is imprisoned within a dense shell. Of course, pain is sure to manifest when the subtle body connects with the network of nerves that runs over the surface of the body. Moreover, the subtle body has to recapture its own dwelling whenever it returns to the body. You already know that the subtle body is somewhat higher than the physical, which is why there is discomfort every time it returns. Once the Subtle World has become a natural continuation of the earthly realm, there will inevitably arise the feeling that the subtle body is constantly separated from the earthly one. It could become an important new task for doctors to differentiate the pains that result from illness and those that arise from the movement of the subtle body within the dense shell. So it is also possible to approach the sensations of the subtle body by following this medical path. In this way one can connect two tasks, the spiritual and the physical.

298. More than anything else, direct sensation of the Invisible World is what transmits an understanding of it. Nothing can help the heart if it does not wish to surrender itself to this feeling and sensation. A careful approach to the phenomena of life shows readiness to apply the experimental method in investigating them. Nobody should think of this assertion as something abstract; rather, one should fully understand just how close the Teaching is to every aspect of life, since

it is rooted in experience. Likewise, one should understand all the rhythms in the alternation of events. The train runs through the fields, but when it enters a tunnel only a child screams about its disappearance. So let us stay calm throughout the multifaceted movement of events.

299. The lower spheres are so polluted that one could say without exaggeration that meteoric dust is being oxidized because of the chemical reactions of psychic energy, which first of all act upon metals. This simple observation can be borne out by paying attention to the metallic objects worn by people of various psychic dispositions. Of course, the pollution of the spheres closest to our planet is disastrous. The lower subtle bodies loiter about like swindlers at a bazaar and thereby prevent the successful formation of a spiral of constructive effort. One has to harbor a special aspiration in order to penetrate beyond the bounds of these dreadful deposits. So we should not believe that there might be thoughts without consequences; even the largest cup can be overfilled! This especially applies to rotation, when gravity holds back many particles of lighter weight. So when We speak about the vital need to purify psychic energy through refinement of thought, We have in mind the purification of the lower spheres. To borrow the language of the Church, it is necessary to conquer the infernal hordes.

300. Today is a good day for good thoughts. If thought contains creative energy, how useful it is to send a good thought out into space. Once humanity agrees to send forth good thoughts simultaneously, the infected atmosphere of the lower spheres will clear up right away. Even if it is only a few times a day, you should make a point of sending forth thoughts not about yourself but about the world. In this way you will get used to aspiration that is free of selfish motivation. Just as humanity's Savior thinks only of the entire world, in emulation of Him we can make use of our thoughts for the development of creative energy. You should not regard the transmission of thought as some sort of supernatural activity. Rather, let it be the food of the spirit, just as fuel is food for a fire during the night. Also, you should simply follow the higher example. The heart will act as a trustworthy timepiece that calls one to thought about everyone and everything. There is no need to sit in tiring meditations; thought about the world is short and reflects the renunciation of self so simply. May all go well with the world!

301. Speak to your friends regarding thought about the world, regarding thought about all the worlds! Let them not be visited by the pernicious thought of the hypocrite: "What does my thought matter to the world?" Anyone who has thought in this way has yet to renounce the self. True, each warrior shoots just one arrow, but if everyone grudges the use of his arrow, the army will end up defenseless. In that case, of what use is the cross of the world?

Who, then, could forget to patrol for the tiger? Do not let thought about the world erase memory of the tiger or of Armageddon.

302. It would be helpful to compile a book about the harm brought on by evil thoughts—helpful for oneself as well as for others. These thoughts are the source of a great many maladies. In the past only mental illnesses were thought to be connected with evil thoughts, but it is now time to discern the vast number of extremely diverse physical illnesses that arise from thought. Not only heart disease but also most afflictions of the stomach and skin are a consequence of destructive thoughts. Similarly, the transmission of

infectious diseases may be a result not only of predisposition but also of thinking. This is not simply a matter of autosuggestion, for one finds cases in which a disease was spread by one person to many. One can see how physical effects run entirely in tandem with spiritual manifestations. In this regard it has been noted that certain organisms unintentionally spread a specific infection without being subject to it themselves. In ancient times people already knew about such carriers of infection, but later that scientific knowledge was forgotten, and everything was attributed to the so-called evil eye.

303. This means that even when dealing with purely physical illnesses one needs to search for the cause in the quality of thought. Therefore, gradually direct the thoughts of the people around you toward good. You already have an example that shows how much pain is caused by maledictions and swear words, even at a great distance. In order to really pay attention, one has to turn one's heart toward the essence of what is happening. Possessed people who contact the aura may especially have an effect, even if the contact is slight. So it is essential to pay close attention to one's very first impression of people, for it is then that the heart is able to convey its sign. It is easy to imagine how possessed people may spread infection quite efficiently, which is why one ought to avoid them.

304. The manifestation of fire is destructive for the physical body, but the fiery element is quite natural for the fiery body. This means that in the expanses of the Subtle World a change must take place in the relationship between fire and the body. In fact, by observing the condition of subtle bodies one can see the boundary beyond which fire's influence becomes beneficial. The higher strata that have been purified of coarse

physical motivations are already experiencing the fiery grace, while the lower cellars of the Subtle World are still subject to the physical sensation of the flame. In addition, the more there remains of the physical husk, the more painful the action of the fire may be. That is where the idea of hellfire comes from. So it makes sense that every piece of true knowledge will direct people toward the higher strata. It is also thoroughly scientific to warn people not to carry feelings of coarse lust into the Subtle World. One can only pity the foolish people who mock the idea of a postmortem state.

305. Let us now descend from the Fiery World to the jaws of the tiger; this also has to be foreseen. Only by avoiding many jaws and hideous masks can one reach the higher strata. So the path upward must pass by many manifestations of hatred, so long as humanity does not clean these cellars by joining together in a harmonious outburst of consciousness.

306. The Teacher can point out the right direction, and sometimes He can forewarn, but seekers must carry out many actions on their own. Moreover, these actions have to be undertaken voluntarily. It is this voluntary striving that contains self-perfection. Any admixture of personal gain or fear will disturb the salutary bond.

307. The dark ones are always hoping that by harming the constructive work they will impede fulfillment of the goal; but they always fail to see that the Existent is indestructible and multifaceted in its conditions. The name of the darkest place can be uttered—yet even Marakara cannot exclude the possibility of Light. It is only necessary to find a way to approach.

308. There exist disturbances of constructive work that actually lead to a new, more refined completion of that work. That is why We are so resolute in expelling

fear, which prevents coworkers from perceiving the happy distribution of all aspects of the work. This same perspective ought to be applied in all of life's situations, for then there can be no defeat. Indeed, a happy combination of parts can only be shifted, not eliminated. But an eye that is clouded over with fear loses its field of vision.

309. Marakara is a terribly oppressive place in the lowest strata of the Subtle World. It is a disturbing place to be, because prana hardly ever reaches there. Even so, it is sometimes necessary to penetrate these Satanic strata.

310. After an attack is discovered, quite often there is an improvement in the overall situation. The enemy passes its verdict and tries to proclaim it, but if the destruction thus proclaimed fails to arise, you are sent new strength by the multitude of attentive eyes around you.

311. The Teacher affirms that a warrior can expect complete victory if only unity in consciousness is maintained. On the other hand, he cannot expect success if he harbors the slightest suspicion of the Teacher. So we have to work together, knowing that everything allowed by the laws of the Universe will be done. Is there anyone, then, who will regard this period as a time of rest? No one will deny that this time is unprecedented, not even someone who does not see far ahead. The warrior has to stand watch as if there were no one to replace him. The Teacher understands that your hearts are also burdened. Every day the world situation grows more complicated. From the perspective of Armageddon, this is entirely natural. A consciousness which insists that Armageddon must be nonsense is just raving, because it fails to see the path ahead.

312. Why must we take into consideration the laws of the Universe? Naturally, because they solve the mystery of Armageddon for us. If we lose the thread of Armageddon, we sink into chaos. And there is no path of ascent on which the thread is not needed. You know about these threads that lead one up the rocks of ascent.

313. The consequences of the Great Battle's beginning first of all affect the heart of humanity. Affirmation of the heart is especially needed now, for without it the unaware heart will not be able to withstand the hurricane of elemental confusion. Therefore, think of the heart as a mediating principle that connects you with the distant worlds. You should be aware of just what it is that burdens the heart most. It is not dramatic events that burden the heart so much as the chain of small specks of everyday dust. It is very important to remember this, because great events may even lead to a special influx of psychic energy. But Armageddon does not just consist of great events. Quite the contrary, during Armageddon a multitude of small events are evaluated, and the poor heart must get used to this downpour of small currents. I say "poor," because in essence the heart already knows the great fiery realms, but for the time being it must be dashed against the rocks of the Earth.

314. You know how near We walk to the flames of the raging fire, how close to the edge of the abyss. You know when a saturated silence means that the battle is intensifying. You feel Our tension. Only people who are foolish and conceited can imagine that above them only hymns resound. A person who has turned his gaze toward Infinity understands: the higher the world, the higher the tension. So prepare people for the unavoidable intensification. This does not mean that the Teaching draws one into a state of tension, but that this increasing pressure is a law of Existence.

To many people anything said about the rhythm of the currents seems like complete nonsense, but you know about these beneficial influences. Be assured that I am close at hand.

315. Calmness means an equilibrium of tension. Unification of consciousness means, first of all, preservation of energy. This important principle is usually forgotten. Once psychophysiology is introduced in place of limited physiology, everyone will be able to understand just how important the economy of energy is.

316. If it acts as a dissonance, a small thought can stop even a giant in his tracks. So many people start to glance back, shudder, change their direction, and otherwise show attention to passing thoughts in all kinds of ways—and without noticing where the thoughts come from. The law of attraction and repulsion through thought will be grasped most easily by musicians, who understand consonance as well as the significance of dissonance, there being one key established for an entire piece. Whoever understands what it means to conduct an entire work for many voices in a single key will all the more readily grasp the meaning of a basic thought, even when the task involved is multifaceted. So the thought underlying constructive work does not impede the manifestation of many ramifications so long as all are in the same key. And the incursion of an alien dissonance will not penetrate deeply if the basic task is solid.

317. Actually, one need only avoid terror and decay, because so long as the foundation remains strong there is no situation that cannot be transformed and yield the very best solution. So the only time one

should not create is when complete stagnation and decadence hold sway. In any case, every impetuous motion is already imbued with the consonance that brings about resolution.

318. I think that people who have visions should be carefully examined by doctors. When this is done, special symptoms will be found in the heart and nerve centers. Just as the cadence in the music of ancient India is far more refined than the harmony of Western music, a heart that is aware of the Subtle World will yield modulations of tone that are incomparably more intricate. Of course, doctors avoid examining healthy people, but that means they are overlooking a precious page in life's book, a page that leads on to the future. Usually all miracles and visions are relegated to the category of "hysteria," but nobody explains what hysteria is. People will say that it is a heightened reaction of the sympathetic nervous system, or they will attribute it to an irritation of the peripheral nerve endings. They will determine a multitude of causes and start applying remedies that would work better on a bullock. But they will not take the trouble to consider whether there might not be higher causes working in these manifestations.

319. A miracle is a manifestation of subtler energies, forces that are not accounted for in schools of chemistry and physics. "Miracle" does not just mean levitation or loss of weight, phenomena that you have witnessed; the same subtler energies are utilized in life more often than people think, and these manifestations, being incomprehensible to the majority, ought to be studied. This is neither necromancy nor spiritualism, but simply the science of the subtler energies. Before us is the human heart, the most sacred treasure-chest of all; we need to turn our ears to it and

approach this highest throne with our hands washed. You have seen cases where careless doctors failed to take advantage of the wondrous evidence provided by a flaming heart. And now they are paying for their blindness.

Miracles are possible, but for them to take place the subtler threads of the heart must be joined. That is why We point out that the unification of consciousness is essential.

320. In ancient times certain mechanical methods were used to strengthen the connection between the heart's activity and the distant worlds. For example, one method was to clasp hands above the head with fingers interlocked—that was how a magnetic circle was formed. People also used to place their hands at the Chalice with fingers interlocked so that the edge of the left palm would lie on the heart. That was a way to strengthen magnetic waves. But now, of course, when we are teaching the expansion of consciousness, we will avoid external, mechanical methods. It is far subtler to act through the inner consciousness. We should sense how a transmission of the consciousness touches the substance of the heart, sending its motion upward, as if drawing it into Infinity. Of course, many of our sensations depend on atmospheric conditions. We may feel depression or sense solemnity, but let us be aware that at these moments the heart has opened the supermundane gates. Only enmity or fear uses the subterranean passages.

321. When shaping his images, a sculptor works on some spots only once, while on other places he focuses a succession of strokes, some severe and some delicate. Likewise, in the Teaching it is often remarked how one has to touch on certain ideas in a variety of ways; and this must be done without repetition, for even the chisel of a sculptor does not repeat the very same motion but only delineates the form required. Just as a sculptor usually gives special care to places that require repeated strokes, you ought to pay particular attention to passages on subjects that have come up more than once. Either their content is especially new to the consciousness, or they are dealing with matters skipped over without much attention. Yet just as a trembling chisel may end up having a decisive significance, an opportunity missed will impart a different meaning to an entire task. When I speak about the heart, am I not speaking about something that contains a multitude of individualities, entities that are calling forth manifestations which can never be repeated? It cannot be otherwise, for the ways in which the subtler energies refract and intersect in various spheres are beyond calculation.

322. One has to constantly emphasize the diversity of subtle manifestations; otherwise people will once again rush to confine these phenomena within the crudest limits, without attempting to sharpen their own focus by paying attention to individual details. Again one should turn to certain fires of the heart. These look purple to some people, but to others they seem violet or lilac; it greatly depends on the condition of the aura as well as the physical health. But these differences do not change the essence of the fires.

323. An individual method is necessary to approach the subtler energies. The main mistake will be to use old measures in approaching something that is far beyond them. Someone who uses scales in approaching an imponderable magnitude is bound to fail; but clearly these higher energies penetrate the whole of human nature and connect it with the higher worlds. It is perfectly evident that one should search for these

higher signs not among people who are infected with diseases but rather among healthy organisms with a subtle quality. Let these refined organisms perceive within themselves the manifestations that are quite obvious to them though inexplicable to others. Let them not be ashamed of seeming ridiculous to some people, so long as they can find an effective way to describe the manifestations of the subtle energies. We can be sure that especially now there are a great many manifestations of the energies deposited in the Subtle World. Like microorganisms, they are almost invisible but their effect is striking.

324. The individual method should not be regarded as unscientific; on the contrary, it allows an accumulative process that makes for a deepening of formulas. Thus, the ancient Vedas clearly noted the similarity of certain nerve centers in the human to those in animals and other life forms. In this way, individual observations provided the initial basis for making systematic classifications. And in just the same way, facts noted by sincere observers will merge into a system. Not so long ago the powers of human observation were directed to spiritualism, in spite of its danger; how much more natural, then, to begin observations on manifestations of an energy that is already known in its crude form. Far from putting the standing of science on shaky ground, this will allow it to expand into new spheres.

325. Isn't giving a blow to the heart like hitting a harp or a zither? Doesn't the resonance of the heart suggest that there are invisible strings which are an extension of the nerves into the subtle state? Isn't it scientific to observe these blows upon the aura, since the eyes, heart, Chalice, and crown of the head clearly receive deflected arrows? But it is noticeable how much more powerfully the heart resonates than any other center. There is a good reason why the heart is called the Sun of Suns. Shouldn't transmission over long distances be regarded as a subtle but perfectly natural occurrence? The realm of so-called hysteria ought to be split into several categories. At present "hysteria" includes everything from possession to refined spirituality. Naturally, this sort of contradictory confusion should not be allowed to stand, for nothing is more unscientific than throwing everything into one pile just to avoid bothering the brain with deliberation. Unless this is corrected, St. Theresa may fall within the boundaries of the possessed, while the nastiest demon will be allowed to come closer to the altar. Agreeing to the confusion of various conditions is impermissible.

326. Any effort to be scientific first of all obliges a person to undertake precise observations. Is it possible to make sweeping generalizations when results contradict each other? Instead, the wealth of reality should impel our thoughts toward a multitude of observations. So first let us gather these observations and not be superficial in our deductions. The advice given by the Teachings is perfectly sufficient. We can now think about refining our receptivity, and thereby we shall come closer to the boundary of the Subtle World.

327. To observe the signs of the Subtle World, it is necessary to exercise attention. Attention has to be developed by various methods. One can select a single voice in a symphony and follow it, or one can recognize several harmonies simultaneously. It is also helpful to learn to recognize the sound of silence. Silence has many subtle voices, and following their rhythm means coming closer to the Subtle World. But when studying silence it is instructive to recognize the dissonance that every physical intrusion brings. There is no better way to find an example of this than by comparing

physical sound with that of the Subtle World. A similar antithesis is also observed in the realm of the sense of smell. But the development of this ability is still rarer. The sense of smell may be a form of nourishment in the Subtle World, so to speak, but obviously in the physical world it is not so highly developed. Of course, as you have noticed, the Subtle World is full of scents. The higher one goes, the more perfect they are. But the lower strata are full of decomposition. If disincarnate beings linger in the lower strata, they clothe themselves in a shell of decomposition. That is why it is very beneficial to get used to flight into still higher strata while one is living in the earthly world.

328. The preparation for contacting the higher strata first of all entails purification of one's consciousness and development of the life of the heart. But these conditions need to be kept in mind. Usually people recall them only in times of idleness or rest; but when these conditions need to be met, they are forgotten and replaced by irritation—and the stench of irritation is dreadful.

329. Who will think of attaining success in the Subtle World if no one is allowed to speak or think about it? A teaching that is ignorant of the Subtle World is no guide, because existence on the earthly plane is not even a hundredth part of the life in the Subtle World. This means it would be beneficial to know about the conditions in the lengthier state of existence. But now a battle is going on in the astral world, and conditions are still more complex.

330. Refinement of the heart's condition calls forth special activity on the part of all the senses. The senses of smell, hearing, sight, and taste act continuously. There is no silence, because once the earthly sounds are still, the echoes of the Subtle World begin to be heard. There is not a moment without smell, for even the purest air is full of fragrances. There is no visual void, for the lights of the Subtle World will not disappear from the open eye—or even the closed eye. Isn't the purest sky full of formations? Similarly, there cannot be a cessation of taste, since the human organism itself is the most powerful laboratory. Regarding touch, you yourself know to what an extent the Subtle World is able to touch someone. So without breaking away from this world, the heart makes us participants in a multitude of subtle manifestations. And if someone insists on the existence of absolute silence, do not think of his heart as refined.

331. Refinement of the heart prompts one to give up eating meat. Moreover, an understanding of the Subtle World not only makes clear the harm of devouring decaying products but also reveals the sort of neighbors that decomposition attracts. Actually, it is difficult to decide which is more harmful, the devouring of meat or the undesirable guests that meat attracts. Though comparatively less harmful, even dried and smoked meats have an odor that attracts hungry beings from the Subtle World, and if those entities are welcomed with vile speech, extremely harmful associations come about. As you have heard, many people eat their food in silence or accompany their meal with worthy conversation. Naturally, no decomposition is permissible; even vegetables should not be allowed to decay. People do not need much: two fruits, some grain, and some milk. That way one may not only purify oneself internally but also get rid of many undesirable neighbors. Don't doctors who are researching ways to fight cancer and gallstones need to pay attention to this basic preventative care? People talk about burning incense and using perfumes, but

certain poisons that kill the consciousness are quite aromatic! This research should not be forgotten.

332. In the Subtle World exist diverse affirmations of the earthly world. Even a prototype of the seasons of the year goes round from the perspective of the Subtle World consciousness. Therefore, images of plants or mountains or the surfaces of bodies of water are not foreign to the Subtle World, though they are in a transformed condition, of course. The heart that knows the Subtle World knows flowers and mountains, snows and seas. Flowers thrive in a profusion of forms, and their colors are indescribably more complex and varied than the earthly pallet. The snows are whiter, more crystalline, and richer than their earthly counterparts. One can begin to discern the entire structure of the Higher World. A person who has thereby accumulated a clear, benevolent consciousness on the earthly plane will also be a good builder in the Subtle World. He will bring along with him not monstrosities but the beautiful proportions and rhythm that answer to the majesty of the Infinite. Is the spirit's duty so overwhelming if it has perfected the heart? Only the luminous awareness of the heart will carry the subtle body into the higher Abodes. So everyone who prepares his heart and uplifts the hearts of those around him is already doing the will of the One who sent him. When people ask in jest if the heart might be an airship since it can rise to lofty heights, tell them that their joke is not far from the truth. Actually, the energy of the heart has such a close resemblance to helium and other gases of the subtlest nature, it is not far from the spiritual truth to imagine the ascension of the heart.

333. Who in his heart cannot understand the beauty of ascension? Who will not sense at heart the burden taken on when one returns to a temporary house, an endangered house, a cramped house? So people should be conscious of the Higher World, in order that they be transported and ascend. Can one gaze out the window of the narrow dwelling without thinking about the higher worlds? The heart will lead us by the path of Christ to the step of Transfiguration. That is how we shall open the doors of the cramped house. Every unification of consciousness already acts to open the doors.

334. Ask an intelligent person what has most often warned him of danger and protected him from making mistakes or deviating. An honest person will say the heart, not the brain or intellect. Only a stupid person will rely on a conventional process of rational deduction. The heart is permeated with straight-knowledge. We articulated this concept quite a while ago, but now we are returning to it on another round of the spiral. We have already passed through the discipline of Heart and Hierarchy, and have pondered upon Infinity. Thus, straight-knowledge emerged not as some sort of vague intuition but as the result of spiritual discipline joined to an understanding of the heart's significance. Lead the disciples along these same lines. First of all cast forth the necessary concept like a far-reaching net, and then carefully draw in the edges of the net so that you completely surround whatever you are seeking. It is not by chance that the symbol of the fisherman casting his net is pointed out so often. The heart is not very easy to catch! It is hard to accept the language of the heart as a reality. Time, devotion, and effort are needed to obtain an understanding of the heart's expression.

335. A person who thinks deeply about the heart even amidst the horrors of anarchy shows that this thought has dwelt with him for a very long time. One can place a great deal of trust in him, because he has come in contact with knowledge and thereby already safeguarded his spirit from the filth of treachery. You can be sure that a person who carries an embryo of treachery does not know about the treasure of the heart. So build up the subtlest understanding layer by layer amidst the horrors of darkness. Great is the heart's ability to hear and see!

336. Reasoning is a sort of antithesis to the heart's ability to comprehend. Reasoning is a kind of magic, but magic is the antithesis of Grace. We must get a firm understanding of magic as well as reasoning, because they are so close to personality, selfishness, and egoism, as it is called. Reasoning arises from the self, while magic sets itself against the Highest. But in the heart's power of comprehension, and also in Grace, there is fundamentally no feeling of self—in other words, there is an absence of the principle that most hinders progress. The porcupine shoots out its quills, and it is hard to get at it from above. Every person who resorts to reasoning deprives himself of the great communion with the Highest. Let us avoid confounding reason and conditioned reasoning. Reason leads to wisdom, in other words, to the heart. But a worm cavils away, even though it crawls with difficulty across people's paths. So let us be persistent when it comes to attainments of the heart. In it lies a precious coffer of ecstasy that gold cannot buy.

337. You have before you the heart, which resonates to every manifestation that affirms the cosmos. What is this, if not universal consciousness! It is by this path that the transformation of life will again be intensified. With this transformation you can observe how these manifestations gradually become regular companions on the path to the future.

Observe how Armageddon unfolds. When the very depths of the Earth are rising in rebellion, one cannot fail to notice an increase in the agitation of the elements. When We call for a deepening of thought, We are offering a means for bringing Chaos into equilibrium. The Teacher is not keeping some secret knowledge to Himself; rather, at the first opportunity He is arming the warriors against Chaos. The madmen are trying to set the forces of Chaos against Us, without themselves knowing how to rein in those forces! People should understand that Chaos manifests not only in the physical convulsions that shake the soil but also in the world of psychic energies. It is not difficult to increase the forms of psychic insanity, but how does one get them under control? The madmen do not realize what poor allies they have; their sole desire is to impede the path of ascent. It is astonishing how they push forward all their destructive measures, as if the only thing they needed was ruins!

338. One requires a great deal of courage to build up the forces of the heart in the midst of destruction. If the seekers were not aware of the vital need for all the worlds to be transformed in this way, they might believe that the heart's attainments are futile. But fortunately, everything that exists needs the heart. Therefore, even in the dust of destruction one should go on building strongholds of the heart.

339. Sūrya-Vidyā, the Solar Knowledge—this was a name sometimes given to the Teaching of the Heart, a name that expressed the fieriness, the sun-like quality, and the centrality of the heart. In fact, anyone who wishes to get to know the heart cannot just approach it as a part of the organism. First of all the seeker should recognize the central nature of the heart and study outward from it, not inward toward it. The solar plexus

will be the antechamber for the Temple of the Heart. The Kundalini will be a laboratory for the heart. The brain and all the nerve centers will be estates for the heart, because nothing can live without the heart! To a certain degree, even the brain can find substitutes. Even the Kundalini can be somewhat nourished by an electrical manifestation, and the solar plexus can be strengthened by blue light. But the heart stands as the Temple of humanity. One cannot conceive of the unification of humanity by means of the brain or the Kundalini, but the radiance of the heart can bring together the most seemingly diverse organisms, and even work over great distances in doing so. This experiment of bringing together hearts over long distances is waiting for workers to carry it out.

The wish to launch lengthy experiments is perfectly correct, because through them one can create another bond between the generations.

340. Some people will dismember, but We shall join together, for a theory of focus emerges in the process of joining. Formerly We brought forward the Hierarchy as the focus, but now one should concentrate on the heart as a channel to the Hierarchy. That way nobody can say that the Hierarchy is not a reality because there is no path to approach it. Indeed, there is the most substantial approach, that in which the heart acts as an intercessor, the same heart that ceaselessly throbs and pulsates lest people forget its existence—the heart that is the most tender of all, the most intense, the most resonant to what is near and what is far.

341. Degeneration, fattiness, and enlargement of the heart occur because of the intolerable conditions of life. Heart disease is rarely the result of karmic causes. Enlargement of the heart may be due to good potentials that go untapped. Of course, fattiness of the heart is an inexcusable condition, for the process of taking on fat can always be arrested at the start. Work is the best antidote for the tendency of the heart to grow fat. At the very least, the basic hygiene of the heart ought to be maintained. Striving to work is the best way to strengthen the heart. Not work but an interruption in the heart's striving is what causes destruction. Certainly, powerful hostile arrows also injure the health, but you know that the balm of Hierarchy can heal the wounds they cause. However, this balm has to be applied on a continual basis. Indeed, it is a serious error to forget the existence of such a medicine.

342. Any betrayal is also harmful. You should not forget that an open betrayal is sometimes easier to deal with than a concealed one. Often a traitor does not even admit to himself that he has committed betrayal. The standard for judging such a subtle betrayal is highly complex! By being aware of the betrayal, the traitor at least partially discharges the tension that he has called forth. Had Judas not acknowledged what he had done, his treachery would have been still more heinous.

343. The fiery body may sometimes manifest itself even through the physical shell. So when the manifestations of the Fire of Space have reached a certain intensity, the fiery body begins to radiate, as it were, in small fires across the surface of the physical body. Only rarely can this subtle, fiery condition be seen. Not only is the eye unable to take in such tiny lights, but the very power of the glance extinguishes these subtle flashes, so to speak. Cosmic manifestations, such as volcanic eruptions and other fiery occurrences, are conducive to the phenomena of the fiery body. This sort of phenomenon has nothing in common with the fires of the aura or external fires, such as St. Elmo's fire. Today Urusvati experienced the fires emanating from the fiery body. Rather than causing pains, cosmic catastrophes affected her fiery body. As a result, she became increasingly aware of various signs of interaction with cosmic phenomena. Eruptions in the microcosm can bring on eruptions of the glands, but may also call forth the fires of the fiery body.

344. In this way it is possible to gradually increase the number of subtle manifestations. I can affirm how easy it is to work where there is unity. The Teaching's calls for unity of consciousness are often in vain, for people consider it to be an idealistic appeal that has no practical application; but in fact such unification is a powerful action equal in strength to many powerful energies. So why place a burden on the subtlest energies, when human beings are armed with such a powerful armor?

345. The opening of the heart is also important in that it discerns cosmic periods. Thus, without the heart, vague presentiments will never become the formulation of actual events. Likewise, unless the heart participates, it will be impossible to sense distant events. For example, right now the total destruction of entire structures in the Subtle World must be greatly affecting the heart. Such destruction is not without its usefulness, because piled up accumulations should not hamper the process of perfection. It should be no surprise that subtle forms may also be destroyed so that they might be replaced by their successors. For such tremendous changes to take place, however, fire must be applied. Such a fiery ablution establishes a new step, but in the physical world it is exceedingly difficult. This concept ought to be gradually expanded; otherwise, even experienced warriors may fall into confusion. And let us be aware of the unprecedented

tension. Let us be sensitive to each other. Our warnings about this special time are not given casually.

346. Nor should one forget that all of the details that come up nowadays take on a very unstable aspect. We cannot demand that people think in the usual way when the very air they breathe is unusual. We have to accept this difficult time and remain steadfast. Consolation lies in our ability to affirm the future in thought. So hold on tight, because nothing is steady except the thread of the heart.

347. Scientists have a major task ahead of them—to determine the relationship between volcanic eruptions and the forms of the Subtle World. But this too will soon become clear.

348. A sensible doctor will advise people to be content with every physical condition and yet show an unquenchable upward striving of the heart. No one should assume that perfect ethics are not in harmony with medicine. Nor should it be assumed that thought alone can keep up one's physical condition. That would be one-sided. We live in a chemical laboratory and form part of it ourselves. When the ancients used to say about a critically ill person, "He must be taken to the Fiery Mountain," they were expressing two things. There was a reminder about the fiery body, which knows no illness; but the expression also has a purely physical meaning, because the fire of volcanic eruptions contains a special combination of energies that can stimulate certain nerve centers. How can it be otherwise, when the flame of the heart responds to the most remote subterranean fires? The degree to which the flame of the heart controls the subterranean current also ought to be studied. Since some organisms belonging to a certain element are able to discern underground waters, then fiery people, naturally, should be able to maintain a confluence with fire. Precisely, it is this element that requires a great deal of observation.

349. The pressure of world events should also be observed. It would be possible to compile data showing an unusual rapid progression. Events are intruding into every aspect of life. Contrary to what people imagine, it is not war per se but the conflict of the elements that makes what we are discussing much more than a fairy tale. It is exactly as it was during former catastrophes, when people were unwilling to take note of what was actually going on.

350. Along with pressure one can also sense a sort of emptiness. This sensation should be dealt with very carefully. Most often this involves a certain protective zone that keeps the heart safe from destructive blows, a kind of protective armor. Seekers should know about this condition. Some people regard it as a separation from reality and are distressed without cause. Others believe that this sensation marks the end of danger and they stop being vigilant. Either approach impedes the flow of energy. But an experienced warrior values this shield that protects his power so effectively. You know that blows to the aura are quite painful for the eyes and ears, but there may also be sensations that feel as if one has sustained a cut or stab wound. These sensations are especially painful on the shoulders, neck, and lower abdomen. They may also be felt upon the opening of wounds—stigmata—when the energy of the heart draws a condensed particle of Fohat to a particular spot and injures the cells of the skin tissues. Indeed, the joining of the heart with the energy of Grace generates the most powerful combination.

351. Chaos is not understood. Some think of it as being separate from the Manifest, while others understand it as a complete abstraction. If people only realized in how many forms Chaos breaks into Existence, they would understand why caution is necessary. Every dissonance, every decomposition is dangerous if not taken care of immediately, for it carries a wave of Chaos in its elements of destruction. So there is no need of telescopes to observe Chaos; humanity can study and sense real Chaos quite close to itself. Indeed, the heart trembles from the presence of Chaos. So once more we can turn to the heart.

352. The persecuted leads, with the persecutors trailing after him; so says the ancient truth about the superiority of the persecuted. To understand it means to enter the path of the persecuted. Many persecutors turned to the path of those they persecuted, for the pursuit upon that path ended up attracting them to it. That is why We prefer the path of the persecuted.

353. The heart thinks, the heart affirms, the heart unifies. One can always recall the significance of the heart, which for so long has been obscured by the brain. The heart will be the first to thrill, the heart will be the first to quiver, the heart will discern a great deal before the reasoning of the brain dares to begin thinking. Could we fail to eliminate the tortuous path of the brain? Could we pass over in silence the heart's most direct attainment, the arrow-like ray that the miraculous heart is capable of emanating? So it is possible to commune with the heart and protect oneself from all the attacks of evil. Only through the heart can one sense the brown gas and arrest the process of asphyxiation in time. For the same reason, too, the victory on the field of Armageddon will belong to the heart. That is why I so strongly advise that you safeguard the heart as a sword that smites any and all evil.

354. From Our point of view, any act of vivisection

performed on the heart is inadmissible; besides, it is almost impossible to heal a heart with such techniques, just as it is impossible to find the Ringse in a living organism. On the other hand, it is possible to observe a number of psychophysiological manifestations during the development of the heart. For example, a fiery heart generates a light spot on its upper tissue which, during an increase in fire, turns almost white. The ancients called this manifestation the "sacred ashes." This has nothing in common with enlargement of the heart, but rather with its refinement. Likewise, one can understand why it is impossible to apply the results of experiments on the animal heart to the human heart. Since the human heart is the throne of consciousness, then naturally the animal heart must differ from it in regard to certain functions. Moreover, any forcing of the heart's activity after the subtle body has separated from the physical would constitute a real crime. Each artificial heartbeat will draw back the subtle body, perpetrating an inadmissible act that causes decomposition and suffering.

355. Rescuing the heart has absolutely nothing to do with vivisection. One can work on the heart with a subtle ray that generates a vibration which manifests as a sort of freezing. So one should handle the human heart with far more delicate methods than cutting it open. Of course, there may be cases where the heart has sustained a wound, and these require special measures.

356. There is a story of how one Yogi, in a moment of tension, lifted up a container full of water and shattered it. When he was asked the reason for this destruction, the Yogi replied, "If I hadn't done that, my heart would have burst." Similar discharges exist under all conditions. The tension of the heart may

become so great that one has to perform some kind of action in space to liberate the necessary conditions from the condensed sphere that is holding them back. Such condensation may occur externally due to outside causes, but it may also arise from within—that is exactly what happens during cosmic disturbances. That is why we should follow the dictates of our hearts with such careful attention. The heart senses and reflects invisible processes to such a degree that one could use it as the basis for writing an entire history of the Invisible. It is difficult to correlate the causes of seismic events with the cataclysms that take place in the Subtle World, but the heart resonates to them as well.

357. To restore a heart that has been affected by various factors, We use vibrations. While Mahavan is able to respond to earthly causes, the vibrations of the Silver Bridge are necessary during disturbances in the Subtle World.

358. You know how slowly the consciousness grows; the transformation of the home of the consciousness—the heart—is likewise a slow process. So it should be accepted that a person who pays no thought to the heart will not succeed in improving his consciousness. True, in its essence the heart is not separate from the higher spheres, but this potential needs to be actualized. How many refractions and distortions occur in a heart not purified by higher thinking! Many valuable transmissions take on an ugly outline simply because the heart has been neglected. What concepts and feelings, the very best and subtlest, will be missing from the forsaken heart! Won't we find enmity nesting in a defiled heart? And let these words not be regarded as abstract comments, for the heart must be educated. It is impossible to build up the brain unless there is

refinement of the heart. The old metaphysics and contemporary psychology attempt to reach the heart, but can any subject reach the heart when the word heart is never mentioned?

359. A special subject ought to be created—Knowledge of the Heart. The simplest maidservant understands the sweetness of speaking about the heart; it would seem to be still simpler, then, for a scholar to expand this concept. Human history itself furnishes tables of the workers of the brain and those of the heart, tables that could be compared. Won't the images of *podvig* and the self-sacrificing heroes found therein provide the surest guidance for perfectment of the heart?

360. Now that I am speaking about the heart, you can understand why We spoke about the Hierarchy before the battle but are affirming the heart during the battle. Truly, only through the heart shall we conquer.

361. A surge of psychic energy may create something like cramps in one's fingertips. One can well understand that the bubbling lava of psychic energy is like that of a volcano, which is why caution is especially necessary. Though drops of My sweat may stream down, burden Me still more!

362. The anguish felt is a reflection of Armageddon. The force of the conflict is certain to weigh upon the heart. Look around you—is there much rejoicing? You may even notice that smiles have grown fewer. Do not feel surprised, for even ignorant minds feel the oppression, though without being aware of its weighty cause. Many people will totally deny this in their words but will still feel a heaviness of heart. Refinement of the heart permits many subtle manifestations—for instance, the touch of the hand of a subtle body and many means of preventing pain.

363. Let us turn once more to the quality of the pulse. We will have to point to this indisputable testimony of the heart's affirmation often and from many angles. It is not measurement of the pulse's frequency so much as observation of its quality that will convey a picture of the heart's vitality. We are on the way to photographing auras, but in the meantime we are already able to begin observing the pulse, not during illness but in times of good health, and we can note what sensations influence the subtle play of the pulse and just how they do so. The aura shows evidence that an illness is present, whereas the quality of the pulse conveys a whole gamut of reactions. And while the aura is something transcendental for the majority of people, the pulse presents a purely physical phenomenon. But with what solicitude and caution must we understand the study of the pulse! Nowadays doctors pay hardly any attention to the quality of the pulse. We shall often return to the study of the pulse when we think about vibrations.

364. Knowledge of the pulse's quality is an indispensable requirement if someone wishes to cure with vibrations, because what else will provide a basis for the application of various vibrations? You yourselves already know how diverse vibrations are and what different effects they produce. It is no exaggeration to say that the heart withstands many dangers thanks to vibrations. So one day we talk about psychic energy, which cures the heart, while the next day we remind people about physical manifestations that one would expect to be within the reach of everyone. The latter subject is also about the heart and its pains; the seeker can overcome these only by the link with the Lord.

365. If you encounter a canting hypocrite, know that he is not of the heart. If you come across someone steeped in superstition, know that he is not of the heart. If you meet someone stricken with terror, know that he is not of the heart. Even so, these uninvited guests will mention the word heart. It is time to expose these humbugs of the heart and get rid of them, so they can no longer play around with human hearts. The heart ought to be studied when it is beclouded with conceit and cruelty. For example, by observing the pulse one can draw closer to the true treasures of the heart. In the same way, one can also discern when the heart has fallen silent and the calls are not reaching it. A great deal of work has been done on transmission of thought at a distance—reading the pulse is useful for this. In its subtlest capacity the pulse is able to detect a thought sent, even before the receiver is aware of it. In this way one can again ascertain the extent to which the subtlest possibilities are latent in the organism, though people have formed only a crude, physical image of them. This coarsening process has already built up over several thousand years, and the lamp of the body is receding from the fire.

366. When you have a sense that you should strive toward something or you have a premonition that something is approaching, do not assume that everything will take place in the immediate future. You often feel that a foundation is being built upon the necessary groundwork. This straight-knowledge has nothing to do with immediate success; on the contrary, it shows to what a degree something greater is taking definite shape. Usually people suffer from their own inability to commeasure, to weigh the relative importance of things. With their preconceived judgments they often impede a stream of events that are already taking shape. Consolation and comfort are not for tomorrow but for the more beautiful times that lie ahead. Still, your straight-knowledge is correct.

367. If someone were to collect in a single book all the forms of behavior harmful to perfectment, he could easily ascertain how simple it is to overcome them. He could see from what small actions this evil accumulates. Is it difficult to give up trivial habits in one's daily life? Is it difficult to suppress the small destructive acts that poison the body? Doesn't a child feel ashamed after his first feeble attempt to lie? Only by habit does a child harden his heart. That is why We call habits the calluses of the soul. Who is unaware of the warnings the heart gives every time an unworthy act is about to be performed? Such actions of the heart transmit the best calls, but often people force the heart to be silent. This is a grave crime, as serious as cutting off the current that is bringing salvation to someone near and dear.

368. Unity is the first sign that the Teaching is not simply empty sound. The Teaching is a light on the dark path. Seekers should understand how often caution is needed, because the megaphone of space amplifies every sound. Petty irritation is worked into a whirlwind, much to the delight of the enemies. They are given a new joy to record: in spite of being granted access to the Teaching, its students are acting like -everyone else.

369. I have already spoken about the importance of harmonized work, which can even prevent wear and tear on machines. It is easy to imagine the beneficial energy emitted by unified work. When harmonized consciousnesses have been gathered into working groups, one can make astonishing observations. Governments should have considered setting up such classifications of work according to consciousness.

Such groupings would have written the most successful page in the book of economics. So instead of taking their cues from obsolete dogmas, people should approach the essence of action.

370. The Constructive Cross is formed when indomitable striving and an understanding of what is right are impelled to meet. Undoubtedly it is just this situation that gets the bile of the dark forces flowing. You know all the epithets with which humanity rewards those who bear a cross, but you also know that bearing a cross is the shortest path. Where there is self-sacrifice people see self-serving, as if they were looking in a mirror that reflects everything backwards.

371. I have already spoken about the significance of the rays and currents that penetrate space. It would seem that such ideas should not be difficult to verify scientifically. Why not examine an atmosphere that has been permeated with every possible ray, an atmosphere forcibly filled to saturation? It could be demonstrated that it is possible to have a condition in which the atmosphere is overflowing. Naturally, this forced over-saturation is sure to produce abnormal results. Human beings cannot be subjected to continuous strokes of lightning or a constant shower of arsenic or some other poison. Besides considering the medical consequences, one should think about the intersection of clashing currents. If even just rotating an object may produce powerful disturbances, what a great impact the refraction of various waves must have on the human heart! But it seems that people do not think about anything bigger or taller than they are.

Naturally, many sicknesses result from something in the atmosphere, but the over-saturation or poisoning of the atmosphere especially affects the heart and the brain's reflexes. Therefore, people should not stir up energies without knowing how far the impact may extend.

372. You are already beginning to think about such subjects as astrophysics and astrochemistry. It would seem to be the right time for people to ponder how the powerful reactions that these fields investigate affect the nature of humanity. Soon a process will begin in which the powerful levers of the distant worlds are brought closer for the betterment of life. But with all that wealth of possibilities, the heart element has to be added to everything. The manifestation of the subtlest energies of the heart transmutes the chemical nature of the rays. It is impossible to imagine a chemical laboratory in which the heart has no role. The destined transformation of life will begin as soon as human thought recognizes the heart as an engine, a motive force—not an egocentric personal instrument but a coworker with the subtlest energies.

373. Isn't it true that unity is something difficult, even though it is prescribed as the one, exclusive means that everyone needs? It is difficult to embrace unity, even temporarily. Isn't it true that it is easy to break away out of irritation? Indeed, it is not difficult to forget about Armageddon and everything else that exists, just to have the satisfaction of venting one's bile. Clearly, it is a long way from irritation to astrochemistry.

The arrows that pierce the heart are not simply the result of a nervous contraction; they are a far more profound manifestation, being more spiritual in their origin. How many of humanity's ills are due to inadequate cooperation! Embracing the concept of cooperation easily leads one to cooperation with the forces of nature. Where is the boundary between the forces of nature and those of spiritualization? The servant of the spirit ought to recognize that the spiritual is present everywhere.

374. Mercy, compassion, pity, love, and all the benevolent efforts that We enjoin, are they not wondrous paths of communion with the highest energies? People should get used to regarding these luminous qualities as actual means for connecting with the higher worlds. Unless these qualities are present, the whole of astrochemistry will be astro-toxin. Since ancient times alchemists have known the significance of the light-bearing, connective substance that issues from the heart. Indeed, the emanations of the heart continuously create a luminous substance that we might call, in a manner of speaking, the "essence of psychic energy." Of course, the opposing side tries to solve this problem in its own manner; but instead of undertaking luminous creativity through the heart, they seek to create through sperm, and this means that they try by that approach to find the unifying substance. I will not repeat its name. The sorcerers of the first three degrees utilize the seminal substance to connect with the spatial energies. There is no use in explaining that their methods, which involve forcing the energies, are not powerful enough and require a lengthy process. They cannot be compared with the fires of the heart!

375. A Yogi whom you know took the most powerful poisons without injury, but died because of a slight delay in applying his heart energy. Immunity is contained in the heart. A Yogi mentally directs the poisons to the heart, which dissolves their effects by partaking of the Spatial Fire. But for this the Yogi has to awaken the fires of the heart, and you know how much time this demands. Of course, the taking of poison must be a gradual process. In the case you are

familiar with, it took seven years for the Yogi to accustom his organism to coordination with the fires of space. Just a single minute's delay gave an edge to the power of the poison. In transferring the consciousness to the heart, not a moment's delay is allowed.

376. Some people feel the heart to be something solitary within them. Such a sensation may be very useful in developing the heart's connective substance. When you desire that the heart transmute a certain influence, you should first of all consciously direct this task to the heart. You will then notice with sensitivity that the heart will be felt as something alien. Neither pain nor pressure, but the sense of being a self-sufficient apparatus will characterize the presence of the heart. That is how it has to feel when the heart is assimilating alien influences in order to transmute them and prevent the poisoning of the entire system.

377. A scientist may ask how one sets about developing the immunity of the heart. The question is an appropriate one. For all its indisputable potential, the heart will not unfold unless there is conscious immunity. Balance between the heart and the consciousness gets the connective substance moving. So to answer the question above, the scientist can begin taking a twofold approach. First, he can purify his consciousness, for the physical ballast in itself does not help the consciousness. Only thought purified by art and liberated from slavery can make it possible for the consciousness to flower. Here I am calling attention to liberation from slavery. Precisely, it is from all kinds of slavery that one must be freed. Regarding the second condition for the scientist, he must feel the heart as an independent apparatus and begin to observe its reactions and reflexes. Then the first heralds of success will

also arise—the stars of light. They will teach the seeker to observe still more.

Also the seeker should learn to be constantly vigilant while performing every task. This flexibility is necessary for those who travel far.

378. In their essence all the various kinds of pranayama aim to kindle the fires of the heart. Of course, among the multitude of people who practice pranayama very few receive positive results. Where does the cause of this failure lie? Naturally, in an unthinking attitude toward the heart. A complex practice is devised, and the consciousness is focused on keeping count or alternating movements—in other words, on external, material methods. But no earthly calculations are able to kindle the wondrous talisman of the heart. Just as solar energy does not exist without the sun, the heart will not kindle unless there is striving to a focus. Thus, it is easier to kindle the heart by a powerful impulse toward a focal point than by relying on mental calculations. Of course, pranayama was wisely established as an auxiliary method for speeding up results. But as soon as the significance of the mantram of the heart was forgotten, pranayama turned into a mechanical means of fighting off the common cold. Therefore, let us remember that the sacred heart is a path to the focus.

379. Because a heart is calm does not mean it is in repose. A burning heart cannot be at rest. Calmness of the heart means firmness and imperturbability. By understanding this, one can attain the tension that leads to Nirvana. But how many stages must one pass through with courage in order to grasp the imperturbability of the heart. It is easy to say fine things while one's surroundings seem to be calm, but one should not seek to temper the heart in a state of inactivity.

Naturally, action does not consist in waving one's arms about, but rather in the tension of the heart.

380. Of course, the battle of the past does not bear comparison with the battle of tomorrow. No one should think that Armageddon is just a commotion in the kitchen. No, the biggest guns are in action, and the swiftest cavalry is taking part. If we compare the recent Great War with Armageddon, it is like comparing Europe with the entire world, as it were. I offer this comparison just in case anyone is thinking that the present time is ordinary and easy. People need to summon all the imperturbability of the heart that they can, in order to find themselves among the ranks of Rigden's forces. Nobody should forget the nature of the time that we are going through.

Right now there is no one who can get by without courage. Only utter madness whispers that everything will fall into place of its own accord—that cannot happen! Being unable to govern by the basic principles, the dark forces have violated them; therefore, we must close ranks and go forward undivided in everything. The warriors should understand that the spiritual tension of the present time is no longer at the level of the Subtle World, but is already approaching the Fiery World. The Teacher is reminding us: not terror but a sense of the majestic should fill the hearts of the warriors of Armageddon.

381. You are sufficiently familiar with the transmission of thought and healing currents over a distance. Yet it is necessary to repeat about this phenomenon again and again, because people are most reluctant to admit the indisputable. Naturally, the transmission of thought has to be accepted, because it is essential to allow entry to what the heart is sending. Even a telegraph clerk may get mixed up in the merely mechanical transmission of messages, which suggests how much subtler the heart's receptivity needs to be. Moreover, you know how easily a thought from the outside flies through the consciousness and is forgotten in spite of the clarity of transmission. The heart must be able to accept such inexpressible words into its depths. It is just as easy to overlook the most powerful healing currents if we resist them in our consciousness. These currents can even shake a person's bed, yet this knocking of the vibrations may be denied. It is also good if the heart shows benevolence in understanding that freezing currents do not arise in the heat unless there is a special cause. To accept these simple, scientifically based phenomena, a person needs not blind faith but just open-minded goodwill.

382. People can learn to gradually accept many subtle manifestations as ordinary conditions in their lives. This also is a transformation of life, and it can lead to the loftiest condition without isolating seekers from the flow of life. You yourselves know how it is possible to converse at a distance, and you have many times experienced an entire battery of all kinds of currents. For that reason you also know how the currents are gradually building up, and how even very dangerous cases are being cured by Our currents over a distance.

383. Among the multitude of currents, the most powerful will be the extremely cooling ones and the most fiery. In Tibet Urusvati experienced the fiery currents and then the cooling ones. For mastery of the fiery currents, the lamas require a comprehensive procedure in which the teacher uses exaggerated expressions, but as you can see, one can reach the same goal directly by way of the heart. The Teacher directs the currents, but the heart of the Teacher is sometimes in

need of the connective substance, at which time the disciple's energy has a special significance. The Teacher is sure to be grateful when the purified energy of the disciple ascends in a powerful spiral. This is called the wheel of cooperation. Likewise, the Teacher is always ready to share his supply of energy, but the disciple must also be prepared to purify his heart.

384. The process that employs cooling currents can be likened to the application of a piece of ice to the body. Naturally, the rhythm of the currents reminds one of a certain type of refrigerator. Such vibratory movement produces not only an outer penetration but an inner one as well.

385. Strive into the future. People should look upon the present time as a bridge across a raging current. There is no need to tether the consciousness to all sorts of conditions full of twists and turns—such stipulations are no more than twigs and stones on the bridge. Human misfortunes are usually just due to delays caused by attention being paid to momentary jolts, which ought to be avoided. Every leader strives to avoid being delayed.

386. In its essence, the heart is an organ of higher action and giving; that is why every act of giving partakes of the nature of the heart. Every positive Teaching enjoins giving. Such an affirmation is truly practical, for without giving, the heart does not endure. Naturally, one has to understand giving in all its justice. Giving should not be understood as just contributing money or donating objects one no longer needs. True giving is of the spirit. Let every heart pour forth streams of spiritual gifts. Not without cause is it said that every beat of the heart is a smile, a tear, and gold. All life flows through the heart. The seeker should be able to give constant work to the heart. Nothing can

refine the heart so perfectly as limitless spiritual giving. Usually spiritual giving is not valued, since anything invisible goes unappreciated. But the source of wealth, whether spiritual or material, is the heart. If only one could bring it into every situation where the heartbeat would be precious.

387. Deodar oil has been called the balsam of the heart. Actually, some substances belong to Nature's heart, and their noble quality is conducive to the purification of the human heart. Rose, musk, and amber are examples of this. I am naming substances with various properties in order to suggest the dimensions of Nature's heart.

388. It is impossible to imagine what a battle is raging! Because their hearts are inactive, people often fail to recognize those spiritually akin to them. There is good reason why the Teaching of the Heart is so essential for the life of the future. How would you cross the boundaries of the worlds without it?

389. Rather than regard the heart as personal property, it is preferable to convince oneself that the heart is not entirely one's own organ but has been granted one for attainment of the highest communion. Perhaps if people began to think of the heart as something on loan from Above they would handle it with greater care.

A certain hermit emerged from his solitude with a message, saying to everyone he met, "You have a heart." When he was asked why he did not talk about mercy, patience, devotion, love, and all the beneficial foundations of life, he replied, "Just so long as we don't forget the heart, the rest will come." Indeed, how can we turn to love if there is nowhere for it to dwell? Or where will patience lodge if its dwelling is closed? So to avoid torturing oneself by seeking virtues that find no application, one has to build a garden for them, a garden that will open up thanks to an understanding of the heart. Let us stand firm on the foundation of the heart, and let us understand that without the heart we are no more than discarded husks.

390. Whoever loves flowers is on the path of the heart. Whoever knows the striving to the heights is on the path of the heart. Whoever thinks with purity is on the path of the heart. Whoever knows of the higher worlds is on the path of the heart. Whoever is ready for Infinity is on the path of the heart. So let us summon these hearts to realization of the Source. It is right to understand the essence of the heart as something that belongs to both the Subtle and the Fiery Worlds. One can perceive worlds through the heart, but not through the intellect. So wisdom is contrary to the intellect, but there is no ban on adorning the intellect with wisdom.

391. Feeling will always prevail over reason. One has to accept this as a truth that cannot be suppressed. Therefore, when we speak about the heart, we are affirming the citadel of feeling. But how distant from lust is the feeling of the heart! The teaching about creative feeling will lead to an understanding of the creativity of thought. Let us not pick apart the domain of feeling, because it is a single field in bloom. We know what grows when feelings are sown, but where are the fruits born of reasoning alone? Reason cannot create if the seed of the heart is not provided. So when we speak of the heart, we are speaking about the Beautiful.

392. I believe one can allow the urgent problems of contemporary life to be resolved through the guidance of the heart, as long as there is knowledge of the basic laws. So I am affirming the essence of a sturdy, beautiful structure.

393. While delving into the Teaching, let us not

forget the battle. It is unusual that in the midst of a battle without precedent we are discussing the wondrous heart. Our conversations might be called an affirmation of calmness.

394. "In the evening he placed the thought upon his heart, and in the morning he rendered his decision." Such was said of the Sage of the Mountains in Persian annals. For many people this is just one more quaint old adage; yet an entire Teaching is conveyed in the maxim, "He placed the thought upon his heart." The thought cannot be transformed anywhere else but on the altar of the heart. Many readers of the book Heart will be wondering whether they have learned anything new and practical. Such people desire a pharmacist's prescription for some patent medicines that will uplift their hearts. For them the order to place a thought upon one's heart is nonsense. In their disarray of consciousness, it is hard for them to separate out a single thought. And in all the twists and turns of their reasoning process, it is impossible for them to discover the heart. But a person who has sensed the altar of the heart will also grasp the discipline of the spirit. We send the calls of the heart to friends who are encountered on the crossroads of the East. We send calls of unity to seekers whose hearts have sensed the music of the spheres. But for a person who regards the spheres as void, the heart is no more than a blood-bag.

395. Who can fail to get serious now when all thinking people realize that the old world is falling into ruin? A downfall, indeed, for there is so much that has yet to be outlived. All elements not commeasurable with the future are being thrown into one Furnace! And the widespread lack of discipline wreaks havoc and leads to decay. People have to summon up all their courage in order to move forward with the thought of the heart. The vibrating energies are aquiver, and one cannot demand precision of the warriors when the general discord has clouded their vision. Overcome anxiety, for the whole world is trembling; do not suppose that you can continue thinking in the same old way. Think only of the future, only of the Teacher!

396. The altar of the heart has been given that name not only as a symbol but also because when placing a thought upon the heart one can feel something like a light pressure upon the upper part of the heart. This sensation is so subtle that someone unaccustomed to subtlety of feelings may not even notice it. But every person with a refined consciousness will clearly sense this pressure of thought energy.

397. Often the projection of willpower is mistaken for the energy of the heart. It is easy to distinguish a command of the will, in which a manifestation of the brain acts through the eye or through currents issuing from the extremities. For the heart to exert its influence, no external method is necessary. One could say that for the past century the West has accepted the methods of the brain because they are obvious, although superficial and imperfect, like anything that requires external methods. Though it has declined in many respects, the East has still preserved the methods of the heart. So in everything let us aspire to the inner—in other words, let us strive to the depths.

398. In order to approach a method of the heart, one first of all has to love the world of the heart; or to put it more precisely, one has to learn to respect everything pertaining to the heart. Many people imagine that there is absolutely no difference between the paths of the brain and the heart. It is difficult for such "brain people" to accept the higher worlds. Likewise, they find it hard to imagine how the Subtle World can be superior to the earthly. The manifestation of the subtle spheres corresponds to the subtle state of the heart. Therefore, a heart that is already resonating to the rhythm of space will know the resonance of the spheres and also the subtle aroma; and the flowers, all resonating to the same vibration, will make obeisance to it. Seeing the flowers of the Subtle World means that one is already ascending to the Beautiful Sphere. It is also possible to see these purified images in a waking state, but for this to happen the flame of the heart is necessary. One can also see the fire of the heart soaring in beauty above it. But for these manifestations to take place, the heart has to be kindled. So the heart is not an abstraction but a bridge to the higher worlds.

399. Defense is still not resistance. Everyone dreams of developing resistance. Insusceptibility is only a weak degree of resistance. Immunity dwells in the heart, and even active resistance does not lie in the brain. Only the energy of the heart makes you invulnerable and carries you over obstacles. So you should remember the heart as a weapon. Indeed, the weapon of Light is the heart! But let people not suspect Us of being opponents of the brain. Let the good plowman, the brain, toil over his sowing. Let him give nurture to the seeds and bring forth a thought that has been refined and sharpened in battle. But the perverted thinking of the brain is what has created the disastrous state of the contemporary world. So let us once again turn to the heart as our judge and leader. Whoever helps those close to him find the path of the heart will be able to find his own path to perfection.

400. You are right to note that we must do many things for ourselves. In this fact lies the reason why help comes at the last moment, for otherwise it would be impossible to perfect the spirit. Likewise, it would be inadmissible for a person to suppress the flow of his own energy if it is proceeding in the right direction. While suicide may be the gravest crime, any suppression of the current of surging energy is harmful in the very same way. Since we are here only for the perfectment of the spirit, let us not suppress the life-bearing energy. The concept of Santana is a broad affirmation of the energy stream.

401. Let us summon up resourcefulness so that we can establish resistance. Each of us must place this thought upon the heart, for otherwise it will not be brought to fulfillment. The main thing is not to let the Instructions go unapplied. Blessed be the dangers, for they teach us unity and resistance. When these qualities have been strengthened by the heart's affirmation, the armor will also be ready. The armor of Mars was prepared and forged by Venus and Vulcan. And so the symbol in a wise myth combines various elements into a concept of life.

At times it is so necessary to unify through silence! Nothing influences the heart so much as intense silence.

402. Just as mantrams and all kinds of prayers are able to sustain an outer rhythm, they can also act as a means of connecting with the Higher World. Many people somehow fail to grasp either the outer or the inner meaning of prayer. The beautiful hymns of the Rig Veda died away because they did not penetrate people's hearts. You can look upon this lack of rhythm as a sign of the final period of the Kali Yuga. Precisely darkness will use any means available to disturb every kind of harmony. Dissonance is the distinguishing feature of all the contemporary arts. You can even observe how consonance and the major key have become characteristic of the old-fashioned, as it were. A composer needs to have a certain courage to go on creating in the consonance of a major key—maestoso! In observing the entire structure of contemporary life one can see a departure from every kind of heroism. And throughout the world a cowardly malice is the mark of those who support darkness and chaos. But the heart calls for construction, for it knows how infectious chaos is. Decay gives rise to more decay.

403. People should understand that a boundary runs between Light and darkness. True, it is a tortuous line, but by following the heart one can unerringly discern the adherents of darkness. Can a person whose heart is dark strive upwards? Will that person reject falsehood and self-love as his life unfolds? Will he overcome fear when facing the future? So recognize that whoever is afraid of the future belongs to darkness—that is the surest touchstone.

404. From the notes of the Mother of Agni Yoga one can see that the reaction brought on by the turmoil is almost like that arising from cosmic upheavals. What could be the matter? Of course, turmoil that causes the fires of a particular hatred to flare up may be as powerful as the subterranean fires. Indeed, there may be long, bloody battles that, being mostly a series of horrors or performances of duty, never attain a special degree of tension. Wars are seldom of equal tension; the overall tension arising from religious or revolutionary turmoil may be incomparably more powerful. That is why tension is measured not by counting the number of rounds fired or the number of enemy troops but by gauging the overall conscious striving of the heart. As I have said, the insurrection of the elements has the same strength, whether it issues from the subterranean fire or the supermundane. But there is no fire stronger than the fire of the heart.

405. The flow of events is carrying away the decrepit old world. Although this period was indicated in all of the scriptures, people are not thinking about what is taking place. They cannot even begin to think about the future. So one should not issue a book unless it indicates the Teaching of the period that has already arrived. One should not assume that something will change the course of the current that people have created. On the distant worlds there is already a feeling of horror about the fiery inevitability, yet the Earth continues to shroud itself in a dark mantle. What once required a century now takes place in five years; a law governs the progression of this acceleration. That is why when I speak of the heart it means that salvation can be found by following this channel. Do you hear? I am speaking again about salvation! Not deliberations, not doubt, not vacillation, but salvation will be the sign of this hour. People need to understand still more firmly just how inappropriate the old measures already are. Only one bridge remains to the higher worlds—the heart. Let us approach the source of the feeling of Light. Let us understand that even the youths in the fiery furnace were not consumed when they ascended by way of the heart. This time is a difficult one!

We shall go on repeating this, not fearing the derision of the ignorant. They lack the slightest notion of the heart's significance.

406. When someone asks you how to get through a difficult hour, say, "Only in expectation, only in striving to the Teacher, or in doing work." And then add, "In fact, in doing all three." Doing work must be like packing all one's valuables in preparation for a distant journey. The quality of work is what opens the gates of the heart.

407. In a fit of hatred someone ailing from a

horrible disease attempted to harm humanity by touching as many objects as possible. That is how the mobility of evil expresses itself. Evil requires no definite personalities, just a general desire to inflict harm. If only goodness would distinguish itself by showing a still greater mobility! If only each person filled with goodness would sow it with every touch! What a multitude of beneficial sparks would be cast into Space and how much easier the battle with evil would become! It is true that human goodness can be quite profound, but it often lacks mobility. This happens because the heart has not been cultivated or educated. The potential of the good heart usually works spasmodically and is far from being always open in readiness. However, it is precisely this spasmodic quality that allows the many assaults of evil, which works like a winnowing fan, blowing out in every direction. Only by donning the impenetrable armor of goodness can a warrior protect himself. It is hardly commendable to have armor that is very solid in back but leaves the heart, of all places, unprotected.

408. The education of the heart must begin at the age of two.

First of all, mother's milk or goat's milk is advisable; employing a wet nurse is a hideous custom. Besides its other advantages, mother's milk is often more digestible and already contains particles of the heart energy, but until now this was not taken into account. Even the simplest people feel the truth more than the cold dogmatists do.

409. Even a commonplace lama understands that the human gaze can kill a mad dog. But the deadly eye cannot be permitted in the West, for an inadmissible fray would begin. So the heart can suggest where to draw the boundaries of what is admissible. But one can train one's gaze without harm by practicing not only with plants but also with insects and animals, commanding them with one's eye.

410. Laws have been established against many crimes, but it is also necessary to have a code of the heart. One should sow the good with every glance, every touch. And the heart will grow in this exercise of goodness. Of course, as you have observed, the activity of the heart arises not from heat so much as from currents of energy. And testing with the smallest manifestations is possible for a refined heart. There is a great deal of betrayal in the world. The refined heart is especially sensitive to this abomination.

411. In the education of the heart the first concept to be put forward is work. From the earliest years labor is established as the one foundation of life, as a process of perfectment. This approach eradicates the notion of labor being selfish, and at the same time the child acquires a broad understanding of work for the common good. Such a concept can already refine the heart a great deal, but later on this expansion of the idea of labor is no longer enough. At that point spatial work for the future is created within the heart. Then there is no negation that can hamper the growth of the work, and the spatial work consciously penetrates the higher spheres. In this state of consciousness the heart receives a durable armor that will even prove useful for the Fiery World. Let us strive to have an armor that is useful everywhere.

412. Even the Highest Beings must be filled with spirit in order to act. The expression be filled is quite precise, for indeed one needs to be filled. This means filling oneself with an abundance of the spirit. But does this not also mean that we must enter into contact with the Hierarchy? Only by drawing the spirit

from the Highest Source do we receive renewal and intensification of the fiery energy. That is why it is not indicated anywhere that a person should withdraw in spirit; on the contrary, seekers should be filled with the power of the spirit that leads to Light. You correctly recalled the experience of standing on the edge of an abyss, recollecting how you contacted a boundary that intensified your energy. Only such crests of the waves will uplift the spirit to a point of fullness. But a person who is focused on himself and thinking about self-assertion will never draw from the Eternal Fire. Let us aim our efforts at carrying out spatial measures. I can welcome you resolute warriors who know of the Phoenix that rises from the ashes.

413. Much that is actually not evil is bad from the perspective of earthly standards. If amphibians exist, why can't there be creatures that dwell both on earth and in fire? Thus, great fish are caught in great nets.

414. The phosphorus tissue has an exact resemblance to the fiery body. Set such a tissue on fire and you will immediately see how the flame flows out in many directions. That is how the fiery body flares up when irritation or shock sets it on fire.

415. Somebody may ask whether a second volume of Heart will be issued. Answer that people like reading the last page without caring about the meaning of the first page. That is why the Teaching needs to be divided into steps. It is especially sad to see that senselessly swallowing the last page only brings harm. The heart requires care and coordination, for without them the phosphorus tissue will ignite.

416. However much the manifestations of the Subtle World are hidden, so many and such diverse people have witnessed them that their existence cannot be denied. And many people know about the existence of the Subtle World not through séances or invocations but through natural vision. Of course, it is very rare that someone sees the Fiery World, but a subtle being is not far from our earthly condition. Many people will not even mention these manifestations because they are ordinary for them. Even the simplest people do not fear them, knowing in their hearts that there is no reason to be afraid. Fear, more than anything else, separates people from the Subtle World. That is how the most natural manifestation is hindered. People also turn to the most inadmissible necromancy, forgetting that all coercion is contrary to nature and harms the flow of the law. But one also should remember that even among the various natural manifestations, spiritual vision unfolds in accordance with the heart. The low consciousness will see the low, but spiritual purification will make higher vision possible. So it is the condition of the heart that will keep the consciousness above ordinary manifestations.

417. Since the new is the oldest, seekers should not fear that something is impossible. Everything is imaginable because everything exists. People should not assume that there is a poverty of creation. It is astonishing how easily science allows itself to be shackled with narrow-minded limitations and gives answers regarding things about which it knows nothing. Children sometimes are more correct in admitting, "I don't know." A frank admission of ignorance is recognized to be the Gates to Knowledge.

418. Even if you succeed in convincing people that the heart partakes of mercy, compassion, and love, the other domains of the heart will remain unintelligible to them. Won't reasoning bring forward a thousand unknowns the moment you begin to speak about cosmogony? And unless there is the courage of the heart, these discussions will lose sight of the higher boundaries. Also, unless the heart takes part, you cannot discuss quality, which lies at the basis of everything that exists. Reasoning rejects quality, but you are already seeing how life is ruined when respect for quality is lacking. Only the heart will take joy in the truth of quality. So let us understand why, after all sorts of complicated calculations, there only remains salvation by the path of the heart. A flame that defies control, the horror of a poison let loose—these can only be faced by the heart. Moreover, one has to begin understanding the heart from the very first steps, because only yesterday the heart was rejected. Nor is this a bad thing, for in a sense it gives one a chance to acquire a new treasure. People are so fond of anything new, and after delving into the integral systems of philosophy, it is fascinating to get a new game—the heart. Children like games that resemble those that grown-ups play.

419. It is all right to ask people to think about the heart at least occasionally. At first one should create a general effort to move in this direction. The planet cannot be maintained by just a hundred hearts. It is necessary that people accept the heart, even partially, as the guide of life.

420. The fiery armor can only be sensed very rarely; the same is true of the rays that form the wings of achievement. Even so, a warrior can be aware of how much this armor is protecting him, although like any fiery manifestation it requires unusual caution. The Mother of Agni Yoga knows that attaining such armor is not at all easy, for earthly conditions are quite remote from lofty fiery manifestations. But when fiery actions take place, the fiery armor makes its presence felt. Of course, if a person's heart is already accustomed to fiery manifestations, he can take part in the fiery battles.

421. A severe time requires powerful armor. People should accept this still more deeply in their hearts. They should accept the scope of the world battle so that they can encourage each other by making collective efforts. Criticism and derision are especially out of place. People need to let their hearts unfold upward, as if they were inspired by the grandeur of a temple. By doing this they can come closer to understanding the dimensions of what is happening.

422. People have found it difficult to grasp the idea that a radio broadcast may be occurring simultaneously all over the world; but the speed and boundless nature of thought are almost beyond the reach of the consciousness. The simplest, most beneficial truths are especially hard to accept. Even the methods used to investigate such laws are often deserving of pity. The monitors posted to make observations in experiments and in transmission of thought may be totally incapable of picking anything up. On the other hand, no questions will be directed to people with sensitive hearts. The difficulty now being faced is that many of the people gathering ostensibly in the name of science are undeserving of trust. Researchers should not be afraid of making mistakes, and the masses ought to be surveyed on a large scale. Naturally, there will be contradictions, but someone who conducts experiments honestly will receive really wide-ranging material nonetheless. The social sciences should conduct extensive research on how the diffusion of thought lays the foundation of human welfare. So in this era when energies are being discovered, observations on thought ought to be carried out.

423. In discussion about the education of the heart

there may arise what seem to be differences of opinion. Some will insist on a cautious attitude toward the heart, while others will recall My words, "Burden Me still more." Deployment of a shield is necessary in response to every evil attempt, but one should take on a still greater burden in the name of the Great Service. So the energy for Service ought to be intensified, because it grows with intensification. Many people are envious of anything that arises from oppression, for they find it especially annoying not to even be noticed by the dark forces. But not many appreciate intensification as a way to develop creative energy. Naturally, no intensification issues from thoughts about murder. During an attack whose objective is annihilation, fiery armor is necessary. Every warrior ought to think about such armor. This will not be a sign of retreat from battle, but a wise precaution. There is no contradiction between burdening the heart and being cautious. A warrior has to be ready for all kinds of attacks, and flexible thinking is necessary for this.

424. It is anything but cowardice to keep a watchful eye on things, especially when you are aware of what Satan has decided to do. Even a giant can be hurt by a small seed cast with harmful intent. So those who seek to harm others will try anything and everything, as they are never sure where evil might not flourish. The success of darkness lies in this sowing of rubbish. People forget how cautious they must be. Evil intent does not just spring forward like a tiger, but also creeps in like a mouse.

425. When observing the workings of the heart, a mediocre mind will face a multitude of perplexities. Such a mind will find it strange that even an extremely refined heart often notes the most powerful events very slightly, but resonates strongly to comparatively minor happenings. There are a number of causes for this, external and internal, and one should make careful distinctions between them. All the counteractions of various currents should be taken into consideration; but at the same time one should also understand all the karmic conditions, which may intensify or diminish the transmission. There is no reason to be distressed if the law governing the heart's reaction cannot be expressed in so many words. Quite the contrary, the diversity of the ancillary circumstances enriches opportunities for making new observations. So even in schools instructors can exercise the attention of the little ones, who are often much more honest and flexible than adults; one need only direct the children's attention to the attractive notion that they take note of their own sensations.

426. Development of the power of observation will lead to fearlessness. We should not be afraid of what is around us. So by making observations, we ourselves will bring to light new structures that only yesterday were imperceptible or invisible. And in doing so, we will be able to accustom ourselves to things that once seemed extremely unusual. What yesterday was forbidden out of ignorance will tomorrow become a participant and inspiration in life.

427. Nobody would believe that you knew so much about what is happening now, nor would anyone believe in the signs that you are accustomed to discerning. However, should one pay attention to people who desire neither to understand nor to accept? You know many followers of the Higher Teachings, but do they carry them out? Quite the contrary, their cruelty of heart and self-adoration are astonishing. It means that reasoning has drowned out the voice of the heart.

428. Cor bovinum, ox heart, is a very common

condition, enlargement of the heart. Many things may cause this, but it is the main cause that concerns us here. Enlargement of the heart may arise from an overabundance of unutilized heart energy. It could be said that the people who suffer from enlargement of the heart did not begin education of their heart in time. The potential of their organ was good, but the heart energy was not applied. Naturally, in essence an enlarged heart is preferable to a fatty one. Indeed, the heart can be called the most individual organ, which is why the methods for educating the heart must be very flexible. From the child's earliest years, attention should be paid to its aversions and predilections. It is stupid to regard aversions, which are often not understood, as silly nonsense. Quite often aversions and predilections reveal the entire structure of the heart, and one can draw very useful conclusions by observing them. But most of all one should beware of a heart that knows neither predilection nor aversion. It means that the heart is asleep. There are many such sleeping hearts, and this condition leads to the disintegration of the spirit. So once again the unfathomably spiritual is connected with physical manifestation.

429. One can consider the most spiritual problems from the standpoint of physical laws, and the neglect of our center—the heart—may be described as truly inhuman. People are not used to paying attention to the sensations of the heart, but it will resonate to absolutely anything.

430. An outflow of heart energy may be voluntary or involuntary. The latter may be aroused by an external entreaty or by the irrepressible generosity of the heart itself. One can imagine how bountiful these generous gifts are and how much strength they use up; but the generosity of the heart is immeasurable, and the flaming heart knows no stinginess. The same principle should be applied to heart transmissions that have been aroused from distant places. On the way to its destination, many similar transmissions fasten onto the call being sent, for like gathers like according to its element. Especially in this way is the flow of energy reinforced. Naturally, you know about the divisibility of the spirit, and you will understand these generous responses of the heart. There is good reason for speaking about economy, for it is needed in everything, even in the transmissions of the heart. This is a very grave time!

431. You may notice people showing an absence of attention, a curious absentmindedness, as it were. While this condition lasts, they are unaware of their surroundings. This may be due to absentmindedness or fattiness of the heart, but one should not reject the possibility that many other higher causes may be at work. The spirit can perform its work at many different times. It does not need intermissions or some sort of preparatory steps; it either senses a need for action or it is summoned. It carries on its distant communications in a variety of ways. There is a factual foundation for the stories of saints who, while seeming to fall into a momentary trance, were extending tremendous spiritual help during that time. Often the "trance" is not noticed by those present or even by the person who enters it. Only the pause in awareness of the surrounding conditions proves that there has been a complete absence. It is impossible to judge how long these absences last, because time has no place in the dimensions of the spirit. But anyone who is aware of having had such an absence can state that something happened that was beyond earthly dimensions. Seekers ought to take note of these absences. One can

gradually come to recognize familiar details emerging quite unexpectedly. The details of the spiritual work will flash by like a fiery arrow, and then droop like a flower lowered into poison. The great labor of the spirit is so remote from the lower, poisoned spheres!

432. A seeker's first duty is to watch his own feelings. Nobody should consider the call for such attention to be an exaggeration; quite the contrary, attention ought to be understood as something that shows respect for a higher prototype. It is time to put an end to the theory that things happen by chance. You noted correctly that even the simplest experiment cannot be repeated. But the individuality of an action is not born of chance; it is the result of the irresistible, sequential operation of the law. So by developing attentiveness the seeker can grow used to respecting reality. You were right in noting that only the new consciousness will provide the future with a firm foundation. In the name of the future, let us learn to concentrate.

433. In undergoing the education of the heart, we grow accustomed to the spheres of the Subtle World without noticing the fact ourselves. This happens not because of some sort of exceptional, miraculous phenomena, but rather through the minute sensations that the sensitized heart starts to discern. While seekers ought to accept this idea about the importance of minute sensations, they should not become dogmatists who delve into doctrines based on petty divisions and subdivisions. The heart will show where the tortuous line runs between the essential and the conditional. Little by little we come to acknowledge that around us there exist a multitude of manifestations that the laws of elementary physics cannot accommodate. Experiences will increase, and an entire spectrum will take shape consisting of the sensations of the Subtle World.

This will be the most obvious thing that happens when we begin to approach the Subtle World. After experiencing these sensations, we will also begin accustoming our physical bodies to the specific features of the next state. By grasping the essence of the Subtle World's laws, we immediately attain to more advanced stages on that plane. We regard it as perfectly natural for people to accustom their consciousnesses to subtle feelings and sensations, and thereby also acquire physical adaptability.

434. By these means the entire psychology of existence will be changed. You are already able to understand that there would be an absence of boredom even if you were to find yourselves in inaccessible caves. You already know an absence of fear, even though you are in the front ranks of Armageddon. You already know patience, even in the midst of the worldwide tempest. In this way many qualities are already entering your lives, bringing with them a string of indestructible accumulations. This is the source of true wealth.

435. It is perfectly legitimate to ask whether psychic experiments might not be greatly hampered by the resistance of the will. Let us answer that this is very much the case; not only a resistant will but also a deadness of the heart creates obstacles. Even with the most effectively designed phenomena, the results are limited by the resistance of those who oppose them. One cannot acquire the ability to levitate or walk on water if resistant forces are present. Even the power to walk through fire or wield the deadly eye will not be completely effective if there is a resistant will. Therefore, My advice about unity has a special meaning. This is not just an ethical instruction but also a practical consideration. Even slight resistance already injures the fabric. So the coworkers need to preserve a sense of solemnity, for this feeling will not permit petty irritations and decay.

436. The theory connected with the winding of psychic energy closely resembles that which underlies the induction coil. So it is that many instruments designed for cruder application may provide essential ideas for experiments with subtle energy; but people need to have their eyes open so they will not be reluctant to make use of unexpected allies and materials.

437. There is a question that particularly concerns people: why didn't the founders of the various spiritual Teachings avoid physical illness? Usually this question is asked by people who themselves are contributing a great deal to such illnesses by harboring suspicion, criticizing others, and opposing spiritual work in multiple ways. But put the person who asks this question in a poisoned room and he will immediately fall ill with a hundred different diseases. Of course, to understand this issue one has to imagine the tension of the organism when it is performing spiritual work. In its desire to help, the organism takes in its surroundings, drawing everything in like a magnet. The transference of another person's illness to oneself is not a fairy tale. During this process one may notice that the pain is not transferred to the same organ or body part, but instead strikes the tensest or weakest centers. It is wrong to think that the pains described in the lives of the great ascetics are exaggerated. Quite the contrary, the intensity and degree of those pains are as varied as humanity itself. But what is it that alleviates these sufferings? Besides the silver thread of the Hierarchy, the heart itself often conveys the sign for the healing ray to begin its work. We often find it astonishing that doctors pay no attention to the people who visit the ill. Perhaps half of the cure would consist not in medicines but in removal of the harmful elements that are brought in such abundance by those who come along with their spiritual contagion.

438. Medicine needs to inquire about people who purify and people who do harm. Unless there is a solution to this problem, it will be impossible to find a way of avoiding many of the most recent diseases. It should not be forgotten that diseases evolve together with races and epochs. But our recorded science is still so young that one cannot really suggest that it make comparisons in this regard. It only knows about a few centuries, but what about the tens of millennia that preceded them? We have become very conceited and forgotten how many things we do not know. But the heart knows the dates, and even an ignorant heart quivers at the approach of the Fiery World.

439. The projection of thought onto a highly sensitive film is quite possible, but to do this a person has to focus the sharpest thinking. The main thing is the quality of thinking. Sound creates rhythms in sand. Thought also generates vibrations, but naturally it is much subtler than sound. That is why it can act not upon coarse grains of sand but upon the most sensitive film. People will not reach such subtlety and concentration any time soon. They substitute amusements for concentration. But was extravagance ordained? Everywhere action was enjoined, but not the chaos of scattering and dissipation.

440. The Teacher is sending forth an understanding of world events. Without the Hierarchy the chaos of events turns into formless puffs of mist. So it has been correctly observed that the present period cannot be brought into a system unless a purification of consciousness takes place. The key movements of the various peoples can be affirmed from the Mountain.

441. Who will encumber himself with the Teaching if his heart has not moved upward? It is not conversation that is necessary, but the introduction of quality into the details of everyday life.

Each day brings some knowledge and a deepening of the heart. It is precisely in this that the accumulation of energy lies. The seeker need only be free of boredom, which, like fear, brings so many things to a standstill.

442. "Do not wish evil on the Blessed One"—thus do the scriptures ordain. This instruction contains great wisdom. Frequently Yogis are accused of being vengeful or retaliating for evil deeds. Of course, this completely contradicts the nature of a Yogi, but the sad consequences of slandering a Yogi appear all the same. This manifestation is not difficult to explain: when the fiery magnet of a heart is sending rays to distant lands, one can imagine how powerful this radiation is. When an enemy's transmission comes into collision with this force, a return blow is inevitable. The situation may even demand extreme tension on the Yogi's part so that the grave consequences for the enemy are somewhat alleviated. But often the ray of the Yogi is speeding to a special destination, and then the enemy has only himself to blame for the consequences.

443. These return blows have had to be witnessed on many occasions. They can be correlated very clearly with the physical condition of the enemy. With these return blows the weakest parts of the attacker are hit. This also explains why in each case it takes a different amount of time for the consequences to emerge. Indeed, rather than taking medicine, it often would be better to focus on eliminating every trace of enmity. So the commandment, "Do not wish evil on the Blessed One," has a vital, almost medical, significance.

444. Among the various sacred pains there is a certain type that is called the "Vina of the Creator," after the Indian lute. The pains of the centers in the throat, shoulders, elbows, extremities, knees, and elsewhere speed out like chords reverberating on a musical instrument. That is how the heart is tuned. Without question, the heart's bond with the Highest remains the sole refuge of humanity. The other forms of Yoga were connected with other cosmic conditions. Now the heart is being cast forth like an anchor in a storm, and it is not difficult to approach the fiery Yoga of the Heart. First, the seeker should sense the great battle and the ominous cloud of destruction that is gathering over the Earth. Second, the seeker should look upon his heart as a refuge. And third, the seeker should be firmly established upon the Hierarchy. It would seem that these conditions are not so hard to meet, but so often we humans prefer side-paths and would even rather practice deceit than turn to the simplest means. Of course, tension of the heart is needed. With good reason the heart was called the "Great Prisoner."

445. Powerful volcanoes are awakening; the fire is seeking an outlet. People are aware of this, but they do not give up a single habit. Likewise, it is hard for them to transfer consciousness to the heart; but one needs to be clad in the best armor for protection from all sorts of poison. Similarly, people fail to foresee national events, but their sequence comes rushing forward with unstoppable force. The battle is not easy; everyone has to muster up all the courage in his heart. That is the only way people will be able to keep up with Us.

446. As the Kali Yuga ends, all processes actually speed up, which is why we should not regard the periods predicted in the past to be unchangeable. As the Kali Yuga ends, even half a century is not a minor period of time. And so Agni Yoga is becoming a bridge to the future. People should firmly understand that the development of spiritual forces, which formerly took decades, is now being accelerated to the highest degree by means of the heart. They can accept Agni Yoga as the rapid evolution of forces. Where whole years were once devoted to the refinement and tempering of the body, now the heart can move the spirit almost immediately. Naturally, the education of the heart is necessary, but this lies in the sphere of feelings, not mechanics. So let us swiftly summon the heart to service for the New World.

447. We understand how a great future is being prepared. Of course, people do not acknowledge Our methods. They do not value the immutable quality of the consciousness that leads forward. They assume that something will succeed by means of the usual accolades and money, but according to Our method it is from tension that Beauty is born. Let us not start belittling a tree whose roots are already growing. That is why one has to exercise such caution when tension has reached an unprecedented level. The approach to life that relies on the heart as the guiding principle is not simply repeating previous Teachings; it also lies in undertaking a true transformation of life.

448. People easily recognize that the lower discipline, Hatha Yoga, has a scientific basis, but they do not even attempt to bring the higher signs into the scope of scientific observations. But of what value are the mechanical siddhis in comparison with the manifestations of the loftiest heart? The siddhis of the body cannot often be applied, while the activity of the heart flows without break. Of course, to observe the subtlest manifestations of the heart, the seeker's attentive power has to be intensified; but serious experiments

also require attentiveness. Wouldn't it be best to get used to paying attention through observing one's heart? Such experiments in attentiveness will not be undertaken in vain. Best of all, they are appropriate for approaching the Subtle World. Once a person has listened to his own heart, he no longer sees any end to observations. The observations begun in a single home will inevitably guide the observer all over the world and also indicate the path to the higher worlds. Why write out a multitude of formulas if one does not wish to apply them in one's life? Contact with the subtler energies refines one's entire being. A person who has entered the fiery path understands the refinement, insightfulness, and vigilance of which I speak.

449. It has been correctly noted that Bhakti Yoga also has an influence on the heart, but the difference lies in the fact that Bhakti Yoga has proceeded along the path of the feeling of love, not showing concern for other sensations of cosmic manifestations and rays that lead one beyond the boundaries of the planet. Only with difficulty can science comprehend the paths of Bhakti Yoga. But now the heart is conducting a twofold labor: the heart is leading to the world of love through the circles of the Subtle World and those of the Fiery World. But the solemnity that I am trying to impart to you leads to the fieriest waves of attainment. Not simple is the grace that reveals itself in the midst of solemn devotion, but the armor of solemnity is beautiful.

450. A Rishi used to send small pieces of linen, palm leaf, or birch bark to the needy and sick. Some who received them scoffed and said, "Isn't it ridiculous to waste energy sending people empty fragments?" Words were the only thing they would acknowledge. But those who were wise took what they had been sent and applied it to the sick part or to their hearts, thereby receiving relief. They understood that the Rishi had placed his hand upon the object sent and suffused it with his psychic energy. There are also known to be images or imprints of hands that were transmitted by mysterious means and only appeared when subjected to heat or light. Of course, an ordinary doctor would rather place faith in some very crude plaster or ointment than admit that the magnetism of objects has significance. One may yet be able to win the doctor's favor by pointing out the importance of fatty deposits; but concerning anything of a higher nature, a dog proves itself to be more understanding. So it is incredibly difficult to instill in the human brain any idea that uplifts human dignity.

451. We do not like to give concrete advice with a narrow range of application. First of all, people do not accept such advice as something to be carried out. People do not like the Fundamentals of the Teachings. They always prefer fakirs or fortunetellers. But even these cherished methods are not regarded as conveying anything that has to be applied. Certainly, people will come seeking advice, but they will not make much effort to understand it and will distort it to the point where it actually leads to harm.

452. It is not just fools who deny everything invisible to them; in their search for facts, scholars also destroy a multitude of useful things along the way. Bias in one's thinking acts like a heavy weight, crushing the life out of everything that has been ordained. Likewise, good advice may be accepted for the time being and then set aside just when the seed is starting to take shape. Who, then, is able to imagine the complexity in the course of the currents? You know how a splendid future is being prepared; but since it

cannot be a return to the primitive, the builders have to get used to there being developments that are plain and clear to Us but not to everyone. We are attaining success in piercing the darkness, and the builders should remember that solemnity is the surest means of fortification.

453. Truly, nothing is repeated in the Universe; but even in the midst of all this diversity, the human heart is the most individual of all. But who will measure this abyss? And who will undertake the task of explaining to the peoples about the heart and then repeating it? Not lawyers, not doctors, not warriors, not priests, but the Sisters of the Great Mountain will take upon themselves the solemn duties of laying one hand upon the aching heart, while pointing with the other hand to boundless Grace. Who, then, will be able to understand the solemnity of love, which unites the silver thread with the citadel of the Highest Heart? That is why We are so intent on sending forth the Sisters to a *podvig* of the heart. It is impossible to reveal the infinitude of the Highest Heart in a way that an unawakened consciousness can comprehend. To understand, you must already have succeeded in acquiring solemnity. In order to avoid disgracing solemnity with anything petty or lacking in co-measurement, you must already have developed solicitude. If these conditions are met, the Service of the Sisters of the Mountain will go forward. And they will protect the hearts of the people from the filth and stench engendered by darkness.

454. In all races, at all times there existed the cult of the heart. Even savages, when devouring living hearts, regarded the heart as a higher power and thereby, in their own way, paid it reverence. But our contemporary era has completely forgotten the Teaching of the Heart and cast it aside. The heart demands a new understanding. Anyone who cites purely scientific facts about the heart must be ready for accusations that he is touting superstition. Dogmatic professionals will make a special effort to defend their miserable existence. One should realize that the battle to secure understanding of the heart will be especially severe. So the dark forces will defend the brain, setting it against the heart. Naturally, this will only distort the situation. The leg has important functions, but there is no need to put food into one's mouth with one's foot. And so in everything goal-fitness comes first.

455. The atmosphere has never been this dense! A person has to be particularly slow-witted not to sense the phenomena that are manifested anywhere one walks. The world's condition cannot possibly be considered normal, but the people of Atlantis also completely failed to see all the striking signs around them. In fact, the Atlanteans went even further by meting out capital punishment to anyone who pointed out the obvious calamities that were occurring. Naturally, this measure only accelerated the destruction. People have never willingly acknowledged that they themselves are the foundation for the transmutation of psychic energy, and so they have no compunctions about misdirecting the flow of this precious power.

456. Truly, the unyielding, unswerving power of the heart creates a tempering process that is suitable for attainment of the Fiery World. It is the flaming heart—not a spasmodic, fitful striving—that guides the consciousness in accord with the higher worlds. Let us manifest solemnity.

457. The flow of heart energy is often felt on the right side of the organism. The energy strikes the Chalice and, of course, from there is reflected to the right side of the organism. The temples, neck, shoulders,

knees, and extremities are registering a sensation that is very similar to the feeling of a physical outflow. The amount of energy thus distributed by the heart is incalculable. That is why the Guide often advises caution. It is difficult to determine in advance just when this outflow will begin, because spatial magnets and sympathies often demand simultaneous transmissions to different parts of the world and various spheres. If demands upon the heart energy could be connected to an electric bell, there would often result an uninterrupted ringing that would vary only in the level of its intensity. Such experiments will surely be performed, but the people conducting them will rarely agree that the heart energy is involved; instead they will attribute the results to some kind of nervous contractions. Not so very long ago, a person might have been burned at the stake for possession of such a "telegraph."

458. In fact, not long ago the potato was regarded as the "devil's apple." Let us not get all puffed up with pride, since similar examples of human ignorance abound even now. The ignorance of savages may even be preferable, because they can be led forward more easily to the possibilities of the distant worlds. Even reincarnation is still regarded as a curiosity or a superstition. All the indications regarding the laws of nature have yet to lead to significant conclusions. I am repeating this not for you but for the timid ignoramuses who attempt to cover crime in a cloak of irresponsibility. How they dread death! In fact, they are even afraid to cross to the other side of the river. Their ignorance needs to be disturbed once in a while. Those who slumber are sometimes in need of a good whack.

459. Those who are sleeping can be easily burned, because they have left the fire burning close by and are unwilling to pay attention to it. Again, this is not being said to you, since you already understand what vigilance means.

460. Not only vibrations but also the substance of the heart provides creative power. This same energy should be valued in all the most miniscule manifestations of life. Even in its minute manifestations life performs a miracle that could be the worthy subject of innumerable books. So directing attention to the physical shell will inevitably end up deepening the attention paid to the action of the heart. The Teaching of the Heart is the teaching of the causes of manifestations. The ancients began transmission of the Teaching by laying their hands upon the heart. Then the Teacher would ask, "Don't you hear it?" and the student would answer, "Yes, I hear." "This is the beating of your heart, but it is only the first rap on the Gates of the Great Heart. If you don't pay attention to the beating of your own heart, then the beat of the Great Heart will deafen you."

That was how the Command was conveyed in simple words; thus, the path to Infinity was transmitted through knowledge of oneself. Is it possible that we have not gone further than the ancients, that we have been unable to picture the path of the tremor, the path of eternal motion? You correctly remarked that the potential of motion is a guarantee that one will reach perfection. That is why a static condition devoid of tension and striving will fail to uplift the thought of humanity.

461. How precious is awareness of the fact that each of our correct judgments enriches space! And how great is our responsibility any time we sully space!

462. Many concepts and conditions cannot be expressed in words. Only a lack of respect for words allows people to frequently chirp away like birds; but if people studied the language of the birds, they would be amazed at its solemnity. There is far greater exaltation in the words of birds than in the twisted judgments that other two-footed creatures voice. There is good reason for my repeating about solemnity, for it is nourishment for the heart! Not in criticism or irritation but in solemnity are we preparing for the great march forward.

The onward march should be understood as service to the Teaching of Life. You yourselves see how events are gathering. You also see that quantity has no significance and often may be nothing but a burden. You yourselves see that events are growing in scope, for even people who lack foresight are beginning to feel astonished at the cosmic manifestations. Count the hours, for there has never been an age so filled with events.

463. Without a doubt, there is a disturbance of climatic conditions, but people just make superficial remarks about sunspots or a shifting of the Earth's axis. The most timid people come forward with those assertions, but they do not even understand what they are saying. Many times the Earth has been visited by calamities that wiped away civilizations and life, and these were preceded by just the same sort of theorizing. Then, too, people were unwilling to notice the signs of disturbance, and they continued carrying on superficial arguments about how to prolong the sapped-out conditions of contemporary life. Now, too, people who harbor a multitude of misconceptions are asking why a heightening of sensitivity and intensification of certain pains seem to be unavoidable when one studies the higher knowledge. If someone explained to them that their heedlessness is making the chosen ones suffer, they would not believe it. They will not accept that they themselves are condensers and transmuters of energy. But when numerous such "apparatuses" are damaged, the distribution of energy is disturbed, and only a few refined hearts take on the pressure that should have been distributed throughout the entire world. The solar natures take upon themselves the pressure of the fiery energy and thus must be responsible for millions of drones.

464. We entrust Our disciples with the task of getting to know the desert as well as the atmosphere of the city. This gives them a chance to compare differences in the pressure of the fiery energy. It is inadmissible for people to gather in great multitudes as long as they do not realize what precious vessels of energy they themselves are. They will not allow thought about the value of their own spirit. That is why the feeling of solemnity is the hardest thing for them to experience. The tremor felt when wings are carrying one in steady ascent is beyond a person's strength if he rejects the value of the spirit. Without a doubt, there is a disturbance of climatic conditions. Isn't humanity's spirit responsible for this dangerous manifestation?

465. The impression that an aura makes on film does not depend on the film itself but rather on the photographer and the subject. Ordinary film of good quality works just fine, but the qualities of the participants and witnesses are especially important. Even if one of the participants has excellent qualities, one should not expect immediate results. To get harmonies, the vina has to be tuned, but people dislike preparatory work more than anything else. And one further condition is necessary: the participants should be able to spend at least one day without feeling the slightest irritation. Imperil eats away at the most essential energy reflexes. An irritable person can be called a shell, in the fullest sense of the word. A single crystal of imperil is able to obscure the most significant results. Imperil should not be thought of as a houseplant; its odor spreads far and wide, and blights every current it touches. So when I warn against irritation, I am not promulgating a dogma but offering therapeutic observations. As with everything, implementation of these instructions should begin with the details.

Certain mechanical methods are also useful in photographing the aura. Before the photograph is taken, it is helpful for the participants to take musk, which stimulates the currents of energy. It is helpful to have a black velvet background and also to manifest solemnity, when possible. Naturally, it would be absurd to crowd the room with curious people who just happened to stop by. The very atmosphere of the room should be purified with eucalyptus oil. Thus, one needs to consider not only the occult conditions but also the purely hygienic ones.

466. Seekers should keep the Chain of the White Forces constantly in their thoughts. Not criticism is needed, but only the future structure. Dazzling is the radiance of the White Chain, extending from the Mountains of Light. These are significant times, when even the humblest of souls discern the majesty of the White Chain. People should follow all the Indications so that grains of irritation will not hamper the power of the White Forces. One might even say it is beautiful to sweep aside everything trifling when titanic bodies are trembling.

467. The hygiene of the heart is premised on good deeds—but good deeds in a broad sense. So "good deeds" do not include inciting people to commit treachery or harbor evil intentions, or encouragement of false prophets, deceivers, cowards, and all the other servants of darkness. Nor do good deeds include shameful negligence or deliberate concealment. Good deeds have in mind the welfare of humanity. In the course of good deeds the heart acquires solemnity, which is like the harmony of the spheres. Actually, good deeds can be discerned as beneficial acts of *podvig*—distinguished by their aptness in fulfilling goals, not by their callousness. It often seems to people that they ought to always be nice and sweet, and this misunderstanding leads to avoidance of responsibility; it is simpler for them not to think too deeply and instead take the easy way out.

468. The heart understands where there is deviation, where curiosity, and where a thirst for knowledge—that is how you should discriminate between those who approach. Do not give the fire to the light-minded, nor entrust the curious with counting the leaves of the Teaching. Many misfortunes arise from trusting people too much, a mistake that is impermissible where treasures are being guarded.

469. People should recognize that Light is a living substance. They should understand that ascent is the one direction destined. It is hard to realize that deficiency is the result of one's own mistakes!

470. Let people recognize that the essence of the heart is an inextinguishable substratum. The term used is unimportant, so long as the essence of the heart is clearly indicated. Thus, people need to grow accustomed to the indisputable concepts that are familiar to all humanity. Those who have been victimized will realize why it is that from ages past Osiris has been slain and had his parts scattered all over the world. If this slaying had not taken place, messengers could not have been sent across the globe. Thus, what is suffering from one perspective is only diffusion from another.

Similarly, the reading of works contained in several volumes can have a deep significance. A person who studies the Teaching is in a different frame of mind when trying to assimilate the content of each book, so a multitude of perspectives emerges. That is why in every book it is wise even briefly to touch on what has previously been covered, so that the reader will have a chance to grasp everything in a similar frame of mind, a similar mood. Moods are the birthplace of various points of view.

471. People look upon the Teaching of the Heart as the one having the least foundation. But could one regard a current of heart energy as something occult? On the contrary, there is nothing as precise as a heartbeat. A sensitive heart impels one to a renewal of consciousness. At least show some respect for the heart and its work.

472. Whether negative or positive, prejudice is wrong. It is contrary to every kind of Yoga, for it cuts off the phenomenal side of ascent. People often confuse prejudice with straight-knowledge, but these qualities are entirely antithetical. Prejudice is the progeny of reasoning, whereas straight-knowledge dwells in the heart. So one should not compare the children of reasoning with the children of the heart. The assumption that they can be placed on the same level is not only erroneous but also harmful, since it belittles the activity of the heart. It can be observed how slabs of prejudice accumulate until a person's entire life turns into a self-erected prison. But since straight-knowledge concerns cosmic truth, it does not contain anything that belittles or narrows. The self-development of straight-knowledge awakens solemnity of feeling. So it is that through various gates we approach the Hall of Solemnity.

473. A person who has not experienced the sacred tremor of solemnity cannot understand the harm that prejudice works. It develops not in great deeds but in each tiny action. Thus, the votary of prejudice wakes up cursing a dream that did not fit into the limitations of his nature. He will spend the entire day criticizing and cursing because he lacks the standards of the heart. And he will fall asleep still criticizing and go off to a realm corresponding to that criticism.

474. The dying out of generations of human and animal life, as well as the depletion of nature's generative forces, indicates the end of the Kali Yuga. This process is taking place before your very eyes, but only a few people take the trouble to notice this cosmic manifestation. There are times when even you ascribe all this to chance, while in fact it is evidence of the stern law that humanity has called into action. It would seem impossible for people to overlook what has been happening these past several years! All the same, they lull themselves with the comforting thought that things went all right yesterday; yet if they come across threatening signs somewhere, they fall into an animal fear. Meanwhile, nobody harkens to words about the heart. Its great salutary substance remains unapplied.

You desire to gather Our discussions for the general welfare; go ahead, but you will be able to count your readers on your fingers. Many will turn the pages of the book and smile at the childish opinions concerning the heart, Armageddon, and the depletion of generative forces. The very same thing has happened many times before, and is sure to happen again. One can only hope that the end of the Kali Yuga does not turn into The End!

475. Even so, it would not take all that many steadfast spirits to change this disastrous situation. A few flaming hearts could rise in selfless vigil and weave a strong protective net. Neither the supernatural nor magic will connect the worlds; that will be done simply by the flaming aspiration of the heart. While I have already spoken about the end of the Kali Yuga, some people are thinking about the centuries that appear to remain. They are not allowing for the possibility of acceleration, although simple chemical experiments demonstrate that reagents can speed processes up.

476. Even the tenderest, most compassionate heart should not be lacking in courage. The heart is a rock on which strongholds are built. Can a stronghold prevail without courage and solemnity? In the most straitened circumstances courage gives breadth to one's outlook and solemnity impels one to the Heights. Seekers should be tireless in their quest for courage and solemnity. Courage may be buried under the rubble of disasters or remain completely undeveloped. It is on the list of qualities that require development. Every accumulation of courage has been tested in the past. It is not hard to ignite the flame of courage when its blade has already experienced battle. People often employ beautiful expressions without being aware of their origins. They rightly say, "Her heart caught fire," or, "His spirit was kindled." So there was a time when people recalled the fire of the heart, but now they are ashamed of this fire. They are first of all ready to explain their beautiful expressions either as superstitions or as fairy-tale fantasies. But on the best occasions let us recall fire, courage, and solemnity. Love, which pure solemnity embraces, is always in need of defense against dark desecrators. Courage is a shield, and fire welds its streams into a fiery sword. I have good reason for affirming courage, for it will strengthen the aspirant's outlook.

477. There are all kinds of armor. The parts of the armor are often joined in a solar disk above the solar plexus. Especially among Eastern arms one commonly encounters this kind of structure. Sometimes it has been attributed to the cult of Mithra, but it is far more ancient. The armor of the solar plexus is what suggested the design for this armor. And the solar plexus dons its armor in time of battle. Now the battle is raging, and naturally your spirit leaps to the frontlines. Warrior and mother, you have done well in forging your armor of courage!

478. Let people smile about Our Advice regarding the heart. The most difficult thing for them will be to accept the dimensions of everything, beginning with their own hearts. But We know how to wait for understanding. And since We are well aware of the way people are, We place confidence in the power of patience. When affirming courage, We will not forget about patience. It is comforting to know that patience overcomes every irritation. In the tension born of patience a special substance is produced which, acting like a powerful antidote, neutralizes even imperil. Of course, being patient does not mean being insensible or callous. Benevolent reactions do not appear while a person is showing criminal indifference. Patience is a conscious state of tension as well as opposition to darkness.

479. At the same time, patience is a source of Grace. Nothing tests the heart so thoroughly as patience. You know the essence of what is happening now. Can you withstand the tension of the spheres unless you have the experience of patience acquired over many ages?

480. If somebody begins to complain about the intangibility of the Subtle World, point out how very wrong that statement is. The wings of the Subtle

World touch people far more frequently than they are given to thinking. It is people themselves who brush off the invisible flies and the invisible web, just as they frequently fight off a persistent thought and then turn around with the question, "Who was calling me?" Life is full of a multitude of subtle but entirely real sensations. Given their physical reality, many of them could even be studied with comparatively crude instruments. As you know, the sensation that there are invisible webs on one's face can often be felt distinctly over a sustained period of time. It would seem that physicians engaged in research in the domain of psychic phenomena ought to consider this sensation to be very significant. Why don't they use various instruments in conducting tests with people who experience such sensations, tests to monitor pulsation, the nature of secretions, the heart, and the receptivity of the skin? The subtle element may also indicate a sort of tremor around the person being observed. So by feeling one's way around, one could start making useful observations; but the main problem is that usually such experiments are carried out intermittently, without iron-hard, unshakeable patience. The Subtle World requires striving, not spasms.

481. When I speak of the touches of the Subtle World, I am not referring to the sensation of a handclasp or a touch that calls attention to something. These latter manifestations may happen unexpectedly and therefore be difficult to observe, whereas the invisible web or a persistent thought can be investigated. Naturally, the Subtle World can be studied not in insane asylums but among healthy people. True, possession does provide a series of manifestations, but the lower spheres must not be made manifest, for they are horribly contagious!

482. Wouldn't it be considered a powerful psychophysical manifestation when a bed, an armchair, and a table shake because of healing vibrations? It is not surprising that such shaking is sometimes mistakenly attributed to the tremors of an earthquake. Skeptics will often insist that the shaking sensation is due to dizziness. The ways that vibrations manifest would also provide material for experiments. Even with primitive instruments one can observe the vibrations of heavy objects. From such crude subjects one can move on to people's organisms, which shake in all their nerve centers. You are aware of these vibrations and accept them as something completely natural, but let us not flatter ourselves with the hope that multitudes of people wish to learn about them. Yet all of the teachings have vibrations in mind and speak about them in a definite way; even primitive teachings have accorded them considerable significance. So when thinking about the heart, let us be sure to remember the great healing power of vibrations.

483. When I talk about caution, I also have vibrations in mind, because many crosscurrents can create poisonous combinations. That is why it is so important to understand where vibrations are coming from and thus be able to accept them with one's heart. Wondrous is the conductor of the heart which, being superior to a telegraph, understands the process of right combination. Awareness of the Hierarchy also leads to this understanding. One must understand consciousness in its very essence.

484. A "black heart" has always been regarded as a symbol of great danger. Only the most unshakeable courage could stand up against this disastrous phenomenon, but such courage was rarely found. The degree of courage is tested by the power of the danger

being confronted, true courage waxing stronger as the intensity of the danger increases. She, Our warrior, knows the degree of courage to which I am referring. When the dark legions attack, all sorts of consequences arise. Injury to a person's essence results in possession, but a purified spirit may fall ill rather than suffer possession. You have read how Our Brother, though he was already of high standing, suffered a long illness due to dark opposition. Such consequences must be kept in mind, because it is a great battle that is raging. Certainly, the impact of the dark arrows can be reduced, but personal caution is still necessary. The same impulse should be directed to accumulation of courage as an antidote to the black poison. Naturally, physical weakening does not mean spiritual weakening; quite the contrary, sometimes physical problems may mean that the expenditure of spiritual riches becomes unlimited.

485. One must be extremely careful during the Great Battle. The chief condition that prompts caution is the certitude that behind one looms the threat of vacillation, which leads to betrayal. Seekers should recall how gradually We revealed the properties of the heart and prepared you for great actions. They should remember once and for all that Our Instructions are not abstract. And they should understand that this Yoga is given in time. Achievement does not mean rolling on the ground or consuming physical poisons; rather, as was said long ago, it is spiritual poison that is consumed by Agni Yogis for the salvation of the world. The black hearts will not understand this Great Service. For them the physical poisons are far more potent than the spiritual. All this has to be repeated tirelessly, for then caution will be joined to courage.

486. There is also danger when an Instruction is

not carried out right away. Even in an ordinary situation if we ask a person to step to the side, he is sure to ask the reason rather than do what we say, or at best he will look around and allow the stone to fall on his head. The same thing happens with unsuccessful students. Their hearts will be silent when they ought to be acting immediately. This is also harmful to the heart itself, for what could be more destructive than failure to carry out commands that the heart gives or receives? Just because the heart is silent does not mean that in its depths the telegraphic signal has not been received. Failure to act on a command is as dangerous as smothering the heart with reasoning! How many cardiac arrests are due to tension arising from unexecuted commands! The conflict between the heart and reasoning is the saddest page in human history.

487. Drinking down poison or being crucified represents a condition that is absolutely necessary for movement upward. It is as if a settling of accounts with lower matter were taking place. So we learn to fly, leaving our heavy shoes far below.

488. Even before he has finished reading the first book, my friend is already asking when the next book will appear. Though he has yet to carry out a single Instruction, my friend wishes to learn when the next piece of advice will be given. Having failed to keep even one secret, my friend demands to be entrusted with still greater ones. So you know how things are going. You know how this "learned man," without having read through the book, is able to assure you that he has known all this since the day he was born. You know how this "unassuming man," though he has not given up a single habit, is able to assure you of his complete regeneration. For this very reason, since time immemorial the usefulness of changing one's habits has been enjoined. Journeying through many lands has a special quality that accustoms the traveler to every sort of condition. Someone who has understood the hearts of many peoples will not get lost among the throngs in the Subtle World. But naturally this is just one of many mechanical methods for enlightening the consciousness; the basic path for strengthening the consciousness runs through the heart.

489. A person who has perceived with his heart will not ask about what comes next before having read what has already been given. So it is that heart perception grants one a charm that gold cannot acquire. The manifestation of the anura, the "heart charm," is valued very highly. It belongs among the qualities that can be accumulated and never eradicated. The anura, the charm of the heart, is also known as the Regal Heart. One can see how this charm begins unfolding from childhood, sometimes even being burdensome to the person who possesses it, for people of differing tensions disrupt its rhythm.

490. When they are looking for a house to rent, even the coarsest people will inspect every corner and express their feelings. Could it be, then, that We would place Our disciples in uninspected quarters? A seeker needs to know about everything in his environment. A seeker should sense all the stratifications of the past before he strives into the future. But when a decision about the future arises, the past falls away, vanishes like a shadow cast by the passing sunset, and only the glow of the sunrise remains to illumine the brow. Some people suspect, without grounds, that Our cooperative efforts are inadequate. Our solicitude for them far exceeds their thought about Us. Try calculating the vast amount of advice wasted and structures left incomplete, and you will be able to imagine how hard it is to fill up the abysses thus created! So even now beautiful strongholds can be built!

491. You see how powerful solemnity is. You see how much can be attained through solemnity. Therefore, you should not simply recommend solemnity—you should demand it as a path to salvation. We have only just entered upon the path of solemnity. If you succeed in staying on it, you will witness miracles. Already for a month now We have been leading you on the solemn path of ascent. In spite of the battle, We are assembling in solemnity. We have cleared all of the impediments that were thrown in our way, and have gathered the fruit of the accumulations of goodness. Above all the attainments of the heart shines solemnity. We sound a summons to solemnity, We ordain it!

492. Increase solemnity ten times over. Increase solemnity just as believers increase the number of their prayer lamps. When we march forward on the path of ascent, entrust your hands to Ours. Hasten to the Summit of the Heart. Soon we will concern ourselves with the "Signs of Fire." Now let Us affirm the qualities of the heart and show how they manifest in life. Intensify your energy for the glory of the Lord, solemnly and courageously!

493. Isn't it a wondrous experience to apply your heart energy over vast distances and thereby help the great cause? You can check the dates and receive perfectly exact confirmation of this. Therefore, it is so important to record the most significant manifestations and sensations. That way you can counteract absurd assertions that find everywhere nothing but chance and coincidence. As for those who do not consciously apply the most important energies, their failure will give rise to harmful results, not only for themselves but for everyone else as well. There is

nothing worse than thinking chaotically or cutting off the currents of energy. Anyone is annoyed when his torch blows out under his nose, and suppression of the heart energy can be called the blowing out of a torch. Do not tire of repeating this. Especially when strong outflows of energy are taking place, it is quite dangerous to break the rhythm by fretting about ordinary affairs. You never know what your energy has been required for, so maintaining solemnity will be the best way to guard against breaks and jagged edges. Especially during Armageddon the usual methods must be discarded. I affirm the greatness of this time, a time for which only solemnity will prove appropriate.

494. You desire salvation and success, but for this there must be harmony in action. You have to understand how destructive it is every time the rhythm is broken. I have already been preparing a decade for this hour of battle. Tell the disobedient that breaking the thread is tantamount to breaking away from the Lord. It is time to remember this once and for all. It is necessary now to cross many bridges quickly, and the treasure must not be squandered! At least for the present, We are demanding that warriors realize the special nature of this time; otherwise, instead of achieving a brilliant victory they may end up being hurled to destruction. We are guiding you to victory, and nobody has the right to impede Us! Now the dark forces will start trying to obstruct you with all sorts of petty details, but it is precisely when dealing with such trivialities that one can easily temper solemnity.

495. At times people are ready to recognize the power of thought, but they do not apply this recognition to themselves. They dream about great thoughts but will not put the small ones in order. They will ask how to set thought into motion. One has to start by disciplining the smallest thoughts; only when that is done can one create a thought that moves mountains. By following this advice about putting small thoughts in order, one begins to bring health to the heart. Do not rely on an assortment of outer pranayamas. The path of Agni Yoga is through the heart, but one must help the heart by putting thoughts in order. Disorderly thoughts are like lice and fleas, for they harm the subtle substance. They often carry deadly poison. Precisely the smallest thoughts smack of madness, and are therefore the main obstacle in bringing the subtle and dense worlds together. How can we persuade friends that they should immediately accept what is being said about small thoughts and put it into action? After all, this only requires a little attention and awareness of responsibility.

496. When the dawn is blazing with battle, thoughts about the future and the Common Good are especially necessary. The scala furiosa—hierarchy of fury—will not affect a heart that has been strengthened by the thought of Service.

497. You will come across the question: why is it on the edge of the abyss that the manifested help comes? There are many causes for this, among them karma and the desire for self-perfection, but from another perspective, the cause is linked to the intensity of the heart energy. Tension of the heart is necessary if one is to cooperate with the Higher Forces, but usually cooperation only begins when that tension has reached an extreme stage. This means that if the heart energy were manifested as it should be, cooperation would take place much sooner. So once more we come to the problem of educating the heart energy. Let us again recall that this education must begin with the slightest sensations and the most ordinary activities.

This condition makes things more difficult, because people usually love to say, "Let me fight a giant, but don't make me catch fleas." But giants are rare, while fleas are countless. The seekers have to pass through these dark hordes and protect the house from them. The poison that a giant -carries is less than that of a flea. Moreover, the appearance of a giant arouses an unusual degree of courage; yet courage is also necessary in fighting flies and fleas, and usually people are plagued by flies, not by giants.

498. Refutation of the Teaching may take many forms. Some people are no more able to accommodate the Teaching than they are to take good advice. But it is far more dangerous when someone understands the value of the Teaching but consciously rejects it, for that person is already in the service of darkness.

The same thing also happens with people whose efforts, previously quite pronounced, suddenly lose steam. This takes place because the education of the heart is lacking. This subject should be taken up in the family and in school. Its status should be more than that of an experiment; it should resolutely lead to the development of memory, attention, patience, and benevolence, and finally should direct the student to observation of the sensations of the heart. That is how solemnity and love of the Beautiful will be firmly implanted. And that is how the boundary between Light and darkness will be defined. Children love Light.

499. Evil creates a substance that is just as dense as good is. Naturally, it is inadmissible to maintain seedbeds of poison in space. So can we not say that the law is just, inasmuch as the sower must reap—in other words, must transmute—what he has generated? It would be unjust to load all of the evil onto the good spirits. Of course, a great spirit quaffs a huge quantity of evil and transmutes it, but even for such a spirit it is not easy to take on the poison of the world. You know how difficult it is to transmute evil from every part of the world! You know the price paid for an outflow of heart energy.

500. The heart was always thought of as the focus of life. Later on, people came to realize the Yoga of Hierarchy in their hearts; in other words, they became aware of the link with the Highest. Now the Yoga of the Subtle and Fiery Worlds has been established; this cooperation of the heart is proving to be a new circumstance in the consciousness of the people. Indeed, we must not remain within the limits of abstract ethics. Events and indisputable circumstances are leading humanity onto new paths, which is why We so ardently advise that people discard the yoke of habit and gain an understanding of our unique times.

Moses delved into the science of Egypt, but he outstripped it with the Ten Commandments. That is how the Yoga of Hierarchy works. Now We are advising the scholars: you should observe the heart with all of your methods, for you are sure to come up against manifestations that you do not understand.

501. We shall suggest to doctors that they look upon every inexplicable manifestation as something originating with the Subtle World; then there will be no errors. Just let them begin to make measurements and compare so-called healthy hearts! I believe it is necessary to understand how unusual these times are and get used to them. And it is necessary to always remember about the battle that is raging.

502. Is it possible that people do not notice the peculiar character of the heat waves, storms, and hurricanes that are taking place? And so you are right in grieving for nature, which is sick because of human madness.

504. In essence, illumination is focused grace; therefore, it ought not to be lethal. Life, however, shows just the opposite to be the case. From what does this perverse result arise? Naturally, it is due not to the light-bearers themselves but to the criminal contagion in the atmosphere around them. So once more life shows to what an extent the conditions people have created fail to conform to their wondrous possibilities. Therefore, let us assiduously speed the spatial calls onward in order to revive the consciousness of people! Many are the efforts We establish to draw their attention to the criminal madness that is running rampant. They wish to disregard the Law of the Universe, but first they need to be aware of the possibilities lost, at the same time knowing that everything can be repaired. We dream of new races, but let us consider why the new race is necessary and ask how every person can help it to come about. First of all, there must be mobility of consciousness. Children have to be taught this winged mobility.

504. Indeed, it will soon be necessary to save ourselves from the disorder of the elements. But even this disaster can be considerably alleviated by education of the heart. We are asking physicians in various countries to engage in research on the heart. There exist sanatoriums for all kinds of ailments, but because education of the heart is lacking, there is no Institute for the Heart. Even ignoramuses do not think of the heart as something insignificant. Meanwhile, cases of heart disease outnumber those of cancer and tuberculosis. There is a need for heart sanatoriums where researchers can carry on the observations that are so urgently necessary. Naturally, these sanatoriums

ought to be situated in diverse climates and at various altitudes. One can imagine how an entire host of scientists would be engaged in the necessary research on theoretical aspects of this issue, also linking it to practical fields like agriculture.

The Institute of the Heart will be the Temple of the future race. And, of course, the Institute of the Heart will take part in the Community of Culture, because the concepts of heart and culture are inseparable.

505. It is shocking how little power of observation people possess. Try gradually filling a room with smoke and observe who notices it first. Usually a state of self-satisfaction instantly changes into despair. The horrible thing is that despair also changes into self-satisfaction. So think of the chief misfortune as that of being caught in oscillations which lack rhythm. We first of all pay attention to the power of observation, which helps in harmonizing the centers.

506. First and foremost, people should have simple respect for psychic energy. They should respect an energy which, like fire, pervades space and condenses in the nerve centers. Even children should remember that this connective energy radiates in every handshake, every glance. In striving to respect psychic energy, one learns to care for this treasure of the heart. It behooves every thinking person to feel respect. Do not be ashamed to speak about respect, since this treasure is squandered by humankind. How can anyone expect the heart energy to manifest if there is no respect for it? The energy will only start manifesting when it is perceived. If the law of justice exists, then everything leading up to the heights ought to be respected.

507. An experienced ruler often lays his hand upon the shoulder or hand of the person with whom he is

speaking. Some do so consciously, but the majority do so without being aware of the fact. Even those who do this consciously do not always know how to make use of this method. They regard the hand as being sufficient in itself, and suppose that the palm of the hand is what communicates the power of thought; very rarely do people realize that the fingertips have stronger radiations. So if a thought is being suggested, the fingers need to be squeezed together, while to receive a reaction from one's partner in conversation, the fingertips ought to be separated. With this method one is able to stir up an entire series of centers to a considerable degree. Within every action are concealed so many possibilities! One just needs to realize them consciously. Consciousness and unconsciousness might be likened to swimming with experience and without it. Certainly, someone might start swimming the first time he goes into the water, but this is a rare occurrence. So it is necessary to abide by the Hierarchy in everything, for it pervades our consciousness visibly and invisibly. It would be sad if consciousness were depicted as something abstract or almost supernatural. Every heartbeat fills us with awareness of existence and a real understanding of Being. Mental fog only arises from a lack of respect for consciousness. These words should be written down in every school. The children may ask, "How can we protect ourselves from lifeless habits?" Then somebody can point out what has been written down about respect.

508. People will ask how to feel the influence of the Teaching in the midst of daily life. Answer: by the smallest things, by every action, every touch. Denial and habit deprive some students of a great deal.

509. Where is the feeling, the substance with which we shall fill the Chalice of Great Service? Let us gather this feeling from the most precious treasures. We shall find elements of it in religious ecstasy, when the heart quivers with the Highest Light. We shall find other elements in the feeling of heartfelt love, where the tear of self-abnegation glistens. We shall find elements amidst the heroic achievements of *podvig*, when power is increased in the name of humanity. We shall find them in the patience of the gardener when he muses on the mystery of the seed. We shall find them in the courage that penetrates the darkness. We shall find them in the smile of a child when it reaches out to a sunbeam. We shall find them amidst all the flights that carry us into the Infinite. The feeling of Great Service is boundless; it must fill the heart, which is forever inexhaustible. The sacred tremor will never become an everyday porridge, but when the tremor left the very best Teachings, they turned into assemblages of empty husks. Thus, in the midst of the battle think about the Chalice of Service and take an oath that the sacred tremor shall not leave you.

510. One must educate the heart. One must fill up the Chalice. One must strive to the resonance of the "Bell"—the Brahmarandhra center. One must kindle the flaming wings of the Fiery World. From the heart we shall go onward to Fire—and we shall go soon!

511. Again you should not be surprised that you are doing good deeds in spirit without always remembering them in body. A generous giver does not count his gifts. It is impossible to enumerate the gifts of the spirit in words. So fiery are many of them that they cannot even be described in words! And so it is that worldly concepts do not contain the subtlest and the highest. One should recall that every hour the flaming heart is performing what people call miracles. So

the heart can create in accordance with the laws of the Universe. Make use of this fiery quality with solemnity.

512. When he wishes to recall something, a nature dweller is sure to shake his head. Within this motion is concealed the age-old thought about the substantiality of ideas. Even a physical motion is required to call hidden memories to the surface, as if it were necessary to shift set objects to other positions. Now that we know about various crystalline deposits, the instinct expressed does not seem so strange; on the contrary, we ought to study the movements of primitive peoples. Among them we shall find not only expressions of cosmic rhythm but also manifestations connected with an understanding of the nerve centers. So in essence a human being knows a great deal that has vanished from the outermost layer of memory. Moreover, travels and changes of residence serve to stir up the memory; many small seeds with great potential are awakened in the memory, like pieces of a kaleidoscope that form new combinations. So motion is able to provide evidence of a perfect, subtle materiality. Moreover, we need to feel how we should offer ourselves to the Highest Hierarchy so that our essence might be of benefit to cosmic motion. Certainly, motion may not be physical at all, but spiritual, for, as you know, there are no boundaries between these domains.

513. I say as much as is necessary and possible. An Instruction should be accepted like a battle command. Right now help is needed; it must include not only unity and solemnity but also the intensification of the heart's striving in Our direction. Seekers should cast away all extraneous thoughts in order to make Our transmissions easier. A flaming heart is deeply significant; it is actually a Cosmic Magnet. The most difficult thing for people is to acknowledge their own cosmic

significance. Nobody is averse to flying off to the heavens, but here on earth, too, a person's significance is great!

514. A simple motion may evoke a memory, but for the attainment of illumination special conditions in the Subtle World are necessary. It may be noted with surprise that sudden illumination does not depend upon rational conditions. Illumination descends when one least expects it. One might even notice a series of the oddest motions, pressures, and thoughts, which seem to be coming from outside. Psychiatrists ought to investigate this condition. They could accumulate valuable observations that would aid in approaching the conditions of the Subtle World. Of course, a sensitive heart will perceive this state of illumination by noting the quality of the pulse. The manifestation of sacred knowledge has nothing in common with somnambulism or spiritualism; illumination is a perfectly natural state. One has only to note these fires of the past and future. In the Subtle World, too, the consciousness must be refined. Therefore, each step in educating the heart opens a gate to the Higher Worlds. We are afraid that this urgent advice may give way to commonplace considerations. Someone will claim, "We knew all this long ago," and will go off to the marketplace. You may call after him, asking why he never ponders the heart or thinks about fire.

515. It is dangerous to feel no responsibility. Being a temporary traveler is also dangerous, for we are all trans-temporal beings propelled to ascent like heavenly bodies rushing onward. Therefore, any deviation or retreat is unnatural, as are crime and evil. Every person ascends according to his or her nature, and responsibility becomes wings, not a burden. But as soon as one wavers, that same responsibility turns

into a millstone around one's neck. Moreover, without responsibility we are unable to cross the ocean of the elements. This is not moralizing, but a lifebelt. A farewell only means a new welcome. We are infinite, not temporary.

516. The outflow of invisible energy during physical drowsiness is a genuine sign that one is taking part in the fight to ward off darkness. Since We may sound a call to battle at any time, special attention ought to be paid to unexpected spells of drowsiness. Likewise, the expenditure of energy should not go unnoticed. It will make away with a great deal of heart energy, so it is only right that one let this energy accumulate again. It is unwise to allow this energy to run out, which is why We remind people that they can relax by changing what they do.

517. The observations on the flowers of the Subtle World are quite revealing, as they show that a flaming heart can have access to the creative work of the Subtle World. Indeed, there it is easy for the conscious spirit to create. It can create without effort by transferring earthly images to a superior form. But this creative work is not limited to one domain; this process also implants better images on Earth.

518. It is no accident that We often speak about the creativity of the Subtle World. Awareness and attentiveness prepare us with a vast field for creative work. It may be noticed that this creativity does not weary one and remains ever inexhaustible—and so the cooperation between the worlds takes place. We are able to refine the forms of the Subtle World. Thus, every store of refinement must be guarded as a treasure. There is less wear on the heart if the environment and people around it do not interfere with these refinements. That is why We so strongly oppose ignorance, which above

all disturbs the ascent of the heart. Naturally, ignorance is an ally of the dark forces.

519. Actually, the fixing of an impression upon the third eye is the foundation of creativity. Not only the ancient Buddhists but also the scriptures of hoary antiquity demanded that the power of observation be trained. A heart that lacks the treasure of observational power dissipates a huge amount of energy where it ought to be showing great caution. A teacher should use the most beautiful objects in developing the students' ability to observe. It is especially inadmissible when a human being just gives things a fleeting glance, which neither notices nor gives out anything. Would it not be an extremely beneficial task for a true scientist to research the chemical composition of a glance?

520. After one feels the pulsations of the world, the tremors of the heart are not frightening. Therefore, a great touchstone should be used in evaluating everything, for unless this is done, it will be impossible to go on existing, and people will sink into a puddle of paltriness. Where Armageddon is thundering forth, a scale that encompasses the entire Universe is needed. Consolation lies in commeasuring everything. One's entire observational power should be applied in evaluating the essence of the Battle. Yet people often view the Battle as nothing more than a street fight, forgetting that there is a battle going on in the mailbox, in a smile full of cunning deception, and in the restraints on Light. The Battle is far more dramatic than worldly people imagine. When I speak about caution, understand it also in seven ways.

521. I am advising every seeker to be ready to fulfill the Command of the Teacher with all his heart. Sometimes the move that is required cannot be revealed. When walking the mountain paths, one can go neither

left nor right, but only straight ahead. One can neither jump into the abyss nor climb up a sheer cliff. The path is one, and its destination is seen from above.

My Counsels are similar to a father's words of farewell to a departing son. The trunk for the voyage must contain the objects needed for everything that happens in life. But the heart is hidden in a secret place, and for a long time I shall be calling after you, "Most of all, guard the secret place!"

522. The language of the Subtle World has no need of words, although it may possess them. Its expression lies in straight-knowledge, in transmission of the subtlest feelings. Thus, the Subtle World must not disturb the music of the spheres by generating disorderly resonances. We should not be surprised about any of this, for even in the corporeal world hearts resonating in harmony transmit a great deal to each other through the language of the heart. Let this language be a constant reminder about the potential of the Subtle World.

523. People should understand what a petty thought is. Like an insect it undermines all of the strongest intentions. The most persevering character weakens from the pricks and stings of small thoughts. This may seem repetitious and boring, but when the time comes for action, people cover themselves with a cloud made from fragments of small thoughts. The noblest decisions are blotted out beneath a layer of shameful thoughts. The main thing that hinders achievement is not doubt so much as the inchoate thoughts born of old habits. I affirm that it will not be difficult to liberate ourselves from habits if we sufficiently project our consciousness into the future. Often people measure the future by the present, thereby clipping the new wings. Even birds know about the change in plumage and accommodate themselves to the corresponding

conditions. During their molting season, when feathers are being shed, birds retreat into the underbrush so they may soar once more when renewed. So let us follow the example of these younger brothers. They can sing us a splendid song of the heart.

524. People are reluctant to imagine how many dangers are taking place around them. How many times have the Higher Forces and participants in the Subtle World saved them! But humanity assumes that if the day has gone by without incident then nothing has threatened. This type of thinking dulls the embryonic sense of gratitude; but without this feeling humanity cannot succeed. Instead of gratitude a demanding attitude appears, and after that a threat. But one will get no further on threats than on stingy-nettles. Pathetic are the threats against the Higher Forces! There is nothing that corrupts more than threats do. The heart dries up from the dust of threats.

525. You know how strongly we oppose every sort of conventional habit, but a distinction should be made between habit and immersion in a feeling that brings salvation. For example, solemnity combines in itself ecstasy, ascent, a shield against evil, and a turning to the Hierarchy. So solemnity is salutary, but it must be perceived and maintained. In the midst of decay and destruction can there be such solemnity? But for the solemn consciousness, destruction does not exist. It is immediately covered with a cupola of re-creation, in all its wondrous refinement. So it is with good reason that the reflection of solemnity is considered luminous. Before departing on a journey, a traveler must stock up on all the necessary provisions. Our friends bring the finest flowers to the travelers. Solemnity blossoms in purple—so let us gather the garlands of the heart.

526. We often send people strong warnings, but

their deafness is astounding. Even what they hear they distort beyond recognition. No astonishment is too strong when one sees how people remain sluggish, even though their own salvation is at stake; it is as if they were only intent on outraging the Higher Forces. I ask that the detestable decisions of the Satanists not be forgotten. I ask that the warriors remember: to defeat evil, they must unite their forces. They should remember this as a Command of the Lords. They should harbor no regrets, for in time of battle warriors must strive only to the future.

527. Notice how distant events affect the Chalice before they affect the heart. This sequence has seldom been noted. Naturally, when the Chalice has been filled, measures must be adopted for the sake of the heart; but all the same, it is the Chalice that comes under tension first. The Chalice demands solemnity in order to be filled to the brim, as it were.

I know how hard it is for a giant to suddenly find himself in the cave of a dwarf! In fact, the intensifying pressure is already condensing the lower strata. Naturally, the feverish heat comes not from the sun, nor the disturbance from the Subtle World; rather, these are the offspring of humanity's will.

528. An old Chinese story tells of a giant who towers above the clouds and a dwarf who enjoys mockery. The giant is depicted as standing with his head in the heavens, while the dwarf ridicules the giant for not seeing the earthly world. But the giant endures all the ridicule, saying, "If I so desired, I could crawl on the earth, but you will never be able to peek above the clouds." So let us be giants of the spirit! If we desire the great good in its entirety, then there will be room for all. The finest examples will provide the consciousness

with new dimensions. A kinship with the giants will help us to peek beyond the clouds.

529. People go up peaks in order to study cosmic rays. Probably they have paid little attention to the composition of the mountain itself. And most likely they have not helped on the experiment by conducting research about their own energies. One can either enhance the experiment or cause disruption by bringing in a disorderly mixture of observers. I am astonished at how much people rely on lifeless instruments while forgetting about the influence of their own living energy. It is worth observing how readings on the most precise instruments fluctuate when they are placed in the hands of different people. Even the most sensitive chronometers work differently in different hands. Naturally, this sort of simple evidence arouses the derision of dwarfs. Could they really have such a low opinion of themselves that they do not admit the existence of their own emanations? Indeed, they do not look upon themselves as cast in the image and likeness of the Divine! Yet even pigs have emanations!

530. Certainly, the ray of the planet can be manifested boundlessly once measures are adopted to purify the atmosphere and a harmonious combination has been established among the participants in the experiment. To put it simply, the human laboratory is far more powerful than people are given to suppose. Therefore, be able to maintain the thread that links up with the Hierarchy, and get used to so-called "unexpectedness." And remember, the Teacher wants to summon you to action in the battle.

531. The waves of anguish do not issue from the apparent causes but from the battle. It is essential that you strive to Us like warriors who keep their eyes fixed on the Banner. Some people will ask why the letters

We wrote fifty years ago are so unlike the writings now being transmitted. But even The Call does not resemble the book Heart, for when The Call was being transmitted there was no Armageddon. Let the inquirers understand that Armageddon changes many of life's circumstances. It is impossible to apply peaceful measures in time of war. This means that seekers must don a coat of armor and, above all, strive to the Lords.

532. People vainly imagine that acts of betrayal and malevolence do not call forth a return blow. Sometimes the return blow may not be immediate, and often it cuts off possibilities without causing any visible consequences. But the law of equilibrium is immutable. A heart should be engraved on the pointer of the scales, because the heart is the judge of balance. So all the warnings against malevolence are not only ethical in nature, they are also valuable as medicine.

533. People are wrong in supposing that a Higher Spirit is no longer sensitive to minor betrayals; on the contrary, sensitivity increases with the purification of the heart. Naturally, as sensitivity grows, so does the power of the heart, but a sensitive nature cannot avoid being poisoned by the enmity around it. So the path of purification can hardly be called the path of stupefaction. People should realize how much easier it is to access the purified heart. Therefore, among the questions that the Mysteries posed was, "Can you be free of the fear of pain?" The heart knows the pain of the world, but it is also aware of the supermundane rays. It is not easy to make these rays evident, yet scholars are able to sense the special cosmic rays that gather around a purified heart. There is good reason why the purified heart is called "the summit." So the purified heart can be used in many experiments, but of course this purified vessel must not be broken. It can be said

that the karma of those who destroy the heart is a horrible one.

534. It is wrong for people to pay no attention to the consequences of eating while irritated or agitated. Very strong poisons form during this unwise activity. Many days must go by before this poison dissolves. People should remember that hunger is far better than harmful food. I advise that a person who is feeling irritated or agitated should take milk in all its forms as a regular antidote. Soda strengthens the effect of the milk. The ability to recognize agitation is in itself a substantial step toward the education of the heart. If agitation occurs, one should be able to render it harmless, but it is often confused with fatigue. At times of agitation let us not forget about musk or certain kinds of phosphorus, the substance that is called sperm oil, and the cod-liver oil and fresh kumis that are popular among northern peoples. Also, you remember to what an extent the Teacher sends rays at night, but even those rays will act more powerfully when one is aware of them. The silence that ancient people kept during meals had a sacred significance. But understanding of the idea of the sacred itself had healing properties. Thus, one often can strengthen the heart and nerves by keeping the goal of eating in mind when partaking of food. We are not gourmets, but every vital activity must be in harmony with its goal. Many prominent people have inadvertently poisoned themselves. Also, the Chinese used to sometimes feed enemies with livers of irritated roosters—people are so full of resourceful tricks. But in the New World everything must be directed toward the Good.

535. Observation of the heart should begin from childhood, so the observer can become aware of certain phases during which the spirit takes possession of the body. Likewise, by constantly observing, one discovers how the close presence of beings from the Subtle World affects the heart. Of course, the occurrence of an inexplicable heartbeat is often due to the influence of the Subtle World. Often the cessation of the pulse may be warning about the danger of possession. Often it is normal for a seven-year-old to already be having tremors of the pulse, which signify that the spirit has completely entered the body. Doctors should have been familiar with such evidence long ago, but instead of making observations they begin prescribing all sorts of narcotics, thereby laying the foundation for an early destruction of the intellect. Such coarse, ignorant methods must not be inflicted on the heart. People should remember that if the heart is the mediator with the higher worlds, the methods of maintaining the heart ought to be refined. It does not make sense to lament the coarsening of humanity and yet neglect the care of its chief organ. The heart of humanity is ailing. So if people wish to avert a catastrophe, they must first of all render healthy the sphere of the heart.

536. Among the various fires of the heart, the brightest is the flame of self-sacrifice. It is this armor that wards off hostile arrows and creates the renowned invulnerability. The fire of courage is only a part of the flame of self-sacrifice. Of course, self-sacrifice does not necessarily mean to offer oneself as a sacrificial victim; rather it corresponds to a readiness to attain victory for the cause of the Higher World. One can also notice that the fire burns low whenever there is the slightest deviation from the Hierarchy. Just as a whirlwind blows out torches, a deviation into the abyss of Chaos ruins the fires of the heart. Isn't it strange to see those who are deviating and those who are marching to victory sitting at one and the same table? In finishing

up their earthly repast together, they seem to be completely alike, but already their spirits dwell in opposite domains. The purified heart senses these oppositions. Often the heart finds it difficult to decide by appearances, but the essence is clear to it.

537. The pure heart affirms the Hierarchy with ease, and its ascent is like the manifestation of Adamant—an invincible diamond. Nothing will ever darken the path of a pure heart; even from a medical point of view a purified heart will have a better future.

538. I confirm that the Teaching is considered by many to be the best path of Light. People must get used to the fact that the giver does not know where the drop of Grace will fall, no more than a rain cloud knows where a raindrop will fall. And so it is at present. Therefore, above all do not get distressed or make shortsighted judgments.

539. You already know why a magnet sometimes used to be placed above the crown of a person's head; but you should not forget the ancient therapy that heals the heart with a magnet, as well as the methods strengthening the nerves and magnetizing them according to the flow of the nervous substance. These ancient treatments ought to be closely examined; more than anything else, they represent a starting point for perceiving rays and energy currents. Naturally, besides the magnetic properties of metals that bring about powerful reactions, there are also many other properties that respond to the mineral basis of the human organism. Placing the metals themselves on the body produces a strong reaction. Certainly, the special properties of different skins must be taken into consideration. Fatty skin deposits can greatly hinder the working of subtle influences, which is why in ancient times efforts were made to eliminate them. Of course, the vegetable oils used in massage have nothing in common with the body's fat deposits. Quite the contrary, vegetable oil dissolves the fat along with its poisons. So it can be seen that in antiquity physical hygiene at times stood at a higher level than nowadays. The ancients distinguished the mineral composition of the water they used for their ablutions, something that people at present almost entirely disregard. Nowadays people would probably laugh if they were told that completely different fragrances were applied to the crown of the head, to the area around the heart, and even to the extremities.

Over many generations, a refined understanding of the needs of the body protected humanity. One might recall, for example, the solicitude with which the Egyptians treated the condition of pregnancy. It is rare nowadays for anyone to pay attention to the tastes or strange predilections of pregnant women. But in ancient times, at the earliest stage of pregnancy a temple physician would refer to astrological data and determine what mineral and vegetable influences would be necessary; and this made childbirth much easier. Nowadays, instead of applying wise measures beforehand, people rely on crude narcotics, for they are unwilling to understand that the bond between mother and child has yet to be severed. At times the heart of the mother is very stressed, and any narcotic also affects the milk. Nature is in need of natural reactions.

540. It should not seem strange to you that the present instructions about the heart are ending with medical advice. Since the heart has been neglected a long time, one has to have some earthly methods ready in addition to the spiritual influences. In any case, while the heart is undergoing tension and stress, thoughts need to be redirected. Like a mountain stream, thoughts change the rhythm of the surroundings. It is unwise to talk about having complete rest when the heart is in tension, primarily because rest does not exist in the first place. Actually, a heart in tension senses the cosmic whirlwinds even more powerfully, and it may be shaken with vibrations. But a change of thought can act like musk by making the current of the nervous substance firm and steady. You already know how the rhythms of the currents change, how during atmospheric tension the vibrations of the currents grow excessively intense and even become prickly. So the old proverb about healing "like with like" comes to the fore. Of course, I am not advising that the patient be placed with his head lowered; rather, a level position is useful. The ability to impart a comfortable position to the patient helps to redirect his thought in a healing direction.

When a great Arabian mathematician was lying ill, his heart almost coming to a standstill, a friend of his was clever enough to start speaking about the solution to an algebraic problem, and the mathematician's heart came back to life. I am citing this example so no one will suppose that petty thoughts can change the heart's condition.

541. I affirm that however small it may be, any motion made in the name of the future breaks through the strata of tension in the atmosphere. All the rubbish from the past that has piled up is cut away by the sword of the future. The shield of the future is the most reliable and beneficial. People should not assume that the future is inaccessible, for it is being created tirelessly and continuously—and the heart is a guarantee of the future.

542. A great deal of information is provided, but

one has to make use of it. This information is applied not by falling into despondency, doubt, or suspicion, but by taking joy in the future. So first of all one has to be careful not to cast aside the tiniest blade of grass that is of use. If even the little ones from the Subtle World come with cooperation, do not drive them off, for they can turn away the arrow of evil. People usually expect great signs, while small helpers are never noticed.

543. People put on a most shameful performance when they pick up a book with the firm intention of disregarding its contents. From this attitude arises the remark, "Everything is old and familiar to me." Yet the simplest advice has gone unapplied. One can even see how the most necessary observations were scorned in order to belittle the Teaching. People can go ahead and indulge in frivolous laughter, but not a single Instruction ought to be ignored. Now we are speaking about the education of the heart, but won't we hear from the stupidest people that they knew about it long ago? Meanwhile, they think more about cutting their nails than about their hearts. The most common cause of heart attacks is precisely a failure to think about the heart. We human beings are ready to give in to any overindulgence rather than show respect for our own hearts as the centers of our existence.

544. You do well in observing the characteristics of Armageddon. You can easily form a notion of the tactics that the dark forces employ. And in doing so, you can also discover weapons of defense. We should especially feel sorry for all the weak-willed ones, who are tossed about in the wind like stalks of grass.

545. The law of free will does not permit prevention of crime at the incipient stage. The law of justice, however, provides an opportunity to prevent the development of harm—as above, so below. You cannot

prevent the inception of criminal thoughts, but you can suppress their development. The cultivation of the heart can suggest when it is possible to go after evil. That is why We so fervently insist upon the Teaching of the Heart. No other center can replace the essence of the heart. The heart has at its disposal the accumulations of the ages stored in the Chalice. Indeed, the salvation of humanity does not lie in the separate siddhis but in the central motive force—in the heart. So one must go beyond divisions and arrive at the root of motion.

546. Every piece of a neighbor's bread is protected by law, but there is no ban on devouring or plundering the forces of the spirit. So out of ignorance all kinds of vampirism are permitted. Indeed, it can be horrifying to observe how forces are plundered and not applied to good purposes. The various kinds of vampires are not plundering these forces in order to do good deeds. At best they swallow up energies out of egoism, and the whole gamut of dark criminality comes later. It is impossible to enumerate all the ways in which the precious energies are abused. But when We advise people to be cautious, they confuse caution and inactivity. And when We speak about the significance of the heart, they explain it away as a superstition. Meanwhile, neither the brain nor the solar plexus nor the Kundalini will signal that one's strength is being devoured. Only the heart gives incessant signs—and usually people are unwilling to recognize them. In our present age it is impermissible for people to have such contempt for the heart's multifaceted activity. Moreover, it is time for them to realize that unless there is understanding, all the signs of the heart will come to naught and disappear.

547. When performed against the will of the patient,

healing exacts a tremendous amount of strength. Even when there is no opposition, a great mass of strength may be dissipated due simply to a lack of understanding. Yet tiring treatment may be successful in spite of the patient's lack of understanding. Many cases could be cited in which Initiates suffered greatly after forcibly healing someone. Naturally, these days the tension and expenditure of energy are unusually great. Therefore, if you feel tension or fatigue, do not be ashamed to lie down. In this time of unprecedented battle, the heart must be protected. This advice is for everybody. One should picture the entire smoky surface of the Earth in order to understand why protective armor is necessary.

548. When agitated, it is better to eat very little. Valerian is good, and of course milk with soda is too. The heart should be eased. It is a mistake to turn to narcotics and alcohol. Of course, through the practice of Yoga agitation should be transformed into exaltation. When We see the causes, the effects, and the possibilities, the vast potential of healing by heart energy becomes clear. But since it is like a drop of some precious substance, let this energy not be squandered in unnecessary action. That is why I am repeating about how necessary it is for healer and patient to be aware of each other during the healing. It is impossible to imagine how powerfully a spark of consciousness elicits a salutary decision. The heart should be trained to acquire consciousness in every action. Look upon this as a law. It is intolerable that a human being should bend like a blade of grass beneath the turbid wave of Tamas. What could not be overcome yesterday must be consciously removed today. One must always watch oneself and welcome the most difficult tasks as

a purifying cloak. A seeker should always act in this way, especially in the days of Armageddon.

549. In all Teachings the family is decreed to be a pillar of the entire future. Indeed, alongside all the other ways it is significant, the family is a nursery of karmic ties. Thus, a Teaching would not be complete unless it affirmed the significance of the family. The family should be regarded as the hearth of awareness and cooperation. One can come across true humaneness in cooperation, and this quality will lead to the realization of the Hierarchy. Karmic laws should not be neglected. These laws may often be invisible to the cross-eyed, but an honest observer is shown convincingly each day how the bonds of karma work. But in essence these bonds ought to be wings. The law has foreseen joy and success, not chains. That is how one should understand this law of life's foundation. But what, if not the heart, will remind us about the karmic dates? It is precisely the heart that will contract and palpitate and open when it senses the wing of the law. So let us once again pay homage to the heart.

550. Christ himself transmitted healing power through his touch. In the very midst of life He gave help through the heart. So people should remember that under the law of the Lords magical invocations involving coercion are all unsuitable. The heart's prayer goes straight forward, not even needing a conventional canon. We see that in invocations the same words were used to address God as to address Satan. Not the words but the feeling of the heart is what works miracles. So even in the days of Armageddon seekers can attain success. All the more reason, then, for them to cast aside everything that stands in the way. Everyone who reads the Teaching can understand through the heart where his path lies.

551. A human being cannot conceal his inner intentions. These may not even be reflected in earthly words, but with the subtle feelings there are no secrets. Usually people do not know how to take in the feelings of the Subtle World. But they do feel a sort of agitation, confusion, or joy, as if there were lying before them some secret document whose significance they could sense without even unsealing it. But with the education of the heart, one can obtain a solid understanding of human intentions that is far from haphazard. Moreover, one can discern not only the meaning of thoughts but also how substantial they are. Isn't it true that very often the heart does not reflect people's intentions because such intentions do not exist in the first place or resemble down being wafted in the wind? Ask the person you are talking with what he desires. The usual response will be a show of confusion. Not having crystallized its aspirations at all, such a heart will fall into confusion in the Subtle World. The Teaching is not a luxury item. It teaches the very minimum that might be expected of those who have been incarnating over millions of years. We will not do anything to check the flighty nature of thought, but we must demand that the heart get its bearings.

552. It is time to take a searching look beyond all the haggling and deception. Human wreckage is standing right before Our eyes. So it should be understood that everyone shares guilt in bringing on Armageddon and therefore nobody can evade it.

553. If, while in Asia, you say that you are feeling tired because of participation in the work in America, no one will understand or believe what you are saying. It is time for humanity to learn to respect the spiritually expanded consciousness. Without resorting to any magic, We take part in work over long distances. We inspire thoughts and we write letters; and so it is that people cooperate with one another far more than they suppose. All the more reason, then, for avoiding every source of ill will. Understanding universal Goodness means one ought to become a kinder person. The heart must accustom itself to the active power of goodness. As experienced warriors, you should recognize the power of good. No evil power is able to overcome good. Let us not think of evil as something intelligent. Cunning is not intelligence; obviously, it does not dwell in the heart. We are affirming the path of knowledge, but let us not pass by goodness in silence, for it is a creative principle.

554. A savage in his prayers mainly pleads that mercy be shown to himself, while wise hermits pray that the entire world be granted Grace—therein lies the difference between the savage and the sage. This should be laid at the foundation of all thoughts. It is neither proper nor useful to plead on one's own behalf. Only a crude heart assumes itself to be the most important. It is much wiser to plead on behalf of the world, in which the pleader will also find a drop full of Blessings. Especially nowadays aspirants should follow the great path, for that is the only way they can find the heart.

555. It is said that many people, even those who have heard about Armageddon, continue to live according to the standards of yesterday. Warn friends about the need to thoroughly understand the tactics of Armageddon. The blind ones desire that things be as before, but this would be like placing flowers on ice.

556. You will not be wonderstruck when I confirm that black magic is proliferating at a remarkable pace. Of course, this is one of the weapons that belong to the opponents of Light. They gather conscious and

unconscious coworkers. Conjurations, grimoires, and all the other things that the dark forces have accumulated are being used far and wide. In addition to the dark centers previously indicated to you, many small circles are springing up, often on the basis of the most primitive rituals. The general harm is considerable. Of course, white magic possesses the most powerful formulas—but above all formulas stands the energy of the heart. Formulas and conjurations all require a mechanical process as preparation, and thus remain within the confines of the lower teachings. But now when the forces of darkness are up in arms, the forces of the heart are opposing them. One can observe that gradually the rituals of white magic were carried to the higher concepts of Fire and the heart. The dark ones do not have access to these strongholds; only a pure heart can act. Only the bond with the Hierarchy of Light can kindle inextinguishable fires. So the opposition of the heart to all the dark forces will be a sign of victory. I am confirming the power of the heart, and you know for yourself how near at hand and powerful this weapon of light is. One cannot approach the fiery domain without the flame of the heart. Initiation by fire is only for the pure of heart.

557. Gone is the time when people could imagine the battle as an event with angels blowing trumpets. You already understand that darkness is calling forth the unmanifested forces of Chaos—in this lies the peculiar magnet of the dark forces. All the rays and currents should be reinforced in opposition to this. You already sense this reinforcement. One has to apply crude currents, so to speak, which are able to penetrate Chaos. There are few who can make out this distinction, because human attention has not been turned in this direction. Even the crudest manifestations are

inaccessible to the consciousness if they escape the notice of the human brain. How much easier the battle would be if humanity were able to respond to the most basic foundations of Being!

558. Fear and irritation are called the gates of darkness. The servants of darkness first of all send fear, in order to confuse the spirit. Any conjuration might open the door to danger, for fear may creep in while the conjuration is being said; that is how the most precise magic can turn into the utmost danger. Therefore, one must be guided by a more reliable approach. An educated heart will first of all root out fear and grasp the harm of irritation. So the heart is the weapon of Light that will put to shame the subterfuges of darkness. As the wise have declared, the heart is ever ready to smite darkness and keep Chaos in check. It is especially sad that many people are unwilling to think about the power of the heart. By taking that attitude, they not only undermine themselves but also bring harm to those close to them. Any treasure that goes unrealized sinks into Chaos and thereby reinforces darkness.

559. He who said, "We see with the eyes of the heart," had in mind not a symbol but a physical law. A consciousness that has been deepened and freed manifests a transformation of all feelings. The most vivid color becomes invisible, the loudest symphony inaudible, the most powerful touch unnoticed, the hottest food unfelt. That is how real the realm of feelings becomes—in the heart. This quality should not be considered an abstraction. Quite the contrary, in it is contained yet another approach to the Subtle World. We make Our disciples practice this transmutation of feelings as one of the clearest ways to refine the heart. By a quite ordinary command of the heart one

can force oneself to not hear or see. In that way a person can learn to pass by the very horrors of the lower spheres. The seeker must make this quality his own, for otherwise a great deal of the protective net will be destroyed to no purpose. Conservation of the precious substance is also a task of the Yogi. One must not go squander accumulations that exert an influence on many people in the vicinity. The basis of cooperation first of all lies in taking responsibility for each other.

560. This mutuality especially manifests at a time of tension. Each aspirant must make every touch subtler, must show the tenderest solicitude. All the burdens of those close to him must be accepted wholeheartedly—that is how an impregnable fortress is created. And that is how to go forward!

561. The great law requires converting the heart from an ethical abstraction into a scientific engine, a motive force. This evolutionary step in understanding the heart has had to be adopted in the days of Armageddon, as this is the only way humanity can be saved. Why are people unwilling to sense their own hearts? They are ready to delve into the nature of all kinds of cosmic formations, but reject what is closest of all. Let them call the heart a machine, so long as they observe all the characteristics of this apparatus. We are not insisting on the moral significance of the heart—it is indisputable. But now the heart is necessary as a bridge of salvation to the Subtle World. It should be declared that realization of the heart's qualities constitutes the most vital step in the world's progress. Nobody has ever before said that such realization means salvation. Let those who remain deaf accept all the consequences! People should be able to understand that now the human heart is lending itself to unusual opportunities for observation. The

catastrophic condition of the Earth's lower spheres is having an impact on the heart's activity. People ought to fear not the old epidemics but the whole sequence of sufferings linked to poor prevention of heart conditions. The worst thing one could do is to regard these warnings as so many vague prophecies. No, these conclusions ought to be accepted as the findings of the most precise laboratory. All the circuitous routes should be rejected. People must accept the foundation of the heart and grasp the significance of the focus. Roving and rambling are inappropriate, and doubts are admissible only when a person has yet to attain an understanding of the heartbeat.

Let the arrival of every significant day be marked by a reminder that understanding of the heart is absolutely undeferrable.

562. Any commanding officer would say it is better to evade the enemy than submit to defeat. Similar caution must be exercised in everything related to the heart energy. And with equal caution We are uniting the inner nuclei of those linked in spirit, in order to avoid having one of the warriors be burdened by the various efforts that connect them all. When we ask you to focus all your forces in one direction, it means that you must be as tense as a bow. You must be able to live in readiness, and this quality also requires considerable training. But do not attempt to use this heart energy for revenge—that is impermissible. Moreover, the Guardians of Karma know the flow of the law. And let us not forget, either, that the heart is able to direct itself to construction. Destruction does not arise from the heart.

When practicing hypnosis, Western scientists sometimes also use the energy of the heart, usually without being aware of the fact; in such cases the hypnosis is especially effective, even if "sleep" is not induced. So in time of spiritual battle a warrior must add a drop of heart energy to everything, and this must be done consciously. It is possible to persuade the heart to act. Such conversations with the heart should not be considered as something childish. Just as a prayer is effective when made consciously, it is possible for us to force the heart to concentrate its energy—and this will be the tensed bow. When the fire of the heart radiates and blazes up with every touch, the call to the heart can fall silent. But during the initial education of the heart, we must rely on the practice of conversing with our center—which is what we may justly call the heart.

563. It is possible to cite an entire list of plants that from ancient times were prescribed in expediting heart energy for the purpose of projecting higher influences. But with the exception of strophanthus, I will not name any of them now, so that they might not be abused. Not only does strophanthus regulate the energy of the heart, it also concentrates it. Therefore, even if there is no apparent need, it may be taken without harm every two weeks. One may take six drops every evening three days in a row. Of course, when there are shocks to the heart, it can be taken twice a day.

564. Astrologically, the two worlds are in approximately the same position. It is evident, therefore, that the main paths by which Armageddon unfolds have been foreseen. One should not dwell on separate operations and activities. The earthly Armageddon is in close synch with the Subtle World. In specific instances it may be unfolding less favorably, but its overall flow was foreseen long ago. That which is most important is being determined in the Subtle World; earthly events are only an echo of the invisible battles. That is why I am calling your attention to the Subtle World.

One should not only remember its existence, but also be imbued with a realization of just how important it is for the events ahead. If the existence of ruthless enemies comes to light, they ought to be looked for there; and when we search for true friends, we will find them there. That world should stand before us as a reality!

565. Far more of the wondrous occurs than people commonly think. Several historical instances could be cited in which prominent persons disappeared without a trace. But those who were unable to hide, for various reasons, pretended to die after having stipulated that they be enclosed in a tight casket heavily strewn with flowers. In the night unknown persons would come, make an exchange, and depart with the apparently dead. One could point to cases in Asia, Egypt, and Greece in which events required this sort of transformation. Of course, history depicts such events in a completely distorted manner. Empty tombs and secret cremations might call to memory a great deal that the worldly-minded do not know. One should use large scales when measuring and not assume that anything is limited. Materia Lucida is quite adequate for any achievement. It is precisely by using large scales that one can develop a great sense of responsibility. There are many paths, but if We are now insisting upon the shortest, it means that events have approached their full measure. It is right to observe the causes of manifestations and their course, but few are those who feel responsibility for what is taking place. I affirm that every point made has an immediate purpose. Since ancient times it has been customary to examine the level of the disciple's observational powers. With this in mind, a seemingly abstract formula was uttered, and it was observed whether the disciple's enquiring mind would be able to look around and find a way to

apply what had been said. The Teaching can deepen one's ability to understand through observation.

566. I advise that one be especially cautious when conducting mechanical experiments upon the aura. A considerable increase in the eye's receptivity can lead to atrophy of the optic nerve. Of course, as with everything, gradual development and long preparation are required. The heart may easily be scorched, and then it will not give rise to a vital experiment. Even poisons may be rendered powerless during a series of assimilations properly performed, but time and constancy are necessary.

567. You can patiently begin the photographic experiment I indicated, but all the details should be noted. This will also be a useful practice in making observations for investigation of the Subtle World. But remember that when the photographs are being taken, the photographer must not look at the subject being photographed. Do not forget about the chemical effect of the glance.

568. Dreams and visions of former lives always have significance. A page from the astral archive flares up, so to speak, reminding one of the very same frame of mind being experienced in the present time. Take, for example, the most recent vision. It arose during a time of fatigue from dealing with people, but the first need that came into view was that of extending aid immediately. This is the very path of the Bodhisattva, on which we forget ourselves in order to help out. Great, indeed, is the energy thus generated; everywhere it is spoken of as love for one's neighbor. Such love does not reckon or calculate, but acts without delay. And so from the depths of the Subtle World emerge the pictures of the past. There was a significant detail in the vision, when the servant of delight blocked the path

of *podvig* but was unable to hinder your aspiration and striving. And once more the vision revealed the tolerance shown to many worldly people whom you have had to encounter again and again. Tolerance and patience are also the path of the Bodhisattva. This path is not in the clouds but here on Earth. The noxious fumes here are heavy, another reason the path of the Bodhisattva is necessary. From a human perspective, these fumes are insignificant, but they sting the heart as salt water stings a wound. Make good use of the mountain air. Do not tire yourselves out; even a diver must not descend when fatigued. Precisely, descent into human filth can be compared to a diver's work. The diver is ready to save the drowning person, but he himself is in need of access to air. I am not exaggerating: you are in need of air during Armageddon. Prana is like food for the heart. You cannot be given aid by any kind of unsavory methods, for the means must correspond to the task at hand. But often people do not acknowledge the language of the heart at all, and tension of the heart becomes necessary—in other words, an expenditure of spiritual treasures. Already, many such treasures have been poured forth to the world. The law of Being dictates that with expenditure the treasures increase, but that does not ease the burden of the heart. Therefore, let us be cautious and remember about the diver.

569. The scientific basis that underlies the power of the human glance means that further research is possible. Once the effect upon the human organism has been investigated, attention ought to be paid to deposits left by the human glance on inanimate objects. If the glance may reach a stage where it has become poisonous, then it might also be able to precipitate its poison upon water and all kinds of objects.

Certainly, the spell cast on water lies not in the rhythm of words but in the power of the glance. And of course its influence may be good or evil. As usual, the evil significance can be detected more easily, as is the case with imperil; but after evil has been discovered, good will also come to light. So it is possible to begin research on how various energies influence each other. When one is equipped with modern instruments, isn't it fascinating to observe the effect of energies on various objects? Ancient legends about chalices of peace or pieces of cloth imbued with blessings take on a different, more rational significance. But observers should be advised not to stop at the initial stages. Let them immediately expand their field of experimentation. Won't observation of the way the human glance and thought penetrate the atmosphere lead them on to many conclusions? And won't it also be instructive to observe the influence of the same energy at various altitudes? They can start with crude manifestations, as was done with the evil eye. But it would be better not to delay observation of the benevolent eye. One can come up with extremely beneficial findings; these are the ones on which people ought to focus.

570. Let the scent of Balu remind you of the health-giving purification of space. Though the lower spheres are very polluted, the emanations of the heights are carrying particles from the deposits of prana. Prana cannot be produced artificially, but its natural deposits purify space.

571. It is useful to observe traces of discipline wherever they may appear. Among the various conscious, collective disciplines, attention should be paid to Japanese Zen monasteries. It is rare for Hierarchy and cooperation to be preserved without compulsion. One should understand discipline to be organized,

voluntary cooperation. Among the various approaches to educating the heart, the voluntary organization of cooperation has great significance. But as long as compulsion is lurking somewhere, there cannot be any conscious cooperation, and the results desired cannot be obtained. And let us be expeditious in understanding cooperation. Where there is disunity, one cannot hope for a blossoming and victory. Let us accept this statement of truth as a Command.

572. One can observe a certain stage of human consciousness in which a person who is asked the question, "What is necessary?" is sure to answer, "Money." So long as the person has not outgrown this money-focused limitation, no spiritual help can be extended him. His consciousness must be directed to more significant values; then help will come, even in a material sense. The law of the highest values has been established throughout Existence. Therefore, it is our own consciousness that determines the wellbeing that we deserve.

573. In measuring the right amount to give, the proper standard is that of love and responsibility. To give too little is contrary to love, but it is no better to give too much. Stinginess is unworthy, but generosity that even leads to betrayal is not in harmony with one's goal. Just as insufficient food leads to starvation, excessive intake leads to poisoning. It can be stated without exaggeration that the number of betrayals has increased considerably due to excessive giving. A Teacher who gives and trusts must pay attention to a multitude of conditions. He must take into consideration not only the individual worthiness of the one who receives but also the qualities of the environment and people around that person, not to mention karmic and astrological conditions. The sensitized

heart whispers how one can come to understand this complex current of conditions. That is why We so greatly value the standard of the heart. The path of the Bodhisattva embraces this standard, the very essence of correct measurement. No reasoned judgment will keep the giving one from going to excess, but the heart knows this heavenly balance.

574. Pay careful attention as to whether the Teacher is obliged to repeat something. You know how much We dislike repeating things; it means that there must be a good reason for a repetition. Perhaps someone depending on external facts would judge that the repetition is superfluous; but let us peek into the depths of our hearts, and we will see how necessary it is. Often the very people who call forth a repetition are the ones who fail to notice it. So repetitions have to be used like medicine—applied until they have conveyed a picture to the brain. A person who carries the Teaching of Life within himself must be ready to keep repeating the same affirmation as long as he sees the foundations shaking. People can accept that the law of the foundations must be put into effect before any other, for nobody can replace the foundations with details.

575. It is right to discuss childhood education, but in these discussions, too, the question of the heart is neglected. In fact, the manifestation of the heartbeat is something children pay close attention to. Actually, it is easiest to tell children about the treasure of the heart. I believe that what children are told will stay with them for their entire lives, as their first step of ascent.

576. The little cork figures used in a familiar electrical experiment remind us, above all, of people without heart. Under the influence of energy currents, the figures are ready to come to life temporarily and even rise up; but as soon as the current stops, the cork

essence takes over, and they stiffen into lifelessness once more. But should humaneness descend only under the influence of an energy current? The heart propels one upward, if it has been opened.

We are not necromancers who bring soulless bodies back to life. The current of the heart must strive upward constantly and independently, and then the spark that arises from meeting with the Hierarchic current will be beneficial. True, one sometimes has to bring cork figures to life in order to perform a specific action, but this will be only a passing action that does not lead them to a true ascent. It is sad to see the corks leap about, sad to foresee the fall that will split them to pieces. It is sad to know that the work done in uplifting them is being wasted, but a heart, in all its boundlessness, has been given to every one of them. So much has been given, so much has been experienced, that it is terrible to return to the level of corks being tossed around! So let us once more think about the solemn ascent that goes constantly onward, an ascent in which one can place full trust in cooperation. Only by taking part in such joint labor can one get used to the diversity of manifestations and come to love it. Few people can understand this, because cosmic diversity frightens a heart that has not been tempered. But how are we to close ourselves off from this startling multiformity? Or rather, how are we to learn to love it and be done forever with the limitations of restricted thinking? In fighting off such thinking, let us use the heart as a shield. Indeed, the shield was held with the left hand. So let us understand the heart to be a protective armament.

577. In works written by the hermits of old, one can find the statement, "Good is a fragrance, evil a poisonous stench." Of course, this observation is usually taken as symbolic, but a deep-thinking physiologist will also understand that an instructive chemical experiment is included in this definition. The transformation of energy into aroma is a very concrete fact. When the fragrance of freesias or violets is evident, one can assume that the physical or subtle energy of a Benevolent Source is nearby. On the other hand, the smell of decay accompanies anything low on the physical plane, as well as on the spiritual. This means that it is possible to detect such a chemical reaction by smell and thereby draw still closer to making a discovery that is both transcendental and physiological. Thus, one has to be able to approach cosmic manifestations consciously. We regard a heightened sense of smell and a purified understanding of it to be signs of a very refined state. Among the senses, smell is one of the most immediate ways of determining what is approaching. Many people will not understand that the heart will be the motive force in refinement of the sense of smell. Whenever a being approaches, a particular mode of the inner sense of smell awakens in the flaming heart. Suffocation of the heart often occurs due to such approaches. Neither a breeze nor purification of the air will help where the very energy of evil is forming a sort of funnel, but goodness does provide relief. Likewise, the feeling in the fingertips not only is a line of defense but also a receiver that picks up hostile transmissions. The incessant battle causes disturbances in the rhythm of the heart, which is why every precaution is useful.

578. People who are ignorant of the situation will ask, "In what way is Armageddon expressing itself if all the dens of evil exist just as they did before?" You should point out that everyone has felt the battle, each in his or her own way. The rise of tension within the

dens indicates each increase in the essence of striving. That is why human oscillations must be handled with great sensitivity. The deaf and dumb sometimes make strange gestures, as their disabilities make it impossible for them to find other modes of expression. But don't people who are ignorant of the heart suffer from similar limitations? One should not laugh at such poverty; rather, in a tolerant way that will not be noticed, one should help the impoverished mind move forward to an image worthy of expression. The same tolerance should be shown toward all ugliness or deformity. The present time requires different conditions in everything we do. In the letters of the Mahatmas now being translated, you can see how Our Guidance, which was undertaken in accordance with the higher plan, was quite remote from all earthly activities. The law of free will does not permit Us to exert direct influence on a person's immediate actions. But now that the conditions of the planet have changed, the standards of the laws are under stress. We have to seek out the criteria governing close guidance, cautiously straining the essence of free will. So the task is becoming very complex. Even the slightest infringement of free will leads to consequences with all kinds of ramifications. The job of coordinating the entrusted missions with karmic conditions might be compared to walking a tightrope, but this rope has to be woven out of the most contrasting materials. What great attention is required in combining the threads according to color and rhythm! With a single unrestrained outburst a coworker might cause a work of long duration to grind to a halt, which is why I am advising special caution. There exists a saying about gathering all the ropes for a journey. You do not know which thread will be needed in an hour of tension. Therefore, keep every option open without judging whether it is great or small. For the Teacher, it is valuable to have the definite certitude that each brief Command he gives will be understood and carried out. So we are advancing toward the language of the heart, which has no need of verbosity.

579. Grasp this once and for all: the so-called gift of discrimination is no gift at all but the result of labor and experience. The ridiculous word intuition is based on nothing but a limited understanding. One can acquire discrimination not through intuition but through many accumulations. To assert that discrimination has no particular cause is like insisting that imagination is not a reflection of previous experiences. The time has come for that which seems to be extremely abstract to enter into the chain of events. Human beings have gone through many situations and have thereby refined their ability to judge. You can be sure that a person who lacks discrimination led a crude existence, which he made no attempt to leave behind, and thus deprived himself of the benefit of perceiving through the heart. The human heart is not young, for its substance is permanent. Some will rejoice in this permanence; in this understanding lies eternal life. Some will rejoice that a person's consciousness is also his own responsibility. That is how the Tablets of Truth become part of life. Do not tire of reading the Teaching of Life as it has appeared over all the ages. The open heart will rejoice in the alternation of rhythm. And with these foundations in place, we shall understand that the motion leading humanity onward cannot be seen in everyday life. In accepting this vast scope, let us also find a path to joy.

580. When speaking to the general public, let us understand that there exists a kind of person who squirms at the very mention of the heart. For such

people the subject may seem childish, or worse, they may believe that they alone have the right to judge about the heart, which results in the formula, "Our hearts, but not yours." That is how the permanent, universal heart is turned into private property. Therefore, let us understand where not to knock. Any vilification of the heart is a blasphemy against the spirit of Truth.

581. If there are sufficient accumulations, it is possible to attain a state of the highest consciousness instantaneously. But in the midst of work, let us not seek out the highest standards. The human spirit advances slowly—let us remember this. Therefore, patience alone is insufficient; let us apply the joy of patience. Let us even regard any sort of instantaneous illumination as being inapplicable. In doing so, we will deepen our conviction in the need for tireless effort in educating the heart.

582. The Brothers of Mercy were able to enter places where the plague was raging without being contaminated, because they had committed their consciousness to Christ irrevocably and indivisibly. Such an exchange of consciousness created flashes of fire with an invincible power to purify. This Western example may call to mind many similar indivisible actions that awaken the fire of the heart's tension. Of course, you know about the ancient custom of striking the chest at times when intensification of consciousness was required. Hermits had a clear purpose in striking themselves on the Chalice with a stone. It was not for the infliction of pain; rather, by using this primitive method they kindled the fire of the heart. The various methods of flagellation and irritation of the skin with hair shirts belong to the same primitive approaches to intensifying the heart, in which pain focuses the person's entire being in one direction. Of course, we shall not fall back on such primitive methods when we realize that the highest protection and ascent are included in indivisibility of aspiration. Through the heart one is able to transmit one's consciousness along the Chain of Hierarchy, thereby increasing one's strength and making oneself invulnerable. It means that for such vital achievements three elements are necessary: the heart, the Hierarchy, and the concept of indivisibility. Let us accustom ourselves to constantly feeling the heart. Then let us not forget to hold the Image of the Teacher in the third eye, and let us understand what indivisibility of aspiration means. The last requirement may often be the most difficult. People do not bother to drive off the bats of abomination darting around them, and thus end up smashing their own aspiration to pieces, even at an incipient stage. The result is a shaggy ball of aspiration that spins round and round, making no progress. One should not keep repeating doleful roulades that contaminate space and prevent one from connecting with the Hierarchy.

A good scientist is writing about immunity, but he fails to consider the heart center's role as a focus of subtle energies. It is in the heart that invulnerability manifests. One might even try striking the Chalice if there is a lack of solemn aspiration, but I do not advise resorting to such primitive methods. It is better to constantly keep in mind the three essential concepts and accept them in all their vitality.

583. To select the best from the worst is also part of an Arhat's task. Often you may find yourself surrounded by the worst on every side, but even then you must find the self-control to select the least harmful. In the midst of the ocean it is not easy to select a better wave, but all the same it is possible.

584. Much of what is quite familiar has yet to be

investigated. Have sweat or saliva been fully examined? We read of poisonous saliva, and we know about beneficial saliva. We have also heard about the diverse properties of perspiration, and yet neither of these secretions has been researched. The sweat of labor and the sweat of overeating will not be the same. The saliva of anger and the saliva of assistance are different, but these are just primitive distinctions. Every human condition produces a particular chemical reaction. In studying the truly cosmic multiplicity of the microcosm, one can come to an understanding of the relationship between the physical and the spiritual worlds. With a developed person, also, the reactions will be varied. One can learn how greatly the sweat of prayer or of lofty, heartfelt aspiration differs from the sweat of mercenary motivation. The sweat of a person who runs to render help is completely different from the sweat of someone hurrying to commit murder. By comparing such contrasting reactions, one can detect the products of psychic energy. Thus, further scientific attainments are on their way. Naturally, the researcher must himself show sufficient sensitivity. He will have to distinguish different emotions and, by means of honest comparisons, set right many confused concepts. Observing the link between secretions and changes in the aura will also enrich the experiment. Moreover, there will be absolutely no need for vivisection and other tortures. The researcher might visit various sites of human activity and, in a natural way free of constraint, gather testimony and other evidence. The most difficult thing to investigate will be the products of prayer and aspiration—in other words, the most significant expressions. But in dealing with these manifestations as well, the researcher will find real treasures if he wishes to. You have noticed evidence of perspiration in connection with the movement of the heart; this is a particularly rare example of the aspiration of the heart. So advise your doctors and scientists to pay attention to the urgent nature of these observations, which are being made at a time when the fiery diseases that We have discussed are increasing. These observations will prove highly useful. One should not forget about the fiery epidemics that are on their way. Numerous reminders are spread throughout the history of humanity. Especially now, when various energies are being widely utilized in spite of a lack of research on their nature and potential side effects, people need to keep in mind that a return blow is possible. Scientists should pay attention to the peculiar nature of many illnesses. One should not just explain them away by claiming that they arise whenever the whirlpool of society condenses. The causes are far deeper, and Our Advice about the education of the heart is very timely.

585. Just think, there is no way that the aura and the constituents of the secretions can be falsified. It is hard for humanity to grasp even a simple fact like that. Questions on such matters have their place even when it is Arhats who are being tested. To see nothing and hear nothing, yet maintain faith up to the highest stage of knowledge—this is a quality of an Arhat. To manifest a heartfelt striving—this is also a quality of an Arhat. To grasp both the great and the small—this is also a quality of an Arhat. Thrift in expending the basic energy is also a quality of an Arhat. Constant desire for the Good is yet another quality of an Arhat. Courage and patience are also qualities of an Arhat. It is ridiculous to think of the essence of an Arhat as being something unearthly. An Arhat evolves on Earth as a Leader of hearts. He offers himself as

a focus around which new formations may develop. His consciousness sees everything, all the seemingly intolerable earthly conditions, but his heart understands how to transmute these obstacles. The small in spirit are in constant fear of battle—or more precisely, the condition that we call battle. But no other word will cover the reality of struggle and success as well as battle does. So a warrior can find a place for his adversary—as a whetstone for sharpening his sword. I think that it is possible for a warrior to send the Teacher his reinforced efforts when together they join battle.

586. With a pledge of leadership one can provide the same collective force that a commander provides on a battlefield. An experienced warrior is not flustered by the fluctuations of success. Pulsation is part of any process of growth; an even setting exists only in a state of no motion. So the living heart is not flat and even. But in times of cosmic tension one may suggest to the heart that it not overstrain itself. The link between the individual heart and the cosmic pulse is quite evident. The Universal Heart could be detected using laboratory methods.

587. A hermit who understood the language of animals noticed, as he was doing his prayers, that a small green snake began to coil about him. This went on for several days. Finally the hermit asked the snake, "What is the reason for your odd behavior?" The snake replied, "It's your concentration that is odd, Rishi, if you were aware of my motions during your prayers!" "Cunning worm," the hermit responded, "do not judge others by your own measure. First the earthly concentration arises, then the subtle, and then the fiery, which embraces both the heavenly and the earthly."

Many people might be told this parable—the coils of the snake are so common! Having become like snakes, people cannot put up with anything beyond their slithering state. They are ready to expend time and effort if only to detect something that, in their opinion, would be disparaging. The worm's standards correspond to that sort of thinking. A person who tries to assert that Yogic achievements do not exist is truly a cunning worm! But it is necessary to bring all the details of Yoga into focus through refinement of the heart—that is how the ancient achievements are being renewed in the rays of the New World. Why limit oneself to earthly attainments? Why forcibly tear oneself away from karmic conditions? Here, too, by receiving the Fiery Baptism the seekers can achieve unification with the Subtle World. They are thus able to strengthen themselves in understanding of the heart and receive the beneficial currents that you feel physically.

588. Regard wealthy prophets with special caution—essentially, they do not exist. True, We cannot let a messenger go hungry, but earthly wealth with all its burdens must not become a "Dragon of the Threshold." Let us remember that Apollonius of Tyana was wealthy, but only so he could give away his riches. Similarly, Our caravans do not carry a load of gold, but they go forward all the same. So let us be together.

589. Many times have I warned you about fear and betrayal; this should be remembered from an evolutionary point of view. All the substances belonging to fear are antithetical to fire. A person who is hiding an embryo of fear within himself must not approach Fire! All the fruits of fear that arise will be reduced to ashes. Therefore, striving to the fiery energy means renouncing every kind of fear. Aspirants must look to the example of the brave hearts who not only do not flee from fiery dragons but actually approach them without fear. Let us remember the vision of September 13th. With great vividness it expresses the impetuosity of the fiery elements and shows how the audacious ones will welcome them. Every vision is sure to have significance.

590. About traitors it must be said with sorrow: they have died forever. The seed of the spirit will not withstand the burden of betrayal—that abomination.

591. Any state of despair signifies a limit. The heart signifies Infinity.

592. To commit suicide means to profane the heart and exist at an extreme stage of ignorance. Likewise, premeditated murder is contrary to the heart.

593. But there is beauty every time somebody takes part in building the New World. This is the true domain of the heart. This longed-for purification of life gives rise to the solemnity that shines forth like an inextinguishable Light.

594. In approaching the Fiery Teaching even once, a person transforms the essence of what he was the day before.

595. Let us get used to understanding the human being not only as an expression of the highest spirit but also as an eternally reactive combination of chemicals. In doing so we shall grow used to understanding the special meaning in the combination of human relationships. The manifestation known as an Arhat is obliged to feel with his heart how he corresponds to the approaching combinations—obliged to feel them spiritually and chemically. By doing so he can avoid many unnecessary conflicts. The flaming heart can sense where there is a true correspondence and the ability to complement each other. Such qualifications ought to be demanded of every leader. He or she must have a heart that is open to heaven and earth. Let us also strengthen ourselves in the thought that we shall establish friendly relations with all people. One of the basic conditions of existence is sincerity, or to put it another way, heartfulness. If this foundation is not sufficiently developed, one can strengthen it by turning to the heart.

596. Since you are finishing the first book about the heart, there needs to be a reminder about certain fundamentals that I have touched on numerous times. The chief requirement for applying heart energy will be the realization that one does not need physical effort in utilizing it. The physical nerve centers also act in response to a command of the brain and the will, but a transmission of the heart is accomplished without any outer tension. The heart can act only when it is spiritually liberated from physical tensions. Let us not forget that the Western school usually follows the path of the brain, while the East, where the foundation has yet to be lost, retains the ancient knowledge that power is contained in the heart. Although healing by means of the heart allows the touch of the hand, it is neither the hands nor the eyes that give help, but rather the emanations of the heart. Distance has no impact on healing through the heart, whereas a transmission by the brain may have to deal with the obstacles created by all sorts of external currents. Training in the command of the heart requires the least amount of effort and adjustment. Pure thinking, constancy, and benevolence bring the heart energy into action. A person's karmic merits may increase the intensity and refinement of his heart, but each time he strives to the Hierarchy, it opens up his heart according to the level of his strength. People should firmly bear in mind that there is but one path to salvation—through the heart. The affirmation of the law of the heart has traversed the entire span of human history. It can be observed how after a few centuries pass people again turn to the one path.

597. Let us not suppose that we have been given little; let us leave this doubt to the insane. A great deal has been given, the heart has been strengthened anew, and fully conscious access to the Hierarchy and the Subtle World has also been granted. But it is only the heart that will lead one to the Fiery World. Let us approach that world without feeling terror; we cannot say "without trepidation," for the quivering beat of the rhythm is unavoidable. But what we feel will be solemnity, not terror.

598. I am charging you to walk with Us through joy and sorrow; it is only in this twofold flame that consciousness is created. Training in consciousness is the Yoga of the Heart. This practice is impossible outside of everyday life; but as you know, it can be continued in the Subtle World. In this way let us draw near to the fiery knowledge.

599. A legend of the Uighurs tells of a giant who captured the Black Dragon and bound him with many chains. The giant left his sister to keep watch on the dragon, and he hurried to the ends of the Earth to announce his victory. But when the giant had reached those distant lands, he heard his sister calling and knew that the dragon was breaking free from the chains. The giant hurried back, but when he saw the seas before him he realized that he would be late if he continued on the same route. So the giant decided to go from one mountain to the next, avoiding the seas, forests, and swamps—that was the only way he could arrive in time. The Black Dragon was breaking free from his last chain when the giant arrived and bound him fast again.

Let us remember this parable and speed along the

summits. Moving from summit to summit will make it easier to encounter all those who dwell in different lands and wear different clothes but live by one heart. That is how we shall reach the threshold of the Fiery Gates.

600. A second book about the Heart may be given, but first let friends and enemies fully assimilate the book now being completed. In his own way—friendly or hostile—every person can draw on the advice about the heart. But even if someone only remembers about the value of Being, he has already helped himself.

For now, let us turn to the foundation of the Fiery World; let us gradually learn to approach it in solemnity and joy.

AGNI YOGA SERIES

Leaves of Morya's Garden I (The Call)   1924
Leaves of Morya's Garden II (Illumination)   1925
New Era Community   1926

Signs of Agni Yoga

Agni Yoga	1929
Infinity I	1930
Infinity II	1930
Hierarchy	1931
Heart	1932
Fiery World I	1933
Fiery World II	1934
Fiery World III	1935
Aum	1936
Brotherhood	1937
Supermundane (in 3 volumes)	1938

Agni Yoga Society
www.agniyoga.org

www.ingramcontent.com/pod-product-compliance
Lightning Source LLC
Chambersburg PA
CBHW071601080526
44588CB00010B/985